HEAVEN'S TIDINGS

A Brief History of the Life of Muhammad, the Final Messenger of God and the Message of the Quran.

"Not for him do I weep. Know I not that he hath gone to that which is better for him than this world? But I weep for the Tidings of Heavens which have been cut off from us."

-Umm Ayman (Baraka)

"There certainly has come to you a Messenger from among yourselves. He is concerned by your suffering, anxious for your well-being, and gracious and merciful to the believers." Quran 9:128

Ifthikar Hassen

Inquiries and Book Orders should be addressed to:

 **Great Writers Media**

Great Writers Media
Email: info@greatwritersmedia.com
Phone: 877-556-0487

ISBN: 979-8-89175-131-6 (sc)
ISBN: 979-8-89175-132-3 (hc)
ISBN: 979-8-89175-130-9 (ebk)

For a mother who sacrificed all that she was able to obtain from God's provision upon her to give her four sons -Ifthikar, Iqbal, Imran and Irshad a sound early education and start in life.

Contents

Illustrations, tables and appendices

INTRODUCTION

In the name of Allah the most Merciful the most Compassionate

T here are few personalities in the history of the world
that have made so many biographers write so much detail with
such minute scrutiny on the life of someone who has impacted
and continues to influence the lives of so many in the world. The biography of the Prophet Muhammad (ﷺ) or "Seerah" has been researched
and written by religious scholars, journalists and historians of all stripes
throughout the ages using authentic and chronologically comprehensive original records that have been preserved since around 150-200
years after the Prophets death. Details of his life in the form of oral
traditions and written records and letters were available to the early
writers like Musa Ibn Uqba (763 CE), Ibn Ishaq (d.768 CE), al-Waqidi
(d.823CE) , Ibn Hisham (d.833 CE), Ibn Shihab (d.742 CE) and al-Tabari
(d.922 CE) in fragmented manuscripts and parchments as early as from
the first two decades after his death. They drew heavily upon earlier
sources, none of which have survived except as quoted by these and
later sources. In fact parts of the manuscript of Hamam Ibn Munabih
who was born 19 AH or eight years after the death of Muhammad and
who was a student of Abu Huraira who in turn was not only a companion of the Prophet but who recorded and wrote the largest collection
of hadeeth or the prophetic traditions were available to the aforementioned scholars and writers.

Hence written hadeeth about Muhammad were available as early
as the first two decades after the Prophet in addition to the extensive
oral traditions. It was through a process of absorption and incorpora-
tion that these now extinct early records are preserved and reflected in
the extant books on the Prophetic biographies mentioned above. The

presence of the written Quran and the traditions of the Prophet and the scientific methodology that was developed in collecting these traditions and the rich and diverse scholarship in the exegesis of the Quran further complemented the biography of the Prophet referred to as the "Seerah". The objective of this book is to present the "Seerah" in a condensed format and minimize the use of historical names of characters other than the most important and relevant to the core Seerah and present it within a framework that might be insightful to both Muslim and non-Muslim readers alike. Most of the content in this book has been referenced from contemporary writings on the Seerah (see bibliography) that are based on the most authentic original early writings and has attempted, God willing, to portray the most significant events, episodes, lessons and milestones during his mission on earth.

To capture the spirit of its title, this condensed biography brings in to context verses from the Quran which have been liberally interspersed throughout the book to place in perspective the integrated and interactive synthesis of the life of the Prophet with God's revelation. The appendices address some of the more contentious and misunderstood concepts in the life of the Prophet and in Islam in general and attempt to place in proper perspective the normative Islamic viewpoint. Several sub-sections and articles addressing important issues and concepts within Islam and the life of Muhammad are interspersed throughout this book, in an attempt to explain and describe them in the light of normative Islamic sciences.

The abundant use of appendices in this book is intended to articulate some of the more controversial and misunderstood aspects of Islam and the Prophet and to examine them again in the light of the normative teachings of Islam. The content in these appendices and the text table inserts in the body of the book reflect the author's interaction over a period of several years with inter-faith groups especially dialogues with Christian groups and attempts to address the questions and misconceptions that surfaced. Hence this book although written for a general audience could also be a reference point for Muslim-Christian dialogue and to clarify some of the most polemic and Islamophobic misunderstandings out there and also reach out in a spirit of mutual cooperation towards a better world.

The section titled 'Towards a productive and meaningful interfaith dialogue between Muslims and Christians' explores insightful concepts proposed by Robert Schedinger in his book "Was Jesus a Muslim?" which looks at interfaith relationships at a meta-religious level that positions the nature of religion itself and its relationship to the larger political, social and economic order as the primary forces of discussion.

The section then goes on to look at Quranic rules of engagement in interfaith relationships and the etiquette of dialogue and highlights key dimensions as propounded by Maria Massi Dakake of George Mason University in an article published in the 'Renovatio' Journal of Zaytuna College where she suggests what one might call a set of Quranic "rules of engagement" for interacting with Jews and Christians in peaceful and dialogic contexts and argue that, from a Quranic perspective, demonstrations of virtue and good manners (adab) in such interactions are ultimately as important as, or perhaps more important than, the eloquence of words and the rigor of arguments.

For those who come from a Christian background, where the Gospel accounts of the life of Jesus plays a major role in faith, it is well to keep in mind that Muhammad plays second fiddle in the Quran. He is enormously important for Islamic religiosity, but his importance stems from his relationship to the Quran. As F.E. Peters in his book 'Judaism, Christianity, and Islam-The classical texts and their interpretation' (1990), states;

"The Christian cannot but study the 'Good News of Jesus Christ", since the sacred work of Jesus is revealed therein, the Muslim reads the "Life of the Prophet of God" simply as an act of piety, revelation lies elsewhere"

Finally, just as God exhorts the readers of the Quran to ponder, reflect, and use the intellect to understand its essence, the 'seerah' or the life of Muhammad (ﷺ), requires reflection and reasoning to derive from it the wisdom, beauty, mercy and justice behind a man who lived a life that epitomised the purpose of life and its physical and spiritual significance.

[The benedictions "peace and blessings be upon him" after the name of Prophet Muhammad, has been inserted in its Arabic equivalent "salallaahu alaihi wasallam" (ﷺ) not exhaustively in all of the places where his name is referred to, and "peace be upon him" after the names of other respected Prophets of God and "may Allah be pleased with him" after respected family members and Companions of the Prophet Muhammad have been omitted for the sake of continuity and clarity for the non-Muslim readers, and it is strongly urged for the Muslim reader to observe sending such salutations on the Prophet at the mention of his blessed name at all instances.]

Toronto 2024

LINE OF PROPHETHOOD- A compressed genealogy through the ages

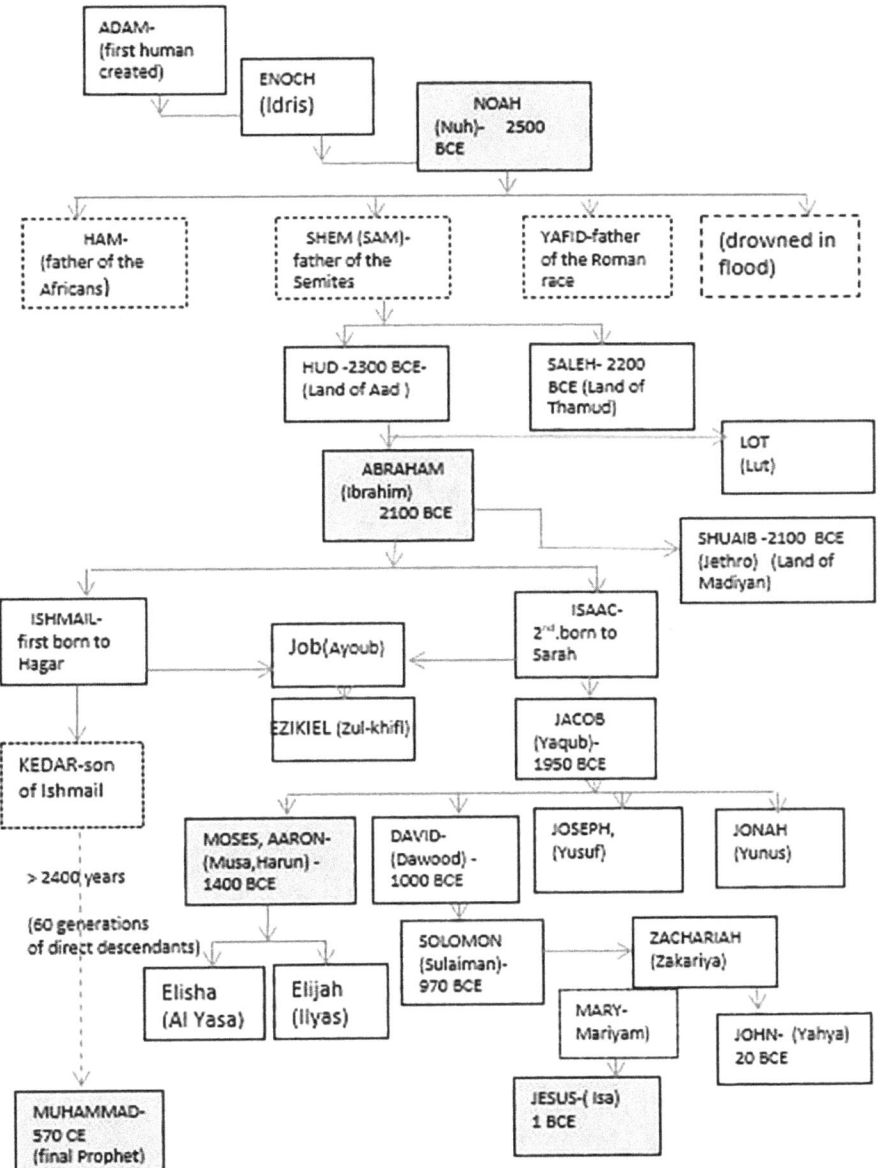

Note: Shaded boxes indicate major or Arch Prophets except for Aaron. Boxes with dashed outline indicate Non-Prophets.

Prophetic Timeline - Milestones

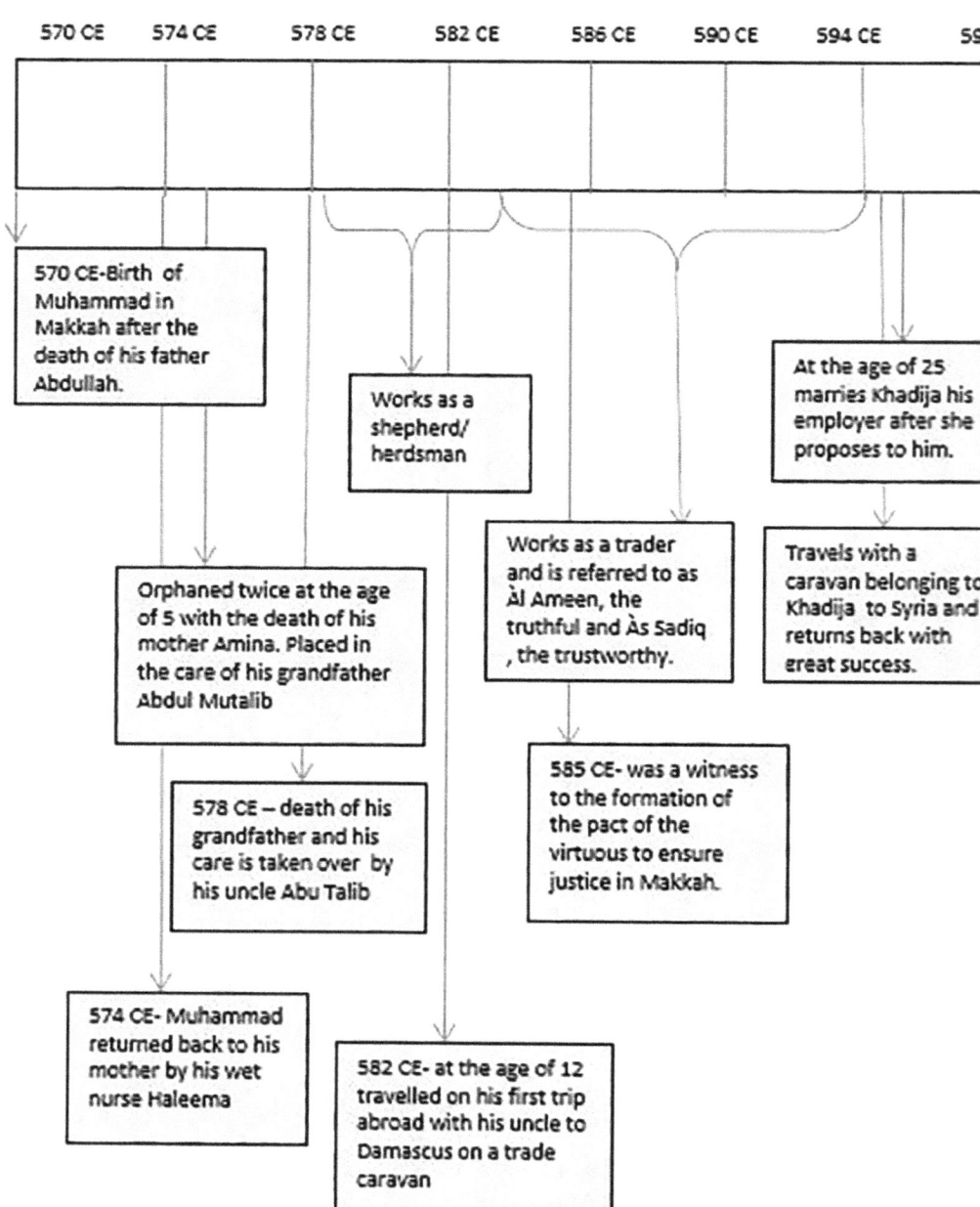

| 570 CE | 574 CE | 578 CE | 582 CE | 586 CE | 590 CE | 594 CE | 598 |

570 CE-Birth of Muhammad in Makkah after the death of his father Abdullah.

Works as a shepherd/ herdsman

At the age of 25 marries Khadija his employer after she proposes to him.

Orphaned twice at the age of 5 with the death of his mother Amina. Placed in the care of his grandfather Abdul Mutalib

Works as a trader and is referred to as Àl Ameen, the truthful and Às Sadiq , the trustworthy.

Travels with a caravan belonging to Khadija to Syria and returns back with great success.

578 CE – death of his grandfather and his care is taken over by his uncle Abu Talib

585 CE- was a witness to the formation of the pact of the virtuous to ensure justice in Makkah.

574 CE- Muhammad returned back to his mother by his wet nurse Haleema

582 CE- at the age of 12 travelled on his first trip abroad with his uncle to Damascus on a trade caravan

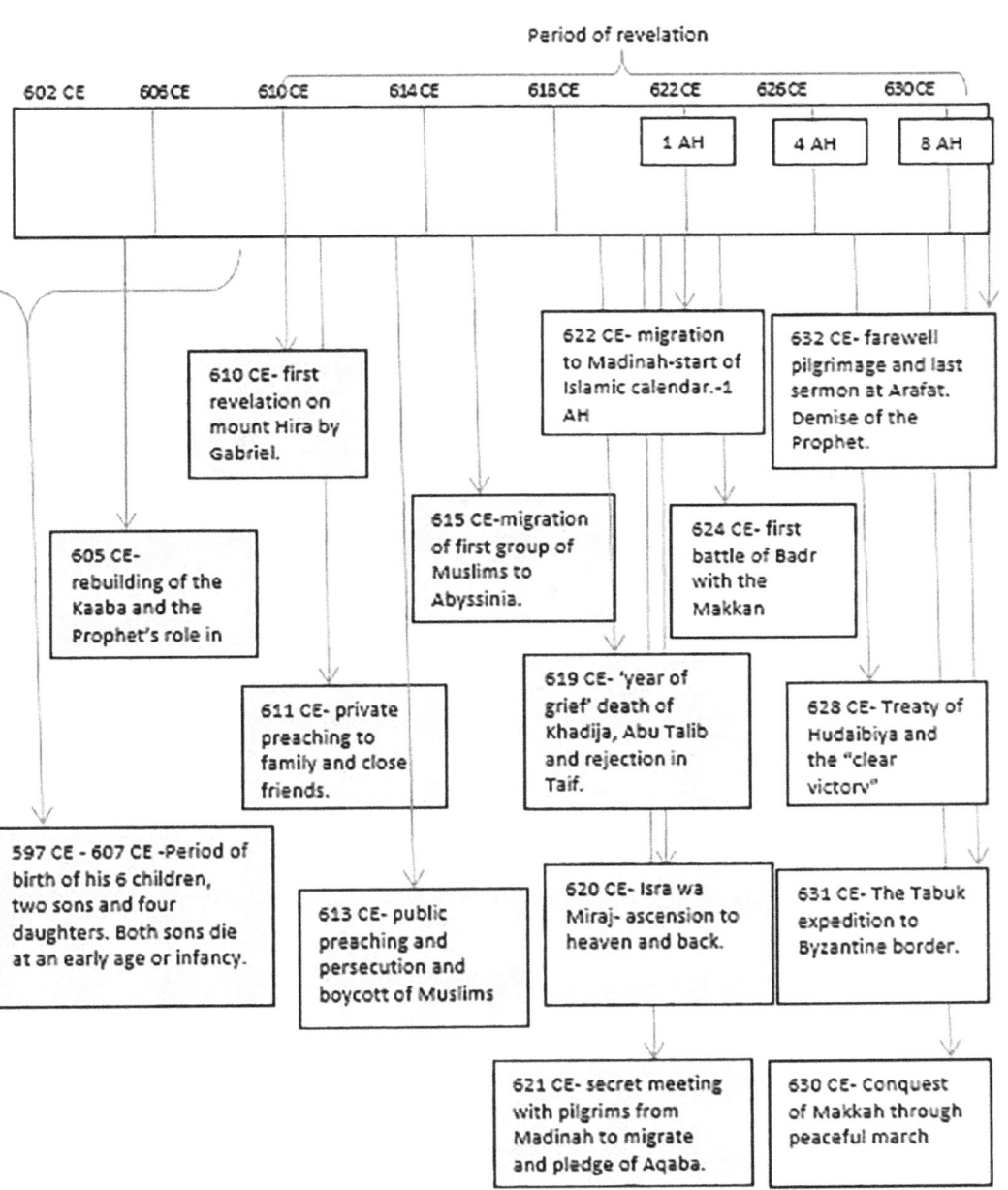

Period of revelation

| 602 CE | 605 CE | 610 CE | 614 CE | 618 CE | 622 CE | 626 CE | 630 CE |

1 AH   4 AH   8 AH

610 CE- first revelation on mount Hira by Gabriel.

622 CE- migration to Madinah-start of Islamic calendar.-1 AH

632 CE- farewell pilgrimage and last sermon at Arafat. Demise of the Prophet.

605 CE- rebuilding of the Kaaba and the Prophet's role in

615 CE-migration of first group of Muslims to Abyssinia.

624 CE- first battle of Badr with the Makkan

611 CE- private preaching to family and close friends.

619 CE- 'year of grief' death of Khadija, Abu Talib and rejection in Taif.

628 CE- Treaty of Hudaibiya and the "clear victory"

597 CE - 607 CE -Period of birth of his 6 children, two sons and four daughters. Both sons die at an early age or infancy.

613 CE- public preaching and persecution and boycott of Muslims

620 CE- Isra wa Miraj- ascension to heaven and back.

631 CE- The Tabuk expedition to Byzantine border.

621 CE- secret meeting with pilgrims from Madinah to migrate and pledge of Aqaba.

630 CE- Conquest of Makkah through peaceful march

Note: The battle of Uhud and the battle of the Trench that took place in 625 and 627 CE and were major milestones have not been shown due to space constraints.

The Ancestry Of Muhammad (ﷺ)

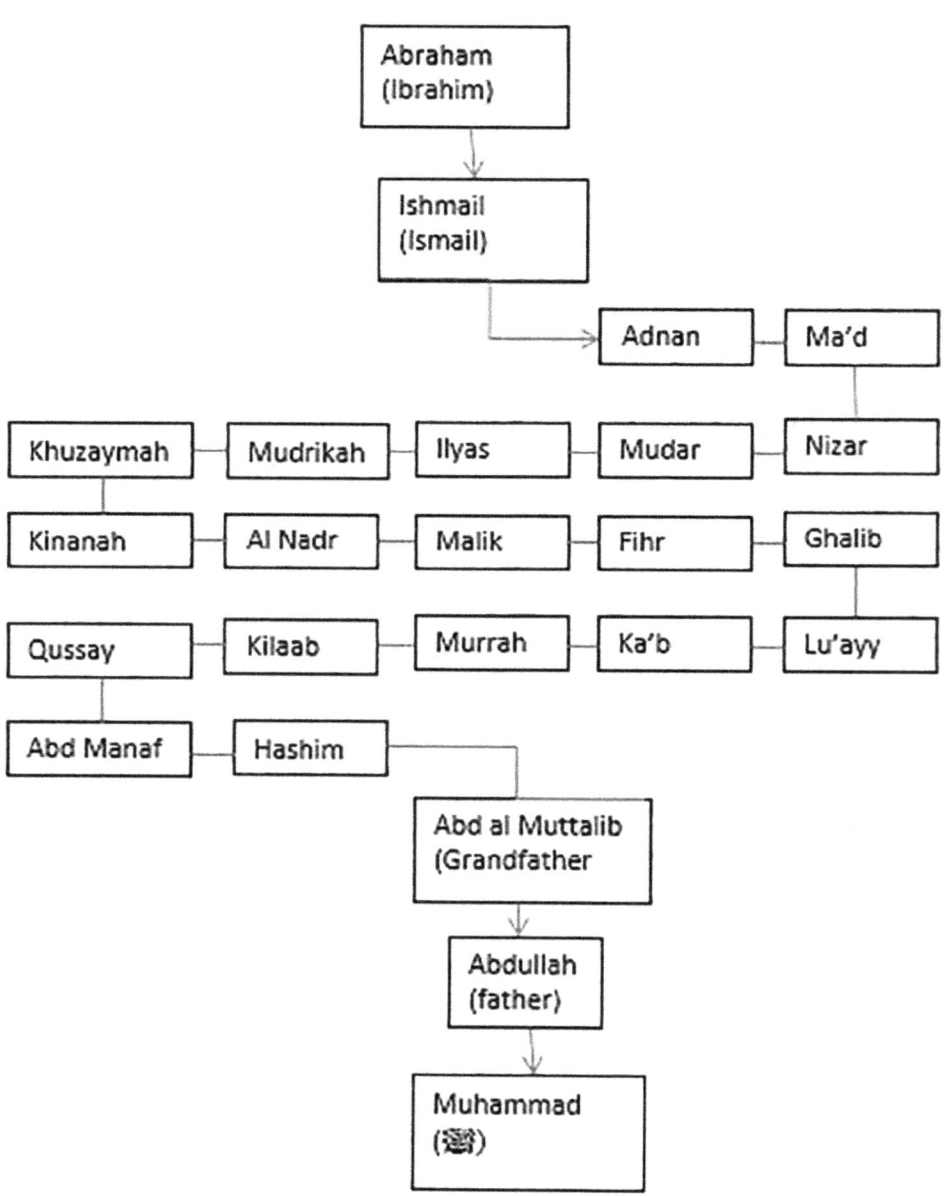

Map of the Middle East in the 6th Century

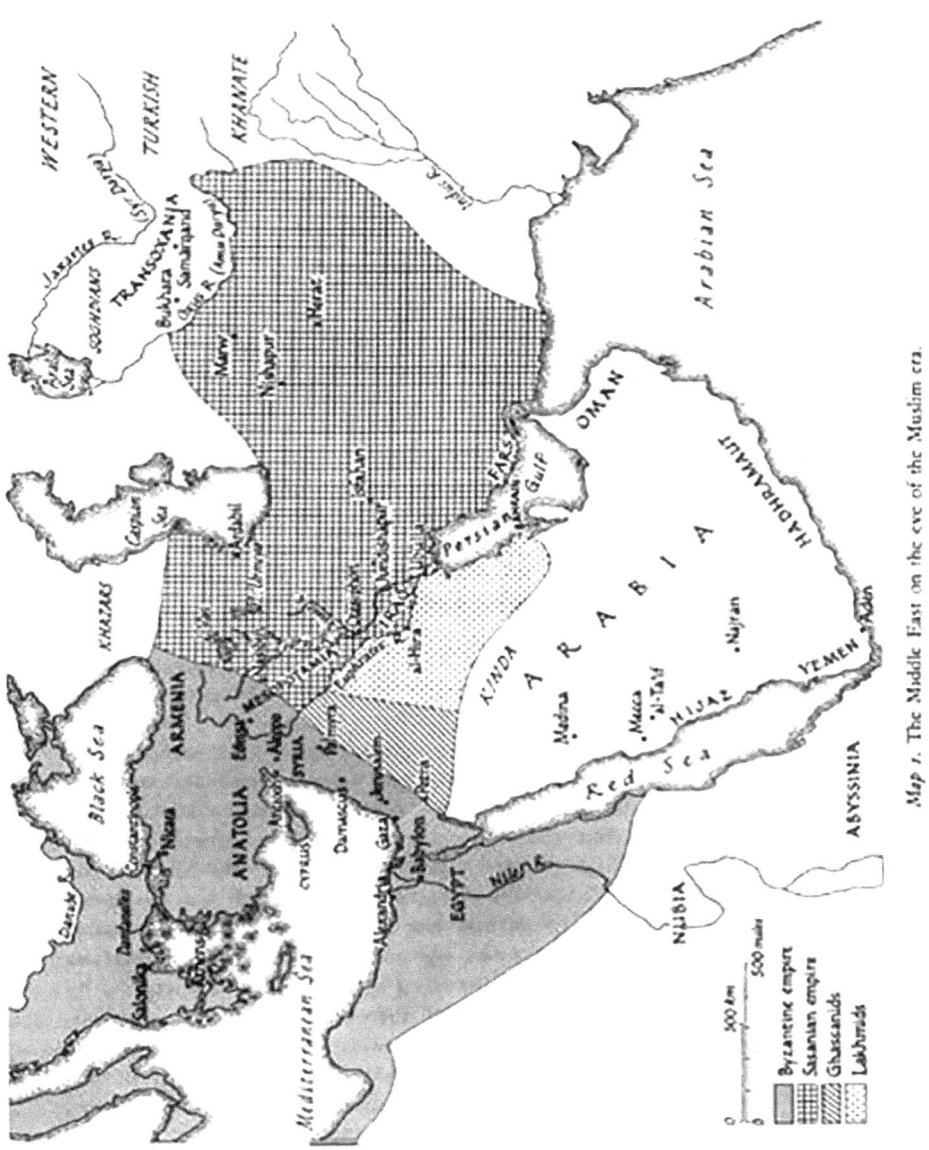

Map 1. The Middle East on the eve of the Muslim era.

Map 2: The Middle East in the Sixth Century AD
until the birth of the Prophet Muhammad

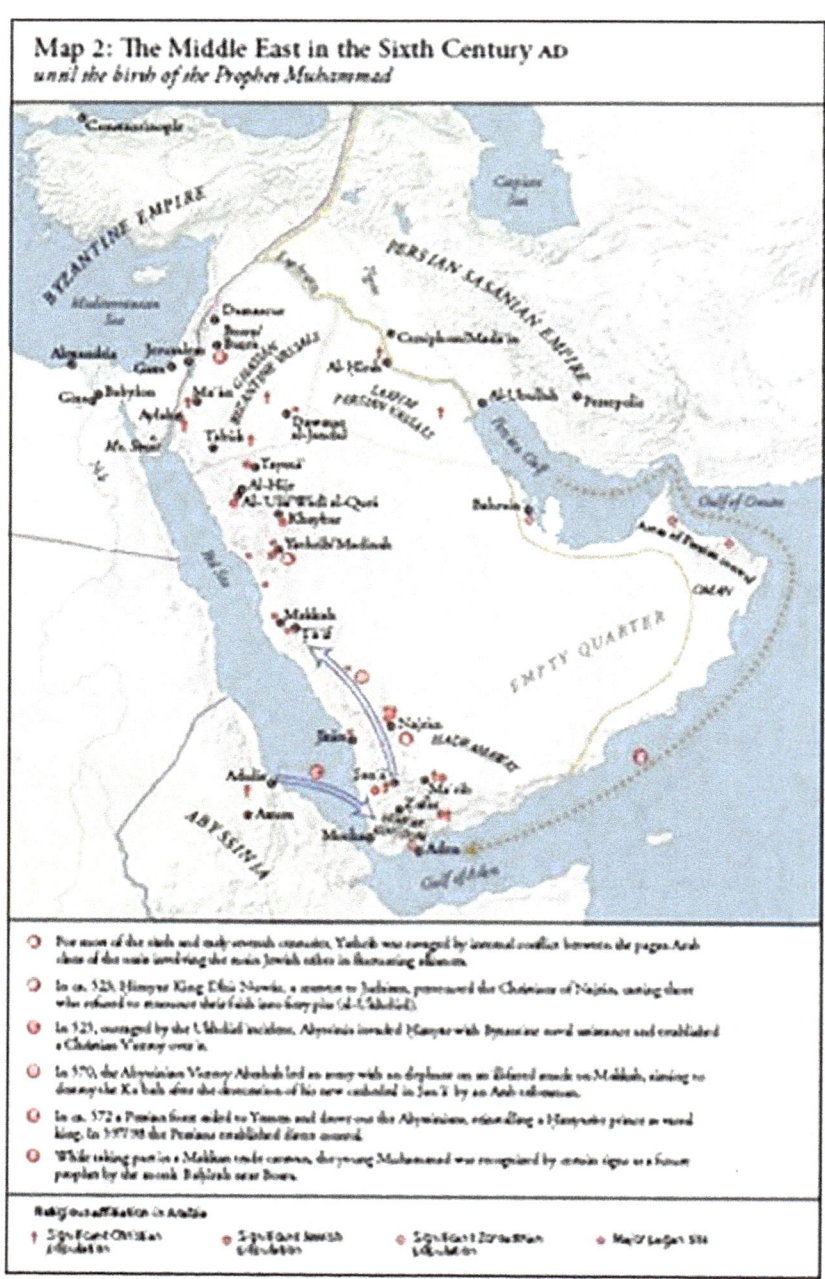

Source: The Study Quran

One

The Perennial Covenant and the Abrahamic legacy

When Abraham left Hagar and the infant Ishmael in the barren desert valley of Makkah as God had ordered, he lifted his hands towards the heavens and supplicated:

"Our Lord! I have settled some of my offspring in a barren valley near Your Sacred House, our Lord! so that they may establish prayer; so make the hearts of 'believing' people incline towards them, and provide them with fruits so perhaps they may be thankful." (14:37)

"Our Lord! Raise from among them a messenger who will recite to them Your revelations, teach them the Book and wisdom and purify them. Indeed, You Alone are the Almighty, All Wise." (2:129)

The Quran then asserts;

"Abraham was neither a Jew nor a Christian; He submitted in all uprightness (Hanif) and was not a polytheist." (3:67)

In the Quran, the Hanifs are seen as primordial monotheists and the Quran associates them with the legacy of Abraham himself. Here is part of the Quran's claim that it represents both a continuation of and a return to the primordial monotheism of Abraham. The Quran simply and accurately states that Abraham lived prior to the existence of a distinct people called Jews, as well as before the emergence of Christians. Yet he too related to the God of the whole world, and it is this primordial form of monotheism that, according to the Quran, has been the message of all the prophets from Adam through the ages—and finally Muhammad (ﷺ).

"He has ordained for you 'believers' the Way which He decreed for Noah, and what We have revealed to you 'O Prophet' and what We decreed for Abraham, Moses, and Jesus. 'Commanding;' Uphold the faith, and make no divisions in it." (Quran 42:13)

The connection between Abraham and Muhammad would be a cornerstone of the Islamic tradition. The ritual of the pilgrimage, for example, recalls the hardships faced by Abraham's wife Hagar, a former handmaiden, and his son Ishmael when they were left in the Arabian Desert. To this day, millions of Muslim pilgrims go to the hills of Safa and Marwa to re-enact Hagar's desperate search for water in the hot torrid sun. The tale of the test that God put before Abraham, to sacrifice his son, is well known to Jews, Muslims, and Christians. Whereas Jews and Christians identified the son as Abraham's younger son, Isaac, Muslims, however, noting that the narrative refers to Abraham's "only son," argue that it must have taken place in the period when he had only one son, that is, Ishmael. Even in the centuries prior to the rise of Islam, Ishmael had already been identified as the ancestor of the Arab peoples, and it is no surprise that when God chose a prophet to deliver the message to the Arabs, it was through Muhammad, a descendant of Abraham through Ishmael—as Jesus had been a descendant through Isaac. Later on, Abraham and Ishmael together established a temple devoted to the One God. This temple, built in the shape of a cube, is remembered as the Kaaba and continues to serve as the spiritual axis of the world for Muslims.

In the words of the Quran:

"Remember we made The House a place of gathering for human-ity and a place of safety. So take the Place of Abraham as a place of prayer. We established a covenant with Abraham and Ishmael that they should sanctify My House for those who circumambulate it, or use it as a retreat, or prostrate themselves in prayer in that place." (2:125)

Pause for reflection- The Covenant of God

God's covenant with mankind to worship only Him and obey Him was continued through the history of prophecy, even though it was repeatedly broken and forgotten. Abraham re-establishes the covenant through the seed of both of his children and builds the Kaaba as a place of worship. The Quran then speaks of the covenant God has made with the followers of Prophet Muhammad , as one of the last verses to be revealed states, "And remember God's Blessing upon you, and his covenant by which He bound you, when you said, 'We hear and we obey', And reverence God. Surely God knows what lies within breasts" (5:7). Reminiscent of Quranic verses addressed to the Children of Israel, this verse follows an explanation of the manner in which Muslims are to purify themselves for prayer. This alludes to the fact that the specific form of prayer revealed through Muhammad is the means by which Muslims are to observe the covenant, as did Jews through the Temple sacrifice and as did Christians through the sacraments.

The basic practices of Islam the 'five pillars' as they are known- testifying to the oneness of God, prayer, charity, fasting and pilgrimage- can thus be seen as means by which human beings return to their primordial nature, the fitrah, where they are ever cognizant of the covenant with God. When observed with sincerity, the rites of Islam like those of Judaism and Christianity serve to re-integrate and reorient the dispersed elements of one's human nature. The rhythm of life thus comes to be fashioned upon the norms that God has ordained for humanity, rather than upon the aberrations that human beings have created for themselves. As particular modes of observance, every religion embodies the fullness of the primordial covenant, the religion of the fitrah, which was the religion of Abraham-devotion and true submission in Islam. For these reasons the Quran emphasizes the eternal principles and fundamental practices that transcend the particularity of each covenant in previous revelations in order to reaffirm what it maintains to be the pure essence of all covenants-full submission to God.

- The Study Quran, A new translation and Commentary - Joseph Lumbard, et al. HarperCollins.

∞

The Arabs lived in the land that today forms the entire Arabian Peninsula, as well as Palestine, Jordan, southern Syria and southern Iraq. Theirs was a tribal society, which considered allegiance to tribe as the paramount bond between various people. Individuals identified themselves as members of a tribe, and the tribe protected and defended its individual members. A tribe could easily go to war against other tribes over a dispute that involved only one or two of its members. In such cases, right and wrong were of secondary importance, as tribal loyalty was supreme.

Long before the advent of the Prophet Muhammad (ﷺ) and even pre-dating Abraham, God sent to the tribes of Arabia three Arabian prophets to the lands of Aad near Yemen, Thaamud and Madiyan in the north beyond Tabuk towards the Gulf of Aqaba. They were Hud, Saleh and Shuaib probably between the period 2300 BCE and 2100 BCE based on the best estimate of historical scholars (see "line of prophet hood" on page 13). According to the narrations in the Quran all these nations were destroyed as they rebelled against God and disobeyed their prophets and rejected the covenant despite being repeatedly warned of a terrible chastisement if they continued in their pagan idolatry and disbelief. Around 2000 BCE, God sent Prophet Abraham to the region that is present day Iraq and through his seed of Ishmael and Isaac fulfilled the prophecies to both the children of Israel through the line of Isaac and to the Arabs through the seed of Ishmael, His greatest Messengers and Prophets culminating in the final Messenger of God, Muhammad.

Although the pre-Islamic Arabs had many virtuous ways, when Muhammad was born, Makkah reeked with oppression and injustice.

The strong oppressed the weak, and trivial arguments would spark horrible tribal wars. The rich oppressed the poor, and men, fearing poverty, would often go calmly into the blue-black desert nights to bury their baby girls alive. Yet, around the Arabian Peninsula, kings and emperors sat upon thrones of pure gold, dressed in rich clothes inlaid with jewels. Like the dusty, red sands that whipped across the scorching desert, the years flew by and there came a time when idolatry again prevailed over Abraham's religion. Only a few followers of the Abrahamic creed referred to as the Hanifs remained, and being so few they could not influence the majority.

Although the Holy House remained a sacred place, idols now polluted its pure structure. Many people had forgotten the religion of Abraham and had again started to worship idols, resorting to the pagan practice of divination and sacrifice of animals at the altars of the idols. Some elements of the pre-Islamic Arab religious worldview can be gleaned from the Quran. They were certainly not atheists or agnostics. If anything, they believed in a well-populated spiritual cosmos. All pre-modern societies had faith in some conception of one or more deities, souls, or forces that transcended the visible level. For the Arabs prior to the rise of Islam, their objection was not that God did not exist, but rather that there were a multiplicity of gods. In fact, the pre-Islamic Arabs did have a view of One God, whose name in Arabic was Allah. Even the Arab Christians and Jews referred to God as Allah. Incidentally, the Aramaic cognate for God is "Elloha" from which "Elohim" is derived.

In their conception, however, Allah was not the only God, merely the Supreme God among them. This conception was similar to that of many tribal societies that had a conception of a High God or Sky God who transcended the lower deities. Likewise, the Arabs held that between Allah and our level of existence stood a whole host of lower deities who acted as intermediaries. Quite often these deities were connected to particular tribes, so that each tribe had its own representation of deity. The Kaaba temple, established by Abraham for the One God, eventually came to be surrounded by some 360 idols—more or less one for every day of the year. The various tribes would bring their icons and idols to the Kaaba during the pilgrimage season, creating a pantheon of tribal deities. The annual rite of pilgrimage brought many pilgrims to Makkah, and during their visits they engaged in trade as well as worship. Pilgrimage and business perfectly intertwined for Makkah. The religion of Makkah was their business.

Pause for reflection - purpose of life.

God reveals in the Quran that there is no nation to which He has not sent a prophet or warner and the essence of their message was simple- believe and worship the one true God and follow my way.

"Indeed, We have sent you with the truth as a bringer of good tidings and a Warner. And there was no nation but that there had passed within it a Warner." (35:24)

A simple enough message of monotheism that through the prism of time gets distorted and split into a myriad of deities and superstitions resulting in the need for yet another prophet or messenger. It is only through the mercy and grace of God that He sends down guidance for our own salvation and to prevent us from self-destructing. Yet mankind is arrogant and ungrateful and driven by his own desires and lust for power and the riches of this world engages in injustice, oppression and bloodshed. Didn't the angels query, **" Why would you O Lord place on earth someone who would spread corruption and bloodshed whilst we glorify and sanctify You?" and God replied "I know that which you do not...." (2:30)**

God who created man as His vice-regent on earth also created him in the best of moulds and taught him the names of all things (intellect) and the capacity to descend to the lowest lows or reach for the highest expression of divine closeness. Hence the purpose of life in the form of the human body and soul we know is for man to exercise his free choice and use his reasoning to elevate himself to the highest potential of his being by embodying and displaying the moral and beautiful attributes that God himself possesses; mercy, compassion, generosity, love, truth- fulness, justice, patience and the like so that he may draw closer to God and experience felicity and tranquility both in this world and the hereaf- ter. A necessary condition for humans to experience and manifest these qualities of excellence is the essence of suffering and pain in this world. Life in this world is a test and the Quran states:

"We will certainly test you with a touch of fear and famine and loss of property, life, and fruits of your toil. Give good news to those who patiently endure." (2:155)

Two

The Orphan, the Trustworthy One the Prophet

T hus, as the darkness of ignorance again spread across the land, a new glimmer of hope flickered on the horizon. This new hope, from the descendants of Ishmail would be fulfilled through the family of Abdul-Muttalib, the chief of the Hashemite clan who belonged to the master tribe Quraysh. His call to resume the religion of Abraham would rock the ungodly societies of Makkah from the foundations of their idol worship to the core of their superstitions.

In this social environment, Muhammad was born in 570 CE. At the time, children who belonged to distinguished families in that society were usually looked after by Bedouin wet nurses, who came to Makkah seeking to take babies home with them. The Makkan families believed that it would be in the best interests of their children to spend their first couple of years in the desert, where the clean air and environment would ensure that they had a healthy start. The Bedouin families received financial help in return for caring for the town children. So, within a few days of his birth, Muhammad was given to the Bedouin woman Haleema, who was to breastfeed and look after him during his infant years.

Makkah and its environs had faced a severe drought over the past year and Haleema and her family were facing great hardship as their camels and goats had very little milk and their riding donkeys and camels were on their last legs and this was another reason why she wanted to take a child from an affluent family so that they would be compensated handsomely. Haleema was initially reluctant to take an orphan under her care as she knew there would not be much money paid but after having no other children to take and not wanting to go back without an infant to nurse she felt sorry for the orphan Muhammad and decided to take him. It is reported in all of the biographies of the Prophet that no sooner had Haleema's family taken custody of Muhammad, her breasts swelled up with milk and their she-camels and goats began to produce milk in abundance and the pastures around their home had green grass once more. Haleema realized the blessed nature of Muhammad and pleaded with his mother Amina to keep him for another two years at the end of the first two years when they are returned back to their parents. She wanted no compensation.

So Muhammad spent his first four years growing up in the clear clean atmosphere of the desert and watching over goats and sheep, sleeping under the stars and learning the pure Arabic of the desert tribes.

The Prophets parents' had been married only a few weeks, when his father, Abdullah, travelled to Syria with the traditional trade caravan that travelled there every year. On his way back he was taken ill. The caravan people left him in Madinah to be nursed by his maternal relatives, but he did not recover, and he died soon afterwards. Muhammad's mother, Amina, died a few years later, when he was only six years of age. A mother's death is keenly felt by a child, but perhaps even more so in young Muhammad's case, as he was with her on a journey that took them to Madinah where they visited his father's grave. The distance from Makkah to Madinah is over 450 kilometres. When they reached al-Abwa, a village that is a little closer to Makkah than to Madinah, Amina was taken ill and died. The child was left to the care of his nursemaid, Umm Ayman, who took him back home. Muhammad's grandfather, Abdal-Muttalib, who then looked after him, but he in turn died when Muhammad was only eight. Such a sequence of loss of immediate and loved relatives is bound to have a profound effect on a young person. Muhammad remembered his mother to his last days. More than fifty years later, he visited her grave in al-Abwa, and as he stood at her grave, he wept in grief. So emotional was the moment that all the companions wept at the sight of the Prophet's passion for his mother. Abdul Muttalib had tenderly placed him in his own home. He was determined to take care of his grandson, who had now lost both his mother and his father. Indeed, Abdul-Muttalib had a burning belief that one day his grandson would hold a special position amongst his people. Perhaps it was the wise, quiet nature of the boy that made Abdul Muttalib feels this particular way about him. However, the little Muhammad had many superior attributes that were very admirable. He was always kind, honest and trustworthy. Moreover, he absolutely hated the idols that occupied Makkah, the drinking of wine and the terrible treatment of slaves. Death had now claimed three of the dearest people to the little boy, making him triply orphaned but God never deserted him. Muhammad's kind uncle, Abu Talib, stepped in and immediately took him into his care, and into his heart. He too noticed the boy's excellent manners, and his love for Muhammad was as deep and pure as Abdul Muttalib's had been. He treated little Muhammad with great respect as he would his own sons. Muhammad grew with youthfulness and his heart filled with goodness opened his mind that had always studied its surroundings which he continued to observe. Yet, Muhammad felt like he was a burden to his kind uncle who had a large family. So he told his uncle that he wanted to go back into the desert to pasture the sheep.

Muhammad had always loved the calm, simple life of the desert and he longed to return to it. So when his uncle agreed to his request, he eagerly went back to the surroundings of his childhood. The temptations of Makkah had no power over the disciplined soul of Muhammad whose prime concern was contemplation. This is not surprising. Far lesser men than Muhammad have also overcome these temptations. He led a life far removed from vice and immorality, and found his pleasures in immersing himself in thought and contemplation.

The Prophet (ﷺ) said "God never sent a prophet except that he was a shepherd". The companions asked "not even you?" This shows most companions didn't even know he was a shepherd. So they thought he would be an exception but the prophet replied "yes I was and I used to tend to the flock of the people of Makkah in return for some pennies".

When he was twelve years old his uncle Abu Talib took Muhammad on his first caravan journey to Syria and back and soon after between the ages of fifteen and twenty, Muhammad took up trading, and his excellent character helped him in his trade. Although he stayed away from the superstitious practices of his people, Muhammad was still active in his community. His excellent character and sound intelligence always motivated the people to accept his opinions and he would often help them solve their problems. Muhammad was an honest man in his business dealings, and eventually people started to call him "Al-Ameen" (The Trustworthy) and "As Sadiq"(The truthful). If anyone wanted to entrust money to someone, the people would tell him, "You should only go to Al-Ameen." He thus made a 'brand' name for himself through these twin virtues which were the foundations of his self- development in his youth. Although later in life he would through God's command go on to change the world, Muhammad started by first changing himself from within with a deep sense of morality, responsibility and accountability.

Whenever the merchants wanted an honest person to handle their trade, people advised them to go to Muhammad. Thus, as the young Muhammad grew up, more people noticed his wonderful qualities, until everyone knew of his truthfulness, honesty, wisdom, and good manners. At the age of fifteen, Muhammad was exposed to and was a witness to a unique pact of social justice in Makkah. Having decided, after an earnest discussion, that it was imperative to found an order of chivalry for the furtherance of justice and the protection of the weak, - following an incident which involved an outsider being treated deceitfully by a Makkan, the leaders of the tribes of Quraysh took part in an oath and Muhammad was present when one of his uncles brought him to the event. Thus at an early age Muhammad appreciated the significance of justice. Muhammad, who took part in the oath and who said in after-years: "I was present in the house of Abdallah ibn Judan at so excellent a pact that I would not exchange my part in it for a herd of red camels; and if now, in Islam, I were summoned unto it, I would gladly respond." Such civic engagement further built his character at an early age as he grew and matured and social justice would be one of the cornerstones of an Islamic community which he would go on to establish later on in life as a prophet of God.

Apparently, he worked for modest wages. However, the best opportunity a young man of his age could have was to join a trade caravan as an agent of one of the Makkan businessmen. Khadijah, a wealthy businesswomen and a widow needed such an agent, and the stories she had heard about Muhammad encouraged her to send him as her agent in the traditional summer trade caravan to Syria. The venture was highly successful, as Muhammad secured handsome profits for Khadijah at both ends of the trip. Khadijah had sent a servant of hers, Mysarah with him, who reported to her on Muhammad's honesty, integrity and business acumen.

The formative years of the Prophet was rife with deeply impressionable experiences through the loss of close family and the lack of any form of material comfort or financial ease. Yet, God placed in the hearts of those who looked after him immense affection for him largely due to his impeccable virtue and mannerisms. He won the hearts and trust of the people of Makkah though he deeply disliked the ways of pagan culture and norms. In fact, as recorded by multiple biographers, Muhammad was under the constant protection of God's guidance even before prophethood. When he was a young boy and working as a shepherd in the hills outside Makkah he had through adolescent curiosity wanted to visit Makkah at night and on multiple occasions he was distracted on his way by singing at a village wedding or a joyous occasion and he stopped to listen and found himself asleep through the night. This saved his young innocent mind from witnessing the debauchery, vice and immorality of pagan night life in Makkah.

Early signs of his prophet hood was seen and exclaimed by a Christian monk named Bahira who lived in a monastery bordering Syria when Muhammad accompanied his uncle on his first trade trip on a caravan when he was twelve years old. The aging monk asked Abu Talib the Prophet's uncle to take the boy back to Makkah quickly from Syria for fear of the Jews who would have tried to kill him if they recognized the signs of prophet hood in young Muhammad. However God had different plans and little did anyone know of the greatness that would come out of him as the seal in the long line of Prophets from God. It had already been written. At a time when dates and the years were not accurately recorded and periods referred to around the occurrence of major events at that time, the year of the birth of the Prophet was etched in the memories of the Arabs at that time who referred to that year as the 'year of the elephants'. It was in the year 570 CE that the Abyssinian ruler in Yemen invaded Makkah with a horde of elephants and failed miserably when God sent a flock of birds with pellets of clay in their beaks that destroyed the elephants to dust.(Quran 105).The Prophet was born 50 days after this event. Scholars' state that it was not the Kaaba that God was protecting but the unborn soul of Muhammad.

∞

As a wealthy widow, Khadijah had no shortage of suitors, including some with favourable social standing, but she had refused them all. Now she realized that she had found her eligible bachelor. Khadijah discreetly proposed marriage with Muhammad, and this was soon accomplished. It is suggested that Muhammad was twenty-five at the time while Khadijah was forty, but this is highly questionable. She gave him two sons and four daughters within ten years, which suggests that she was in the prime of her life. This means that she could not have been much over thirty. Indeed, a report by Ibn Abbas, the Prophet's cousin, tells us that she was twenty-eight.

This was a very happy marriage, and Muhammad continued to manage Khadijah's business and the family lacked for nothing. He was a model husband and she was a very caring and loving wife. She was not disappointed in her choice: she had found a man of great integrity, who was well respected by his people for his honesty, courage and friendly temperament. Khadijah had six children from him: Al Qasim, Zaynab, Ruqayyah, Umm Kulthum, Fatimah and Abdullah. However, death called on Muhammad once again, and much to their sadness, both of their sons, Al-Qaasim and Abdullah died in infancy and both Khadija and Muhammad bore this and accepted God's Will with patience. Although they could not know what the future would bring, Muhammad would prove to be the great man that Khadija knew him to be, and Khadijah would be his tower of support and comfort. The Prophet once said about his relationship with Khadija "I was nourished by her love".

The condition of the Makkans deeply bothered Muhammad. He always hated the practice of worshiping idols and he never ate the slaughtered meat from their altars. He rejected their superstitious practices, and avoided their wine drinking parties and adulterous practices. He loathed the treatment of the weak and the arrogance of the powerful. He detested hearing people swear by 'Al-Laat' and 'Al-'Uzzah', and their idol festivals disgusted him, forcing him to seek refuge in the caves high above Makkah. There, he silently meditated on the problems of his society and wondered what the solution could be. In the year 605 CE a heavy storm in Makkah damaged the Kaaba extensively and after the pagan

Makkans restored it and came to the point where the black stone had to be placed in its corner, each of the three major tribes claimed the right to do it. To avoid a quarrel they decided that the first person to walk to the Kaaba at that time would lift and place the stone and as they waited it was Muhammad who walked in and they all agreed he was the right person to do it. Muhammad however showed his innate ability to unite the hearts of people by getting the tribal leaders to place a thick cloth on the ground and place the stone on it and then lift the stone to its place with each holding onto a corner of the cloth including Muhammad who held the fourth corner. A truly symbolic moment of solidarity for the Makkans but a more significant event for Muhammad who would soon receive revelation as the last Messenger of God in fulfillment of the prophecy in the earlier scriptures of a Prophet to come after Jesus who would be like unto Moses and from the brethren of Isaac, which is Ishmael the forefather of the Arabs who placed the black meteoritic stone together with his father Abraham in the corner of the first house they built for the worship of the One true God.

He often spent many hours alone, thinking about creation, divinity and morality as they swirled through his mind. One of his favorite places to think was in a remote little cave, high in the mountains above Makkah, called Hira. He would often escape the busy scenes of Makkah, taking food and water with him and go to the cave to ponder, especially during the holy month of Ramadan. There, free from the daily distractions of family and work, he continued to observe nature and the universe as the last rays of the setting sun played upon the summit of mount Hira and Makkah lay immersed beneath in the darkness of night and ignorance. The love for solitude, introspection, meditation and contemplation is a gift from God to His Prophets and Muhammad's heart found happiness in and yearned for the closeness to his Creator and soon enough the world would witness one of its most momentous moments in time when the flicker from the light of purity of the 'fitra' or the innate human self is touched upon by the majestic holiness of God's all-encompassing light to illuminate the universe with the radiance of "light upon light".

Khadija did not become the wife who would stop working to look after the family home. On the contrary, Khadija's wealth enabled the Prophet to spread his message without having to perform the kind of traditional work done by other Prophets in the past. Khadija also provided moral support. Her business continued to provide the financial underpinnings of their marriage and of the Prophets' mission for the length of their life together." This unique marital/commercial relationship in the 7th century underlines the shared responsibility between married partners in jointly being responsible for the financial and moral wellbeing of a family.

The tale of two slaves

On the day of his marriage, Muhammad set free Barakah, the faithful slave he had inherited from his father; and on the same day Khadijah made him a gift of one of her own slaves, a youth of fifteen named Zayd. As to Barakah, they married her to a man of Yathrib to whom she bore a son, after whom she came to be known as Umm Ayman, the mother of Ayman. As to Zayd. several years had now passed since Zayd had been taken by some horsemen, who had carried the boy off and sold him into slavery. Harithah, his father, had searched for him in vain; nor had Zayd seen any travellers from his hometown to send a message home. But the Kaaba drew pilgrims from all parts of Arabia, and one day during the holy season, several months after he had become Muhammad's slave, he saw some men and women of his own tribe and clan in the streets of Makkah and he was able to send a message home. On hearing the good news his father Harithah at once set off for Makkah and going to Muhammad he begged him to allow them to ransom Zayd, for as high a price as he might ask. "Let him choose," said Muhammad, "and if he chooses you, he is yours without ransom; and if he chooses me, I am not the man to set any other above him who chooses me." Then he called Zayd and asked him if he knew the two men. "This is my father," said the youth. "Me thou knowest," said Muhammad, "and thou hast seen my companionship unto thee, so choose thou between me and them." But Zayd's choice was already made and he said at once: "I would not choose any man in preference to thee. Thou art unto me as my father and my mother". Zayd's father was shocked at the response of his son and his choice of slavery over freedom and he resigned himself to his son' wishes. Muhammad immediately announced publicly that Zayd would from that day be his adopted son and no more a slave.

∞

As he approached forty, Muhammad was a well-established family man. He was a highly respected figure in his tribe and in the Makkah community in general. His kindness was always forthcoming and his readiness to help anyone in need was assured. Then the great moment that changed the course of history arrived. He was sleeping in the Cave of Ḥira in the hills surrounding Makkah, when the Archangel Jibreel (Gabriel or Ruh-al Quds, the Holy Spirit) came to him asking him to read. Muhammad was unlettered, and he replied that he could not read. The Angel pressed on his chest until he was almost out of breath, before releasing him and telling him again to read. Again he said he could not. This pattern was repeated twice. After the third time, the angel told him:

"Read in the name of your Lord who created man out of a clot. Read; for your Lord is the most Bountiful One, who has taught the use of the pen, taught man what he did not know." (96:1-5)

He recited these words after the Angel, who thereupon left him; and he said; "It was as though the words were written on my heart." But he feared that this might mean he had become a jinn-inspired poet or a man possessed. On his way back from the mountain, Gabriel appeared to him in the sky which the Prophet described as covering the sky from the horizon upwards and his vision was in every direction he turned his eye to. The voice of the angel exclaimed "You O' Muhammad are the Messenger of God and I am Gabriel the Archangel". As soon as this was all over he ran home to his wife trembling and asked her to cover him up, which she did. When he regained his composure, he told her what he saw. She reassured him that nothing evil could happen to him, because "you are faithful to your trust, kind to your kinsfolk and you always tell the truth."

After this momentous experience Muhammad faced a period of silence and quiet during his nights of contemplation at Hira and he longed for the divine countenance of Archangel Gabriel or the holy spirit once again. This interregnum some reports say lasted a few days and others upto forty days before Gabriel appeared to Muhammad a second time whilst he was walking back from mount Hira, the majestic vision of the Holy Spirit filled the sky above as he beckoned to Muhammad declaring again who he was , the Messenger and Prophet of God. Once again the experience overwhelmed Muhammad and he hurried back home and called out to his wife Khadija, "cover me, cover me", as the holy essence permeated every cell of his human body and soul in a transformative expression of divine Will.

"O you who covers himself [with a garment]. Arise and warn. And your Lord glorify. And your clothing purify. And uncleanliness avoid. And give not a thing so that you may have more. And be patient for the sake of your Lord."
(74:1-7)

The Call to Truth Alone Oh, what divine majesty, what peace of mind, what joy of heart and exaltation to the soul! Muhammad's fears dissolved and his dread was dissipated. He was overjoyed with this fresh evidence of his Lord's blessing and fell down in worship to God and praise of Him. There was no more reason to fear that God was displeased with him, and there was no cause for his dread. God had now taken him under His protection and removed from him every doubt and fear.

and soon other verses followed:

"You enfolded one! Stand in prayer at night, all but a small part of it, half of it, or a little less, or add to it. Recite the Quran calmly and distinctly. We shall bestow on you a weighty message. The night hours are strongest of tread and most upright of speech. During the day you have a long chain of things to attend to. Therefore, remember your Lord's name and devote yourself wholeheartedly to Him. He is the Lord of the east and the west. There is no deity other than Him. Take Him for your guardian." (73:1-9)

Here were the early nascent revelations to call people to truth and to fortify oneself with prayer. On God's instructions Muhammad began his mission in private, speaking to individuals who were close to him and who he could trust entirely. A family unit of Muslims was soon built which included his freed slave, Zayd, Khadija, his wife, and Ali, the Prophet's young cousin whom he had taken into his home to ease his uncle's burden as Makkah went through hard times. Abu Bakr, the Prophet's close friend, also accepted Islam without hesitation. Through the efforts of Abu Bakr other recruits soon followed, including the Prophet's daughters, his uncle Abu Talib`s wife and five more who were fellow tribesman from Quraysh, save one who worked as a shepherd.

A small Muslim community thus came into existence and they formed the vanguard of the early Muslim converts who went on to play major roles in the future course of history. Although the advocacy of the new faith continued in private, the Quraysh elders noticed that something was going on. However, they did not bother to look into this, as they assumed it could represent no danger to their established social order. When the Quraysh men saw the Prophet going about with his followers they used to say with sarcasm, "there goes that lad from Bani Hashim who claims that he receives messages from the Heavens".

Pause for reflection

The pure human reaction and response of the Prophet is brought into focus during this momentous event of spiritual revelation of Majesterium by the Holy Spirit Jibreel (Gabriel). Allah describes the Quran as such a weighty thing that if it was revealed upon a mountain it would have reduced it to dust. Just ponder upon the impact it would have had on the Prophets mind, body and soul when it was impressed upon his heart! The angel Gabriel pressing on his chest three times would have been a physical manifestation of a spiritual reality whereby Muhammad's mind, body and soul is emptied out of its earthly essence to receive the holy words of God. The incidents reported and recorded of this event are so purely human and natural and devoid of myth and fantasy. He did not float down from the mountain with a halo on top of his head but reacted in an utterly human fashion as he began to wonder what was happening to him and feared the worst until he was reassured again by the continuation of revelation from God which exonerated him from being possessed or being crazy.

The very first word of revelation "Iqra" or "read" that Muhammad who was not literate received would go on to define the greatest miracle bestowed upon a prophet of God who over the next 23 years of his life would receive and recite a revelation that would not only be the final divine testament but convey the clear, pure and eternal words of Allah plain and without contradiction or crookedness, error or conjecture nor myth and confusion.

"The initial revelation to Muhammad literally echoes the prophecy in Deuteronomy 18:18, where God says: *'I will raise them up a Prophet from among their bretheren, like unto thee, and will put my words in his mouth; and he shall speak to them all that I shall command them'.* It is also mentioned in the book of Isaiah 29:12, *'And the book is delivered to him that is not learned, saying Read this, I pray thee: and he saith, I am not learned'.*"

∞

Three years later the group of followers had reached around twenty and the revelations that came in that period primarily addressed the oneness of God, the stories of the early Prophets and their people, the hereafter and the foundations of belief and comprised mainly of the shorter chapters of the Quran with 10 to 20 verses in each. The small group of disciples memorized every word that was revealed and that would be revealed over the next twenty years and would go on to become legendary and the backbone of the early community of believers. The Prophet (ﷺ) was now instructed to make his message public and then Angel Jibreel brought down the revelation:

"And warn, [O Muhammad], your closest kindred. And lower Thy wing over the Faithful who follow Thee. And if they disobey thee, then say: 'I verily am clear of your doings'
And put thy trust in the Mighty, the Merciful."
(Quran 26: 214-220).

As he was to prove throughout his career, he never shrank from the fulfilment of a duty. Therefore, he addressed his immediate Hashim clan, and invited them for a meal. He spoke in a voice that exuded the sanctity of the divine call and the promise of salvation and as he addressed them he made certain to meet the eye of each one and turned his full body and face when he did so:
"O sons of 'Abdal-Muttalib, I know of no Arab who has come to his people with a nobler message than mine. I bring you the best of this world and the next. God has commanded me to call you unto Him. Which of you, then, will help me in this, and be my brother and my successor among you?
The gathering fell silent possibly shocked and dumbfounded by the sincerity and conviction of his words and only the thirteen-year-old boy Ali rose up to answer by stating that he would be the Prophet's helper. Surely even they recognized that there was something radical and indeed anti-traditional at work. What Muhammad had stated represented a "revolution" vis-a-vis their own cultural norms, according to

39

which they were expected to follow in the "ways of the forefathers." He compassionately appealed to them to accept Islam, as this would save them from the social ills that plagued their materialistic way of life and give them a future life to look forward to. Abu Lahab who was also an uncle of the Prophet stood up. "I swear by Allah that this is a terrible thing. You must stop him before the others do", he demanded. However, Abu Talib ignored Abu Lahab and again replied,

"I swear by Allah to protect Muhammad as long as I live."

Muhammad also addressed all the clans of the Quraysh, standing on Al-Safā hill, near the Kaaba, he implored them to accept the oneness of God and turn away from idolatry and that he was the Messenger of God and that everyone would be accountable for their deeds in the life to come after death which would make them enter heaven or face punishment in hell.

As he listened to the Messenger of God in amazement, Abu Lahab angrily responded. "Perish you all the day! This is what you called us here for?" It was a very difficult situation for the Messenger of God when some of his own family members would not accept his Call to Salvation. He had tried to rescue them with love and faithfulness, from their own destruction. His own uncle responded with hatred, rejection and threats. Fortunately, Abu Talib had fostered great love and affection for his nephew. He had raised Muhammad in his own home and had loved him like one of his own children. He was proud of his nephew's truthfulness, honesty and fine manners, and he was determined to protect and defend him.

As the Messenger of God continued to call people to Islam, anger and turmoil grew throughout Makkah. Now, the Quraysh recognized that Islam was a direct threat to their oppressive way of life, their wealth and their powerful status in the area. During this time Muhammad continued to preach his call, and he gradually gained more followers in Makkah. The aristocracy of Makkah kept a watchful and concerned eye on the growing movement. Recognizing the challenge not just to their religion but indeed to their social customs, they went to Abu Talib,- Ali's father and Muhammad's uncle—and stated: "By God, we cannot endure that our fathers should be reviled, our customs mocked and our gods insulted. Until you rid us of him we will fight the both of you until one side perishes"

Abu Talib, who had not at this point adopted the faith of Muhammad, went to his nephew and spoke to him out of his concern: "O son of my brother, spare me, and spare thyself. Lay not upon me a burden greater than I can bear." Muhammad's response was legendary:

"I swear by God, if they put the sun in my right hand and the moon in my left on condition that I abandon this course before He has made it victorious, or I have perished therein, I would not abandon it"

Abu Talib, moved by the sincerity of his nephew, rose up with tears in his eyes and pledged his support. As an elder of the tribe, Abu Talib could provide some moral support and protection for his beleaguered nephew, but even he could not always protect the Prophet.

Islam called people to worship Allah alone; therefore, they worried that no one would come to the Kaaba to make pilgrimage to the idols anymore. Islam called to equal treatment of all people, but they wanted to remain above all people. In light of these initial threats, they became determined to smother the Message before it could spread. Yet, they had a great problem on their hands-the bearer of this Message was an upright member of the community.

Everyone agreed that Muhammad was an honest, truthful man, with the best manners and human values. How could they discredit him while he was of such a virtuous character? Finally, they decided to go to Abu Talib and demand that he stop his nephew or they hand him over to them and they would give him a replacement for Muhammad! Abu Talib rejected outright their requests and demands and refused to give up his nephew to them.

They would follow at the heels of Muhammad shouting, "O men, do not listen to him for he is a liar. As the pilgrimage season drew closer, the Quraysh became more and more anxious. They were concerned that Muhammad would preach to the pilgrims who came to pay tribute to the idols, and they were determined to prevent the pilgrims from accepting his Call. Together, they all tried to think of how they could discredit Muhammad so that no one would accept his Message. Some suggested that they call him a fortune teller; some suggested that they say he was a mad man. Some insisted he be called a poet because the

Revelations he recited, rhymed, and others insisted that he be called a magician. However, they all recognized Muhammad's pure character and deep down they all knew that he was none of these things.

Yet, with their livelihood at stake, they were determined to defame the Messenger. They decided that they should say that he practiced magic like the people of the past. With that resolved, they all set out to disrupt Muhammad while he tried to tell the pilgrims about Islam.

Abu Lahab, the sworn enemy of Islam, would say; "He is an apostate."

Yet, this did not deter Muhammad. No matter what they said about him, he continued to preach to people about Islam. So the disbelievers continued in their efforts to prevent him in his Mission.

They laughed at the converts and made fun of them and they called the Messenger a magician and warned everyone to stay away from his magic and lies. Yet, Muhammad went on with his mission. Their evil eyes burned with hatred for him and they would trip him and laugh when he fell. Yet, Muhammad went on with his mission. Seething with hatred, they attacked the Message he brought, calling the Revelations tales from the past that someone had told him. Yet, the Messenger continued to strive in spreading Islam. The matter seemed hopeless. It seemed like nothing could stop Muhammad from calling people to Islam.

Then, the disbelievers devised a new plan. They invited Muhammad (ﷺ) to worship their god for one year, with the promise that the following year, they would worship his one God Allah. Immediately, God responded and revealed the verses of Surah Al-Kaafiroon (The disbelievers)

"Say, "O disbelievers, I do not worship what you worship, nor will you worship what I worship, Nor will I be a worshipper of what you worship, Nor will you be a worshipper of what I worship, for you is your religion and for me is mine." (109:1-6)

They asked, "Why don't you change Mount Safa and Mount Marwah into gold? Why don't you cause the book of which you speak so much to fall down from heaven already written? Why don't you cause Gabriel to appear to all of us and speak to us as he spoke to you? Why don't you resurrect the dead and remove these mountains which bound and enclose the city of Makkah? Why don't you cause a water fountain to spring whose water is sweeter than that of Zamzam?" Whether serious or in ridicule, all these questions and demands were answered once and for all by revelation. God commanded Muhammad,

"Say: `I have no power whatever to bring advantage or avoid disadvantage. What God wills, that will happen. If it were given me to tell the future I would have used such knowledge to my own advantage. But I am only a man sent to warn you, and a messenger to convey a divine message that you may believe." (Quran 7:188)

A concerted effort was made by the Quraysh to prevent anyone they could from listening to Muhammad. This was true both within and outside Makkah, as people from across the Arabian Peninsula who frequented Makkah for worship and trade began to come in contact with him and the message of Islam. An elite Makkan and highly influential businessman initiated a smear campaign against Muhammad at a council of tribal leaders. In it, he devised a plan to accuse Muhammad of being a magician as a way to warn the public against the mesmerizing effect his words had on those who heard him recite the Quran.

The zeal and thoroughness with which the pagan Makkans carried out their false propaganda and misinformation about the Prophet (ﷺ) was probably the first recorded instance of "Islamophobia" on a public scale or the equivalent of present day social media smear campaigns. Despite all the falsehood and hate, the message of the Quran when it entered the hearts of people, whatever their predisposition, it moved them towards declaring the `Shahadah` or the declaration of the oneness of God and Muhammad as His Messenger. This was the case with Abu Dharr who was a highwayman and Tufayl who was an acclaimed poet, both of them despite being warned of the Prophet's `sorcery` they approached the Prophet and on hearing a few verses being recited from the Quran , they had no hesitation in becoming Muslims. Tufayl in fact was so zealous to convert his entire tribe and when they refused he returned disappointed to Makkah and asked the Prophet to curse all of them to which the Prophet of God said, ``I shall pray for their guidance and return to them and deal gently and kindly with them.``

Pause for reflection

All that Muhammad wanted from the Quraysh is that he be allowed to preach the word of God, he did not want to force it on anyone nor did he desire fame and position. The Quraysh realized that the combination of the excellent character of the Prophet and the eloquence, reason and simplicity of the Quranic message would soon sway everyone in Makkah and those visiting Makkah to become Muslims. This would have destroyed the very fabric of their pagan rituals and superstitions and their status as the master tribe in Arabia. More importantly it would have destroyed their commercial base and the wealth they accrued using the Kaaba as the hub of pagan worship and pilgrimage in Arabia. In 7th Century, Arabia the Arabs had developed poetry into an art form and took great pride in their ability to compose and recite it. However in the verses of the Quran they heard something greater than poetry, a message that challenged their way of life and promised salvation to those who embraced the new faith.

The eloquence and sublime beauty of the Quranic verses were so empowering and appealing to the rational mind and the human heart, that the chieftains of the pagans used to secretly make their way to the Kaaba at the dead of night to listen to the Prophet recite the Quran. Scurrying back home before the light of dawn so that no one spots them they used to bump in to each other and guiltily look down and head home without saying a word. This happened over three consecutive days before they decided and swore never to do it again lest they be discovered and the news spread throughout Makkah and created a mass interest in Islam. It was the sheer arrogance and pride in their ways and stubborn refusal to change or listen to a higher call that was their ruin.

As the Quran itself described their condition "deaf, dumb and blind they will never return to the path of righteousness..."

Over the 23 year period the Quran was revealed in, it not only provided a roadmap and guidance for the spiritual and material life in this world for all of humanity, but produced a sublime yet convincing thematic message that incorporated a vision, affirmation, motivation and inspiration for the Prophet to strengthen his heart and through that medium fortify and nurture the hearts of all of humanity who believed in its message.

Concept of `Shahada` or `Declaration of faith` in Islam

The phrase `There is no God but Allah and Muhammad is the Messenger of God` is the formal statement uttered by anyone who wishes to embrace Islam and is probably the single most oft repeated statement uttered by millions of Muslims every day in their daily liturgies. This statement is made up of two parts, the Unity of God and the Mercy of God. The first part declares the absolute nature of the unity of God, that He is one without partner and is infinite and there is nothing like unto Him. The second part is His Mercy which manifests in Him sending down His guidance to mankind through His final Messenger. The first part is absolute, static and ontological whereas the second part is dynamic and salvational. God states in the Quran that Muhammad was sent as a mercy to the entire universe so that humanity will not be lost and find the path that leads to eternal life in paradise. Hence the two components of the *'attestation of faith'* are at once distinct and complimentary: the first acknowledges the essential truth of the Message of all previous prophecies (the fact that your Lord God is One), while the second accepts the message of the last Prophet, Muhammad as laid out in the creed of Islam. The defining importance of the first part of the 'shahadah' is captured in chapter 112 of the Quran titled 'Ihklas' or purity of faith.

"Say He is God, the One and Only. God the Eternal, the Absolute. He begets not nor is He begotten. And there is none like unto Him."

A holistic concept of the first part of the Tawhid can be described through its intrinsic elements of Rububiyyah (His Lordship); Uluhiyyah (Him being the center of all devotion); Asma wal Sifat (His attributes and Names as given by Him). Tawhid-ul-Rububiyyah is to believe in Allah's Omnipotence; He Alone is the Originator of creation, maintenance, life, death, etc. As for Tawhid-ul-Uluhiyyah, it is the sincerity of devotional acts e.g. Salah (Prayer), Sawm (Fast), Zakah (obligatory charity), pilgrimage etc. Tawhid-ul-Asma' wal-Sifat is to talk of Allah's Names and Attributes in the same manner He and His Prophet (ﷺ) did; giving Him the same Names and Attributes He calls Himself therewith free from comparison, likening Allah's Attributes to those of His Creation, distortion of the meaning or denial of Allah's Attributes (like the Omniscient and Omnipotent).

Concept of `Shahada`` or declaration of faith

True and sincere Tawhid thus is an integral combination of all its elements.

Islam, thus is a strictly monotheistic religion. Its central and unifying principle, upon which the combined elements off its creed and ritual practices are founded is known as *Tawhid, which means the 'uniqueness or singularity of God'*. Hence by declaring the tawhid, one embraces a creed (aqidah), principles (usul), rituals (ibadat), obligations (wajibat), prohibitions (muharramat) and a moral code (akhlaq).

This oneness or unity of God is the central thrust and theme of all the Abrahamic faiths and of the prophets sent by God to any nation anywhere on earth.

The Great Commandment is a name used in the New Testament to describe the first of two commandments cited by Jesus in Matthew 22:35–40, Mark 12:28–34, and Luke 10:27a. In Mark, when asked "which is the great commandment in the law?", the Greek New Testament reports that Jesus answered, "Hear, O Israel! The Lord Our God, The Lord is One; Thou shalt love thy Lord, thy God with all thy heart, and with all thy soul, and with all thy mind".

In the Old Testament, Deuteronomy 6 states:

"Hear, O Israel: $_3$ The LORD our God, the LORD is one!, "You shall love the LORD your God with all your heart, $_,$ with all your soul, and with all your strength. "And $_,$ these words which I command you today shall be in your heart. "You shall teach them diligently to your children, and shall talk of them when you sit in your house, when you walk by the way, when you lie down, and when you rise up. $_,$ "You shall bind them as a sign on your hand, and they shall be as frontlets between your eyes., "You shall write them on the doorposts of your house and on your gates``.

As if through divine scriptural obedience, the Muslims take great pride and a sense of aesthetic and spiritual fulfillment in adorning their homes with Quranic calligraphy that echo the oneness of God, His divine attributes and the eternal words of scripture.

Three

Rejection, Tribulation and Grief

During the fourth year of the call (614 CE), the disbelievers realized that all their attempts to stamp out Islam had failed. Thus, they decided to take more serious steps once and for all, to rid themselves of Islam's threat. They decided to use any means necessary to torture and persecute the followers of Islam. The Quraysh knew that this new approach would be easy to execute as many of the converts were poor, weak slaves, who had readily accepted the Islamic principles of justice and equality. However, the disbelievers were not sure this approach would work for Muhammad who was still under the protection of his uncle, Abu Talib. Still, they were determined to try everything possible to rid themselves of the Muslims, Muhammad and Islam.

Eventually, Abu Lahab became more severe in his attacks towards his nephew. He flung rocks at him, and was so cruel that he even mocked the Messenger of Allah when his second son, Al-Qasim died. Once when the Messenger was in prostration in front of the Kaaba, Abu Lahab threw on him the entrails of a slaughtered camel and the youngest daughter of the Prophet, Fathima had to come rushing out to help him up as the new converts were afraid to help for fear of torture.

Yet, the most horrific forms of torture were carried out to the poor, weak converts. Bilal, the black slave from Abyssinia who had no lineage or kith or kin in Makkah was severely beaten by his master, dragged through the streets of Makkah, starved, and left in the scorching desert sun with boulders upon his chest, pinning him to the ground. Yet, he maintained his belief in the Oneness of Allah and never asked for mercy.

He would only say, Allah is One" after witnessing one such torture session, Abu Bakr purchased Bilal and freed him. This was probably the first instance in history of an action in direct support of "Black lives matter". Bilal went on to become the first caller to prayer in the Prophet's mosque as he had a powerful melodious voice and used to always sit close to the Prophet later after migrating to Madinah. Another companion of the Prophet, Amaar who was from a slave family with his mother and father endured unspeakable torture at the hands of the Quraysh.

They were often dressed in armor and made to lie on the blistering desert sand and were severely beaten. Sometimes, they even put Amaar, who was just fifteen years of age at that time on hot, burning embers. Still, the Messenger always comforted them.

"Be patient,"he said; 'Verily you will find your abode in Paradise." Eventually, Yasir, Amaar's father died from his injuries and the cruel Abu Jahl himself stabbed Amaar's mother, Sumayyah, to death whilst she was lying on the hot sand with her hands and feet tied to stakes. Thus, making the first martyr in Islam to be a woman. Ammar escaped death by declaring that he believed in the idols and came rushing to the Prophet soon after and said that he had sinned but he really did not mean what he said and that he was a Muslim. Muhammad assured and comforted him and told him if they ask you again tell them the same. God then revealed the following verses:

"Who so is forced to disbelieve after believing, while his heart is convinced of the Faith, he shall be forgiven." (16:106)

Unfortunately and sadly non-Muslim polemics use this instance in history to claim that Islam allows lying in general to hide the truth. It is evident to any honest person that this incident is purely in context to a life threatening situation and persecution and in no way or manner implies that Muslims are given the permission to lie in a general sense. However, many of the converts who were not slaves were tortured by their own family members. Uthmaan bin 'Affaan's (who became the third rightly guided caliph) uncle used to wrap him in palm fiber and light a fire under him. In spite of the constant persecution they endured, the Muslim converts remained steadfast. Although the Messenger of Allah openly displayed his belief and devotion, he thought it best to meet the converts secretly to avoid further abuse from the Quraysh.

Therefore, in the fifth year of his mission, Muhammad started to use the house of Al-Arqam, a young convert, as a secret meeting place. Daar Al-Arqam, as it was called, offered the converts safety and security because it was located high on the mountain of As Safaa.

There, Muhammad instructed the new converts in the Quran, and in Islamic rituals and wisdom to a group of around fifty Muslims largely made up of the slaves, the poor and the oppressed all inspired by a simple message of the one true God of mercy, compassion, love and justice.

As for Muhammad himself, the abuse he suffered from the idolaters of Quraysh was brutal. They spared no opportunity to demonize him, divorced his daughters, and exiled and starved his entire clan for three years. As for physical assault, they strangled him from behind when he prayed in public, Abu Jahl ordered camel intestines to be dumped over him while he prostrated, Utayba bin. Abi Lahab spat at him, and others beat him unconscious.

This overall situation continued to deteriorate. The hardliners among the Quraysh had been able to wrestle the initiative and impose biting sanctions on the Muslim community, and they wanted to expand this. The resort to sanctions was also prompted by the conversion of Umar (who would become the second caliph of the Islamic state) to the new faith. Umar was a tower of strength to the Quraysh and feared and respected by all and his acceptance of Islam badly eroded the position of the Quraysh and boosted the morale of the faithful. They managed to carry the entire Quraysh with them in imposing a total economic and social boycott against the Hashemite clan. They wrote down terms that specified that no one in the Quraysh would have any commercial dealings with any Hashemite, not even selling them food, and that no marriage with them would be agreed upon until they handed Muhammad to the Quraysh. The Hāshimites would not agree to such humiliation, and both the Muslims and the unbelievers among them endured the boycott with patience. Not everybody in the Quraysh was happy with the boycott, but they had to go ahead with it so as not to breach the traditions of their tribal society. Hence, the boycott lasted three years, until five people from different clans of the Quraysh successfully plotted its abrogation but not before the boycott had taken its toll and placed undue suffering on the early Muslims through physical and social deprivation.

For ten long years since Muhammad received revelation, Khadija his wife had willingly and lovingly supported the Prophet in his mission. Her wealth which she had made through her international trade caravans had all but depleted in the cause of spreading the message of God. Yet she stood steadfast in her faith and commitment to the mission of her husband. She used to cook almost every day as the Prophet invited people to eat at his house and took the opportunity to invite them to the message of God yet very few changed their ways. The negative propaganda of the likes of Abu Jahal, Abu Lahab and Walid Al Mughira who were the "high priests" of pagan ways had made the Makkans deaf, dumb and blind to the message of God and many never returned to the truth before their death. A very close parallel in history to these events was when Jesus (peace be upon him) together with his handful of disciples entered Jerusalem and called upon the Saducees, Pharisees and the Jews to turn away from their evil ways of oppression in the temple and accept his messianic message and the corrupt priests collaborated with the Roman authorities to have Jesus crucified-in their belief-for blasphemy.

Pause for reflection

Pained by the visible suffering of his followers and unable to protect them from harm, Muhammad was at the same time grieved at not being able to convince the community at large—among whom were many of his own clan members. Despite this, his strategy was a deliberate one: to continue to invite people, choosing to appeal to their sense of morality and reason over the potentially far more destructive use of force. When seen through the lens of a tribal society, any one of the provocations of Quraysh would have been sufficient cause for war between the tribes involved. Yet, we see unprecedented individual and collective self-control, conviction, and perseverance that can only be realized with great spiritual and moral foresight; this foresight was the foundation of a leadership strategy for reform that Muhammad was carefully building at this stage in Makkah. This came at a time in which he and his followers had not been given divine permission to take up arms—even as a means of defense. As the Muslims were a minority living in a city that was largely hostile toward them, war would have destroyed the few who had joined the ranks of the Muslims, as well as any chance of establishing this fledgling community.

"How the Prophet Muhammad rose above enmity and insult"-Mohammed El Shinawy and Omer Suleiman, Yaqeen Research Institute.-2017

∞

Makkah and Madinah, the Hejaz, where Muhammad grew up and had his prophetic career, was surrounded by two empires, the Eastern Roman (Byzantine) and the Persian (Sassanid Empire).

In the year 603 CE, when Muhammad would have been probably in his thirties, the two went to war. It was a brutal war that lasted for twenty-six years and was the 7th century equivalent of a "world war." It took place in central Asia, in the Balkans, in the Near East, and Syria Palestine and Egypt were swept up in it as well. The Persians, for much of that period, won victory after victory against the Eastern Romans, whose capital was in Constantinople but who had much of what we now call the Middle East under their rule. They had Syria, Palestine, Transjordan, Egypt, Tunisia, but much of that was taken away from them by the Persians.

All that was happening while the Quran was being recited by the Prophet to his contemporaries. And Surah al-Rūm, the chapter of Rome, is explicit in mentioning these events:

"The Roman Empire has been defeated in a land close by; but they (even) after (this) defeat of theirs will soon be victorious within a few years.

With Allah is the Decision in the Past and in the Future: on that Day shall the Believers rejoice With the help of Allah.

He helps whom He will and He is Exalted in Might Most Merciful.

(It is) the promise of Allah. Never does Allah depart from His promise: but most men understand not." (30:2-6)

This Quranic prophecy was revealed around 616 CE when the Muslims were being subjected to their worst persecution by the pagan Makkans and it was not until the year 624 CE that the Roman Byzantines under the leadership of Heraclius were victorious over the Persians. Remarkably, it was in the same year that the Muslims were victorious over the pagans in their first battle at Badr after their migration to Madinah. This prophecy in the Quran also demonstrates the divine authorship of the Quran as who could promise that the Romans would be victorious after their humiliating defeat earlier except through the Wisdom of the All-knowing and Almighty God. These twin victories of the Romans and the Muslims over the pagan beliefs of the Persians and Makkans was an occasion for the believers (both Muslims and Christians) to rejoice as it was a victory of the forces of light over darkness. The Muslims considered the Christian Romans as believers and followers of Jesus and hence as true people of the book (the message of Islam was in its nascent stages and had probably not reached the Romans fully) whereas the Jews in Arabia who rejected Jesus as a prophet of God were looked upon as betraying the scriptures that were given to them by Moses.

The Jews in Madinah at that time were deeply saddened and dismayed at the defeat of the Persians as they viewed the Romans being responsible for destroying their temples and synagogues and causing them to exile out of their Jewish homeland in Palestine. This dichotomous viewpoint probably played a major role in the animus shown by the Jews to the Muslims who openly rejoiced at the victory of the Romans. The pagan Arabs for their part were equally dismayed by the defeat of the Persians whom they saw as co-religionists as the Persian beliefs in Magianism and Zoroastrianism believed in more than a single God and worshipped fire in their rituals.

Why is the Quran full of these stories about the past, both the Arabian past and the biblical past? It's because these are stories that are meaningful to the Prophet's audience and the Quran is trying to make a point by using these figures in a symbolic way.

During the preparation for the battle of the Trench by the Muslims against the confederate army of the Makkan pagans, Prophet Muhammad (ﷺ) prophesised that both the empires of Persia and Byzantine shall come under Muslim rule and so it did soon after his death. Hence it was God's plan that the two mighty empires that straddled the Muslims in the Arabian Peninsula and clashed so violently over 23 years would become part of the Islamic empire and the crown jewel of the Byzantine empire, Constantinople would also come under Muslim rule in the 15th century CE.

The Persian invasion of Roman territory from 603 forward threatened the independence of western Arabia where Muhammad was based. The Sassanian conquest of Jerusalem in 614 struck contemporaries as apocalyptic and the eventual fulfilment of the Quranic prophecy that the Romans will triumph within a few years and the believers will rejoice, though popularly interpreted as rejoicing over the Roman victory, is more alluding to the rejoicing over the Muslim victory at Badr which happened at the exact same time, a fantastic prophecy which only God could have foretold. In fact a reliable narration states that AbuBakr, who would be the first Caliph of Islam, took a wager with a non-muslim Arab that within 2-3 years the Persians would be defeated, based on this Quranic prophecy and when Muhammad heard of this, he said make it longer around 9 years, and that is what transpired. The Quran repeatedly instructs Believers to "repel evil with good", pardon their persecutors, and wish peace on those who harassed them. These verses have as their greater context the outbreak of struggles among Christians, Jews, Zoroastrians, and a remnant of pagans who were partisans in the clash of empires raging around them. Muhammad in these years resembles much more the Jesus of the Sermon on the Mount than is usually admitted.

The Prophet in those years of pagan attacks did not abandon his options for peace but moved toward a doctrine of just war similar to that of Cicero late antique Christian thinkers. He repeatedly sued for peace with a bellicose Makkah but when that failed, he organized Madinah for self-defence in the face of a determined pagan foe. The Quran insists that aggressive warfare is wrong and that if the enemy seeks an armistice, Muslims are bound to accept the entreaty. The disallowing of aggressive war and search for a resolution even in the midst of violent conflict justifies the title "prophet of peace", even if Muhammad was occasionally forced into a defensive campaign. The Quran contains a doctrine of just war but not of holy war and does not use the word Jihad with the latter connotation. It views war as an unfortunate necessity when innocents and the freedom of conscience are threatened. It strictly forbids vigilantism and equates pre-meditated killing of non-combatants with genocide, paraphrasing in this regard Jewish commentaries on the Bible in the Jerusalem Talmud.

Pause for reflection

The Quran read judiciously alongside later histories, suggests that during Muhammad's lifetime, Islam spread peacefully in the major cities of western Arabia. The soft power of the Quran's spiritual message has typically been underestimated in most treatments of this period. The image of Muhammad and very early Islam that emerges from a careful reading of the Quran on peace related themes contradicts not only widely held Western views but even much of the later Muslim histographical tradition. This finding should come as no surprise. Life in medieval feudal societies did not encourage pacific theologies, and Muslims in later empires lost touch with the realities of the early century. What if we read Jesus's life and thought only through the lens of Pope Urban II, who launched the sanguinary Crusades in the Holy Land with the cry, "God has Willed it!".

Even today many scholars of early Islam seem unduly deferential to later medieval interpreters. Others radically reject all information in those sources, treating Muslim histories differently from Byzantine or Carolingian chronicles , once again condemning non- Europeans to being a people without a history. The Quran tells us about that history if we will listen to it, and it tells us what is plausible in the later biographies of the Prophet.

(Excerpt from "Muhammad-prophet of peace amid the clash of Empires " by Juan Cole 2018)

"Believers, when you fight in the way of God, be discerning, Do not say to one who greets you with "Peace"," You are not a Believer"! You aspire to the goods of this world, but with God are many riches. You were like them in the past, but God conferred His favour on you. So scrutinize carefully, God is aware of all you do" - (Quran: 4:94).

"Fight in the path of God those who enter into combat against you, but do not commit aggression. God does not love aggressors"- (Quran 2:190)

"If they incline towards peace, you must incline towards it, Trust in God - He is all hearing and omniscient"- (Quran 8:61)

∞

In 615 CE, two years after having gone public, Muhammad (ﷺ) advised many of his followers to immigrate to Abyssinia, a country ruled by a just king where he believed they may have a safe haven. A total of eighty-three men and nineteen women immigrated to Abyssinia, in two groups at separate times where they were given asylum by Negus, its king. These represented about half the Muslim community in Makkah at the time. The Quraysh pursued the immigrants all the way to Abyssinia and approached the Christian King Negus to hand them over as they were rebels and were the cause of an insurrection. The king asked the Muslims what they had to say and Jafar, the cousin of the Prophet spoke out one of the most eloquent pieces of oration in Islamic history.

"O King! we were plunged in the depth of ignorance and barbarism; we adored idols, we lived unchastely, we ate the dead bodies of animals, and we spoke abominations, we disregarded every feeling of humanity, and the duties of hospitality and neighbourhood were neglected; we knew no law but that of the strong, when Allah raised among us a man, of whose birth, truthfulness, honesty, and purity we were aware; and he called to the Oneness of Allah ,and taught us not to associate anything with Him. "He forbade us the worship of idols; and he enjoined us to speak the truth, to be faithful to our trusts, to be merciful and to regard the rights of the neighbors and kith and kin; he forbade us to speak evil of women, or to eat the substance of orphans; he ordered us to flee from the vices, and to abstain from evil; to offer prayers, to render alms, and to observe fast. "We have believed in him, we have accepted his teachings and his injunctions to worship Allah, and not to associate anything with Him, and we have allowed what He has allowed, and prohibited what He has prohibited.

"For this reason, our people have risen against us, have persecuted us in order to make us forsake the worship of Allah and return to the worship of idols and other abominations. They have tortured and injured us, until finding no safety we sought refuge in your land and we hope you will protect us from this oppression."

King Negus was visibly moved and he asked the Muslims whether they could recite some of the revelation that your Prophet claims to have received, to which Jaafar responded by reciting the verses from the chapter Mary and about the birth of Jesus and the accusations of the people about her chastity.

"Then she pointed to him. They said, "How shall we speak to one who is yet a child in the cradle?" He said, "Truly I am a servant of God. He has given me the Book and made me a prophet.

He has made me blessed wheresoever I may be, and has enjoined upon me prayer and almsgiving so long as I live, and [has made me] dutiful toward my mother. And He has not made me domineering, wretched. Peace be upon me the day I was born, the day I die, and the day I am raised alive!" (19:29-33)

The King was moved to tears and declared that the same spirit that descended upon Jesus has visited your Prophet and the difference between us is as thin as this, and he drew a line on the floor with his staff. He welcomed the Muslims with open arms saying; "Blessed be you and blessed be your Master" and refused to hand over to the Quraysh any of them. The Negus of Abyssinia whose name was Ashaama formally embraced Islam when he received a letter in 628CE from the Prophet which in addition to inviting the Negus to Islam requested him to arrange for the return of the Muslim migrants and through proxy marry Umm Habibah whose husband had died in Abyssinia, to the Prophet.

These Muslims had lived in Abyssinia for over twelve years before returning to Madinah after the mass migration to Madinah. King Negus died during the lifetime of the Prophet and they exchanged many messages and gifts and the Prophet prayed the funeral prayer for Muslims for Negus in his mosque in Madinah.

Ibn Saad narrates that in the Rajab of the 5th year of Prophet Hood, the small group of Companions totalling seventy had emigrated to Abyssinia. Then, when in the Ramadan of the same year the news spread that the Prophet had recited Surah An-Najm (chapter 56) publicly in the assembly of the Quraysh around the Kaaba and the whole assembly, including the believers as well as the disbelievers, had fallen down in prostration with him. When the emigrants to Abyssinia heard this news they formed the impression that the disbelievers of Makkah had become Muslims. Thereupon, some of them returned to Makkah in the same year, only to learn that the news was wrong and the conflict between Islam and disbelief was raging as furiously as before. Other reliable reports indicate that they returned due to the conversion of Umar who was a tower of strength in the Makkan community and also due to the fact that the Negus, ruler of Abyssinia was facing a civil conflict. Consequently, the second emigration to Abyssinia took place, in which many more people left Makkah. Interestingly, this incident surrounding the return of the immigrants and their subsequent return back to Abyssinia with a larger number of Muslims, followed the controversy of the "Satanic verses" (see inset below) that were falsely attributed to Muhammad.

Pause for reflection

In the course of bringing spiritual salvation to his people and to all mankind, Muhammad and his followers suffered great harm. They were subjected to many travails of body and spirit, to emigration, to alienation from peers and relatives, and they bore these sacrifices with gallantry and patience. It was as if the more his people harmed Muhammad, the stronger became his love for them and the greater his desire and care to bring about their salvation. Resurrection and the day of judgment were the supreme ideas to which they were to give their attention if they were to be saved from their idolatry and evil deeds. Consequently, in the first years of Muhammad's prophethood, revelation constantly repeated divine threats and warnings that the Makkans might open their eyes and recognize the veracity of resurrection and the Day of Judgment. It was this constant assault by revelation which, in final analysis, had inflamed the terrible war between Muhammad and Makkah whose rage did not subside until God had given victory to Islam, His religion, over the religions of man. Scholars have studied the strategic prophetic wisdom behind the Abyssinian migration and are of the opinion that the Prophet was making a longer term contingent plan of keeping a core group of Muslims secure from any murderous intent of the pagans so that they could become the nucleus of a community of believers in the future if the pagans did succeed in eliminating the Muslims in Makkah.

The case of the Satanic verses

It must be stated at the outset that the phrase 'satanic verses' does not appear anywhere in the normative Islamic literature and is a phrase coined first by Sir William Muir a Scottish, non-Muslim orientalist who researched Islamic history. In summary, the story basically states that when the Prophet was leading the prayer one time near the Kaaba, he was reciting chapter 53:19-20 and then immediately after he recited those verses, he said *"those are the high-flying cranes and indeed their intercession is to be hoped for"*, referring to the idols that were around the Kaaba and venerated as the daughters of God. The fact remains that these 'rogue' verses were never part of the written or memorized Quran and only existed in the figment of the imagination of those who fabricated it. It is alleged that the Quraysh tribe were so thrilled that the Prophet spoke so positively about their Gods that they also prostrated with the Muslims after he recited those verses. Critics of Islam are being disingenuous with their use of the Satanic Verses story as they use A PARTICULAR version from WEAK narrations whilst overlooking the AUTHENTIC version (which has no mention of 'Satanic Verses' and also overlooking the other weak versions which contradict the version they use to criticise Islam. This is not intellectually honest. All the six books of accepted canonized hadith and the most original writings on the life of the Prophet by Ibn Ishaq and Ibn Hisham do not have any reference to this story.

However, it is found in some Islamic texts that narrated and recoded every 'hadith' more as a source of reference for academic purposes rather than for correct and authentic narrations. In fact Sahih Bukhari, which is the most authentic book of hadith collection narrates the true version of the incident as reported by Ibn Abbas who was a companion and cousin of the Prophet, that the reason for the Quraysh pagans prostrating was due to the captivating eloquence of the verses of surah 'Najm' and the command by God at the end of the chapter to prostrate to Him, which so overwhelmed both believers and non-believers alike as it appealed to their human frailty and innate goodness. *(fitra)*.

Antagonists of Islam and the Prophet use this story to falsely give credence to their absurd theory that the Quranic source could have been satanically inspired. One of the weak apocryphal versions of the story narrates that the Satan's voice interjected the revelation that was streaming through to the Prophet through the archangel Gabriel and caused the Prophet to utter these verses hence opening the possibility that the Quran revelation could have been influenced by the promptings of the Satan. However, God himself reveals in chapter 22 verse 52 as follows:

"And we did not send a Messenger or a Prophet before you but when he recited, Satan threw in his recitation. But Allah abolishes that which Satan throws, then Allah will establish His verses. And Allah is All Knower, All wise." - (22:52)

Here is a clear unequivocal statement in the Quran that the machinations of the Satan cannot overcome or distort prophetic revelation and that truth will prevail. This promise and guarantee by God only applies to the true Prophets and messengers of God and not to the many false prophets and apostles who appeared soon after the death of His true Prophets. There are defining moments in religious history where despite warnings by the Prophets whilst they were alive, false apostles have claimed to have heard the presumed voice of God (i.e. promptings of the Satan) which made them distort and corrupt the entire scripture and faith of God and launch their own version of satanically inspired religious writings. These satanic promptings are sometimes heard only by the false apostle and at times by those accompanying them as disciples or followers. The Satan is never consistent and exposes and betrays himself to the God fearing and righteous through his convoluted and paganist rituals and beliefs that compromise the Oneness of God and the principles of monotheism.

The story of the 'satanic verses' reported by more than one biographer, pointed to by more than one exegete of the Quran, and singled out and repeated by a number of western Orientalists is a story whose incoherence is evident upon the least scrutiny. It contradicts the infallibility of every prophet in conveying the message of his Lord. All the more wonder, therefore, that some Muslim scholars have accepted it as true. Ibn Ishaq, for his part, did not hesitate at all to declare it a fabrication by the Zindiqs [Non-Muslims concealing their unbelief, falsely pretending that they are members of the ummah; mostly Zoroastrians and Manicheans]. The story of the satanic verses, therefore, is absolutely devoid of foundation. It is utterly unrelated to the return of the Muslims from Abyssinia as proposed by Sir Muir, the immigrants returned after the conversion of `Umar, the strengthening of Islam with the same tribal solidarity with which he used to fight Islam hitherto, and the compulsion of Quraysh to enter into an armistice with the Muslims. Moreover, the Muslims' return from Abyssinia was partly due to the revolution which had broken out in that country and to their consequent fear of losing the Negus's protection.

∞

The ninth year (619 CE) of the Prophet's mission was approaching its end when the boycott was ended. The boycott ended not because of the Quraysh accepting the Prophet's message or the Muslims giving in to the pagan beliefs and ways but due to several tribes and clans within the Quraysh realizing the injustice of the boycott and breaking its conditions until the boycott became irrelevant and non-enforcing. However, there was no sign that the Quraysh would moderate its stance of opposition to Islam. Abu Ṭalib continued to protect Muhammad (ﷺ), although he decided not to become a Muslim.

Abu Talib, however had reached an old age and a few months later he became ill. A number of the chiefs of the clans went to him, requesting him to negotiate some accommodation between them and the Prophet. They offered Muhammad kingship over the Quraysh which was unprecedented in their tribal history but the Prophet (ﷺ) insisted that he could not change God's message and in turn promised them they could be rulers in God's name over the kingdoms of Byzantine and Persia and enter the gardens of Paradise in the hereafter, they only had to believe in God's Oneness and shun idolatry and refrain from injustice and sin. They mocked at his words and this was the last attempt at any sort of accommodation. Soon afterwards, Abu Ṭalib died, and a few weeks later, Khadijah too suddenly passed away. Thus, the Prophet was deprived of the care and support he received from his uncle in his public life and from his wife at home. His companions reported that they did not see the Prophet smile for several months after the death of Khadija and several months after, sensing his loneliness a marriage broker brought a proposal of a middle aged widow named Sawdah with five children whose husband had become a Muslim, migrated to Abyssinia and had died and Muhammad agreed to the proposal and got married for the second time. The situation was becoming even more difficult for him as Abu Lahab his pagan uncle and enemy had given a deadline of a few weeks before he would withdraw tribal protection for Muhammad which would mean if he made any wrong move, he would be at the mercy of tribal injustice or would have to fight for himself. The Prophet thought of taking his message to new areas. He travelled to Taif, a city nestled in the hills about sixty kilometers south of Makkah, with Zaid his adopted son. Taif a mountainous town referred to as the summer capital of the Hejaz due to its milder climate was where the major tribe of Thaqīf lived. He first spoke to its chiefs who ridiculed his invitation to the truth and rejected him, thereafter he spent about a week in Taif exhorting its common people to turn to God but only to be faced with a very hostile reception. The chiefs of the Thaqīf set their slaves to chase him out of their town, and they hurled stones and other objects against him, he bled from his legs and feet until his sandals were soaked in blood and Zayd had a deep gash on his head; they finally took refuge in a garden belonging to two brothers, who were chiefs of a prominent clan of Quraysh.

These brothers though unbelievers, were sympathetic to their tribesman, sending him a plate of grapes through a slave of theirs named Addas who happened to be a follower of Jesus. When Addas gave the grapes to the Prophet who accepted it as a gift and began to eat them by mentioning the name of Allah, Addas was shocked and asked the Prophet who he was as no one he knows in Arabia mentions the name of God before eating. Muhammad explained to Addas that he is a Messenger of God and these are the ways of the Prophets and inquired where he was from, to which Addas replied that he came from the distant city of Nineveh, (in modern day Iraq) which was under the Byzantine empire ruled by Heraclius the Roman Christian emperor at that time. Visibly surprised the Prophet responded, ``that is the city of my brother Yunus (Jonah), who was also a prophet of Allah and was in the belly of the whale``. Addas realized that the person before him had to be a prophet as no one in this part of the world could know about Jonah which he had heard from his scriptures back home and he had also heard of a prophet who would come to Arabia soon. He bent over and kissed the feet of Muhammad just as Jesus had done to one of his disciples in humility and accepted the message of God that the Prophet had come to preach to the people of Taif.

There is a profound symbolism in the Prophet's mission to Taif. He went to Taif to teach the message of God to the chiefs of the tribe and they rejected him and then he went to the ordinary folks who too shunned him and drove the Prophet out of the city physically abusing him. On his way out of Taif, God sends to him a slave with a bowl of grapes and in the ensuing conversation the slave accepts Islam. Just like in Makkah it was not the elite and the rich who accepted his message at first but the poor and oppressed whose hearts are open. A more profound symbolic sign in the countenance of Addas and his acceptance of Islam, was in the realm of the prophetic fraternity where God sends to the persecuted Muhammad a believer from the land of prophet Jonah or Yunus, as if to remind the Prophet of the trials and story of Jonah which would have resonated with Muhammad at that time of distress. When the people of Nineveh rejected the call to worship the one God and the message of Jonah and literally made him leave that land he found himself in the belly of the whale after being thrown overboard from the ship that he was sailing out of Nineveh. Jonah repents for abandoning his mission and is miraculously coughed out ashore from the belly of the whale, returns to Nineveh where the people eventually accept him and the message from God that he preached. Muhammad who is beaten and chased out of Taif responds by supplicating to God of his helplessness and prays in the hope that soon in the near future the people of Taif would become Muslims.

Eventually, the Prophet walked away from Taif, returning to Makkah, but he felt he could not enter the city without tribal protection. He sent word to some of the tribal chiefs to provide him protection, and a distant uncle Mutim, who was still an unbeliever, provided him with protected entry. This happened after two other tribal chiefs had refused to give the Prophet protection. Before reaching Makkah, the Prophet sat down to reflect on his situation and pray. He appealed most passionately for God's support in one of his most heartfelt supplications:

"To You, My Lord, I complain of my weakness, lack of support and the humiliation I am made to receive. Most Compassionate and Merciful! You are the Lord of the weak, and You are my Lord. To whom do You leave me? To a distant person who receives me with hostility? Or to an enemy to whom You have given power over me? If You are not displeased with me, I do not care what I face. I would, however, be much happier with Your mercy. I seek refuge in the light of Your face by which all darkness is dispelled and both this life and the life

to come are put on their right courses against incurring Your wrath or being the subject of Your anger. To You I submit, until I earn Your pleasure. Everything is powerless without Your support.

Aisha the wife of the Prophet reported that she once asked the Prophet, "Have you encountered a day harder than the Day of Uḥud?" The Prophet said, "Your tribe has troubled me very much, and the worst was the day of Aqaba when I presented myself to Abd Kulaal in Taif and he did not respond to what I sought. I eventually departed, overwhelmed with grief, and I could not relax until I found myself at a tree where I lifted my head towards the sky to see a cloud shading me. I looked up and saw Gabriel in it. He called out to me, saying, 'Allah has heard your people's speech to you and how they have replied, and Allah has sent the Angel of the Mountains to you that you may order him to do whatever you wish to these people.' The Angel of the Mountains greeted me and said, 'O Muhammad, order what you wish, and if you like, I will let the two mountains fall upon them.' I said, 'No, rather I hope that Allah will bring from their descendants people who will worship Allah alone without associating partners with Him."The very fact that he prayed for the future guidance for the people of Taif despite their hostility towards him exemplified the description in the Quran of the Prophet; "A mercy unto all mankind"

Four

A Celestial Journey and an Earthly Exile

The year 620 CE was to witness the beginning of a trans-formation in the fortunes of Islam and its Prophet. First, he was taken on a night journey, when the angel Jibreel (Gabriel) came to him, bringing a heavenly steed named 'Buraq' (lightning) that travelled at high speed. Gabriel took the Prophet to Jerusalem, where he met all the earlier Prophets. He led a congregational prayer, and they all joined in. This was a symbol of the unity of God's messages, brought to their fullness by the message of the Quran.

"Exalted Is He who took His Servant by night from al-Masjid al-Haram to al Masjid al-Aqsa, whose surroundings We have blessed,
to show him of Our signs .... " (17: 1)

Gabriel offered Muhammad two bowls; one filled with milk, the other with wine and requested him to choose one. At this point in time wine had not yet been prohibited by God. The Prophet chose the bowl with milk and Jibreel informed him that he had chosen wisely and his followers will receive salvation and will be ennobled by the purity of the 'fitra' or the primordial goodness innate to humans. Symbolically, Mohammad chose the pure form of nature over what is a corrupted form of nature. From Jerusalem, Jibreel took him up to the heavens and as they proceeded through the heavens, Muhammad (ﷺ) met and was greeted by Adam, Jesus (Isa) & John (Yahya), Joseph (Yusuf), Idris (Enoch), Aaron (Haroun) & Moses and finally Abraham as they traversed through the seven heavens. They came to a point where Jibreel told Muhammad (ﷺ) that he had no permission to go beyond that point and the Prophet said "then I was caused to ascend forth". The Prophet describes an ascension that lifted him to the very presence of God and the most prestigious honor of standing before his Lord separated only by the "Holy veil of light".

One of the companions, Abu Durr asked the Prophet "Did you see your Lord?" and the Prophet recalls:

"By Allah's leave, as a sign of His mercy toward me and the perfection of His favor to me, that floated me into the [presence of the] Lord of the Throne, a thing too stupendous for the tongue to tell of or the imagination to picture. My sight was so dazzled by it that I feared blindness. Therefore I shut my eyes, which was by Allah's good favor. When I thus veiled my sight Allah shifted my sight [from my eyes] to my heart, so with my heart I began to look at what I had been looking at with my eyes. It was a light so bright in its scintillation that I despair of ever describing to you what I saw of his majesty. Then I besought my Lord to complete his favor to me by granting me the boon of having a steadfast vision of Him with my heart. This my Lord did, giving me that favor, so I gazed at him with my heart till it was steady and I had a steady vision of Him."

At the time when Muhammad was in the presence of God, three gifts were conferred to His Messenger: the five daily ritual prayers; direct revelation of the last two verses of the second chapter of the Quran and thirdly promised salvation for his followers as long as they do not ascribe partners to God. The ritual prayers became a cornerstone of the observance of the primordial covenant with God and its overarching importance in the life of a Muslim was defined by the fact that God directly commanded the Prophet in His presence the observance of the daily prayers.

On his descent down from the heavens Muhammad was shown glimpses of the wonders of Paradise and the torment of Hell and he met and conversed with the other prophets. The entire miraculous journey was of special significance for the Prophet as he was a witness to the unseen. It also clearly established the brotherhood and commonality of the message of the Prophets and Messengers of God and the concept of monotheistic pluralism among the Abrahamic faiths. On his return from Jerusalem back to Makkah on the 'Buraak' , Muhammad saw three caravans heading to Makkah and he even stopped to drink water from one of them. When he arrived in Makkah he went back to sleep in the Haram and woke up in the morning to relate his miraculous journey to Jerusalem and the heavens.

When news of Muhammad's miraculous Night Journey and Ascension reached the ears of the disbelievers, Makkah erupted in disbelief. Now, the Quraysh had another reason to mock the Muslims. After all, who could possibly travel through space, much less to Jerusalem and to the heavens? "Impossible," they said. Yet, when they quizzed him with questions about Jerusalem, to prove that he had not gone there, he astonished them by describing the Mosque in detail, although he had not ever traveled there before. He was even able to tell them about the location of their caravans and camels that he had passed as he journeyed that night. Although the disbelievers knew the Prophet to be the most honest person, they laughed and refused to believe him, instead, they went to Abu Bakr, "Muhammad claims that he went to Jerusalem and returned in one night," they sneered, but, to their surprise, Abu Bakr replied, yes, I accept it, if he said it."

Hence the reason why Abu Bakr was given the title of As-Sideeq (verifier of the truth). The true Muslims believed the prophet.They knew that with God everything is possible. If God created the heavens and the earth so surely he could take His Messenger to the heavens. Besides, if the Muslims believe that Jesus was taken up to heaven alive in body and soul and shall return at the end times, then why can't Muhammad be taken up to the divine and return in one night ?

The Ascension or Miraj is referred to in the Quran in sura Najm:

"By the Star. When it set, your companion is neither gone astray nor deluded. He does not speak of his own desire; it is but a Revelation which is sent down to him. One mighty in power has taught him, who is endowed with great wisdom. He stood poised in front when he was on the uppermost horizon. (53:1-8)....The heart belied not what he saw. Do you then dispute with him concerning what he sees (with the eyes)?" (53:11-12)..... The sight was neither dazzled nor it exceeded the limit, and he saw of the greatest Signs of his Lord." (53:17-18)

The Isra and Miraj was the greatest miracle that was personal to the Prophet and though others did not witness it, the account of the journey and the details of the caravans he saw on the way and the description of Jerusalem he gave were so true and real that the Makkans were dumbfounded. Abu Jahal, the Prophets arch enemy exclaimed "this is evident sorcery!" The Prophet referred to the experience he had in the presence of his Lord as "the Light of thy countenance" in his supplications. Almost all scholars of Islam consider the 'Night Journey' to be a real physical experience by the Prophet. Although science has advanced significantly and human knowledge about the mysteries of space, time and multiple dimensions and universes are now within the understandable realm of human comprehension, we are still limited by our human nature to penetrate all the mysteries of the relationships between the body, soul, time and the cosmos. The significance of the Prophet's meeting with the earlier prophets of God underlines the universal brotherhood of prophet hood and the monotheistic pluralism that Islam espouses when the Quran states in the last two verses of chapter two which translate both as a promise and assurance by God and a cry and allegiance to God by mankind.

"The Messenger has believed in what was revealed to him from his Lord, and [so have] the believers. All of them have believed in Allah and His angels and His books and His messengers, [saying], "We make no distinction between any of His messengers." And they say, "We hear and we obey. [We seek] Your forgiveness, our Lord, and to You is the [final] destination.

Allah does not charge a soul except [with that within] its capacity. It will have [the consequence of] what [good] it has gained, and it will bear [the consequence of] what [evil] it has earned. "Our Lord, do not impose blame upon us if we have forgotten or erred. Our Lord, and lay not upon us a burden like that which You laid upon those before us. Our Lord, and burden us not with that which we have no ability to bear. And pardon us; and forgive us; and have mercy upon us. You are our protector, so give us victory over the disbelieving people."- (2:285-286)

∞

Muhammad's willingness to report his night journey, given his hostile audience, was a mark of his strengthened and well-founded confidence in the truth of his message. He continued to preach with fresh zeal. By the time the next pilgrimage season approached, the Prophet was more determined than ever to carry his message to people outside Makkah, despite the growing difficulties he was facing. The pilgrimage season of 620 CE brought him a breath of hope and fresh air, as he met six pilgrims from Yathrib (later to be called Madinah). The Arab community in Yathrib was largely a farming community, and they lived side by side with a large Jewish community. The Jews used to boast of their monotheistic religion, telling the Arabs that they anticipated the emergence of a new Prophet who would be permitted to fight and use arms against his opponents. When trouble emerged between Arabs and Jews, the latter would threaten the Arabs, saying that they would follow the new Prophet and cause the Arabs to suffer a crushing defeat. Those six Arabs from Yathrib sat with the Prophet and listened to his exposition of his message and to his recitation of the Quran. They were highly impressed and declared their acceptance of Islam. The Arabs of Yathrib belonged to two main tribes, the Aws and the Khazraj, who were often in war with each other. Those six told the Prophet: "We have left our people in a terrible state of division and enmity. If God brings about their unity through you, no one will be more honourable than you." They promised to explain their new faith to their fellow tribesmen and to meet the Prophet again in the next pilgrimage season.

They kept their promise, bringing with them six others in this second meeting; all twelve pledged themselves as firm believers in Islam. The terms of the pledge were: "We believe in God and associate no partner with Him. We shall not steal, commit adultery, kill our children, assert a falsehood with regard to the parenthood of our children, or disobey the Prophet in anything reasonable. "In this meeting, there was a discussion of the needs of the newly formed Muslim community in Yathrib. The Prophet sent one of his most learned companions Musab ibn Umair with them to teach new Muslims the principles of Islam and the Quran.

Musab was also to organize the efforts of advocacy of Islam among the people of Yathrib. His mission was very successful, and Islam spread rapidly in Yathrib, with whole clans converting to the new faith.

On his return to Makkah ten months later, Muṣab reported to the Prophet that the city offered a good base for Islam.

The pilgrimage season of the following year (622 CE), which was the thirteenth since the start of Islam, witnessed an unprecedented step in Arabia. The Prophet met with seventy-three men and two women from Yathrib, who were all Muslims. They were part of the pilgrimage contingent from the city. Under the cover of the night, they came out stealthily from their camp in Mina to meet the Prophet. They pledged to support him and declared themselves ready to make whatever sacrifices they would need to make. They asserted that they would fight anyone who would oppose him, and that they welcomed all Muslims in Makkah to come over to Yathrib, where they would share with them all they have. They agreed that together they would form a community separate from others, with the bond of Islam making them all a single nation (an Ummah). Their only condition was that this new treaty would come into force once Muhammad had arrived in Yathrib.

Pause for reflection:

Though guided and inspired by God, the Prophet did his groundwork and made sure that Yathrib would be a suitable city to take his followers to and accordingly planned the transition and ensured that the hosts were ready and willing. In fact Muhammad had approached numerous tribes seeking a suitable place to migrate. He did not simply jump on a camel and lead the Muslims out into an unknown and untested city. The second wave of migration of Muslims out of Makkah totalled around eighty. This shows the clear foresight and forward planning of the Prophet and his judicious leadership style. He once said in an authentic narration 'tie your camel and trust in God'. It's vital to appreciate that the 'Hijra' was not just a flight but a divine plan to establish Islam as a complete way of life and a plan for change where the Prophet arrived not as a refugee but as a de-facto ruler. It was a civilizational project and a springboard for launching the complete Dheen or religion.

∞

Madinah glistened like a jewel on the hot, dry sands of ignorance, and the Messenger of God gave his followers permission to migrate there. However, Muhammad was deeply concerned for his followers. He knew that the Quraysh would do anything to prevent them from leaving Makkah. Therefore, he warned them to leave secretly without drawing too much attention to themselves. Apart from the dangers of being caught by the Quraysh, the Makkan Muslims would be forced to leave their wealth and relations behind, and they would have to endure a horrendous journey, full of dangers; like robbers and wild animals. Regardless of the difficulties that lay ahead for the Muslims, the reward of being able to practice their religion in peace, was well worth the risk. Thus, the Muslims prepared for the long journey which came to be known as the Hijra which marked the beginning of the Islamic calendar.

Over the next three months all Muslims who could do so immigrated from Makkah to Yathrib. They travelled in small groups, taking with them only some small items they could carry. They abandoned their homes and businesses, and deserted their clans. Only those who were physically prevented from travelling stayed behind. The Prophet remained in Makkah with Abu Bakr and 'Ali, his cousin, until he received instructions from God to go. In the meantime, the Quraysh realized what was going on and feared the worst.

At an emergency meeting, the chiefs of the clans considered all options and decided to move immediately to kill the Prophet. The plot was to choose a brave young man from each clan so as to share in the responsibility for the assassination. This method was agreed upon so that the Hāshimites would realize that they could not fight the rest of the Quraysh on their own. They would then accept blood money in compensation.

While Abu Bakr sent for their guide to Madinah, the Messenger met with his young cousin, Ali bin Abi Talib, and told him the entire story how the Quraysh were plotting to kill him that night, and Allah had given him permission to migrate and that he planned to leave Makkah with Abu Bakr. Surely, young Ali yearned to go with his beloved Prophet but he had to stay behind to return some things for the Messenger of God. On the night of the migration God *revealed the following verse:*

"And [remember, O Muhammad], when those who disbelieved plotted against you to restrain you or kill you or evict you [from Makkah]. But they plan, and Allah plans. And Allah is the best of planners." (8:30)

The Prophet went directly to Abu Bakr's house. Then, the two companions immediately disappeared into the dark still night. Meanwhile, the Quraysh's young men kept vigil at the Messenger's house, waiting for the attack. Then someone informed them to their utter disbelief and astonishment that Muhammad had already left Makkah.

That was impossible! Immediately, they rushed into the house and lifted the green blanket. There, to their surprise and amazement, was young Ali in the Messenger's bed. All of Makkah was in an uproar -Muhammad was gone. The Messenger of God knew very well that as soon as daylight appeared, the Quraysh would be hunting for them. He knew that they would get every tracker and tribe to help locate them. He was also sure that they would search the road north of Makkah, which was the conventional route to Madinah. Instead, he and Abu Bakr headed towards the south, along a deserted road that led to Yemen. When they had gone a little way beyond the precincts of Makkah, the Prophet halted his camel, and looking back he said:

"Of all God's earth, thou art the dearest place unto me and the dearest unto God, and had not my people driven me out from thee I would not have left thee." They walked for five long miles until they reached a rugged, rocky mountain of Thawr where they rested and hid over the next three days until the search thinned off. The Quran refers to this moment and incident in time:

"If ye help not (your leader), (it is no matter): for Allah did indeed help him, when the Unbelievers drove him out: he had no more than one companion; they two were in the cave, and he said to his companion, "Have no fear, for Allah is with us": then Allah sent down His peace upon him, and strengthened him with forces which ye saw not, and

humbled to the depths the word of the Unbelievers. But the word of Allah is exalted to the heights: for Allah is Exalted in Might, Wise." (9:40)

The Quraysh put out a reward of hundred camels for their capture dead or alive but the Prophet managed to escape his would-be assassins and took every precaution to mislead them and with God's grace he arrived in Madinah after two weeks, where he received a very warm welcome. He immediately set about organizing his new community, which consisted of the Muhajirun (the immigrants from Makkah), and the Anṣaar (supporters who were the Muslims from Yathrib) which was henceforth called God's Messenger's city, or Madinah for short.

The 'Hijra' or exile was a profound physical, emotional and spiritual trauma for Muhammad and the Muslims. It meant leaving behind their motherland, the hometown of their people; the land of their ancestors. In a tribal society there was no greater punishment than to be banished from your land of birth. The tribe never took that step even for the worst criminal, of putting him beyond the security of the tribe. Yet they did it for Muhammad who had committed no crime. The concept of Hijra therefore has both a figurative and a literal meaning. Figuratively to make Hijra is to leave what God dislikes and do what He likes. Hijra is to bring about positive changes in your life that reflect obedience to God and to His Messenger. Figuratively speaking Hijra is to emigrate from the state of sin to the state of obedience to Allah. This type of Hijra is mandatory on all Muslims; to consciously move from all kinds of disobedience to the obedience of Allah. Literally speaking Hijra is to move from a place of evil to a place which is better.

True to his mantle and spirit of leadership as the Messenger and Prophet of God, Muhammad took four measures of great importance on arriving in Yathrib;

1. He built a mosque to serve as a place of worship, a school where Muslims learnt the details of their faith, a meeting place, and a place for government.
2. He established a strong bond of brotherhood between the Muhājirūn and the Anṣār, making one of each group a brother

of one of the other group. This brotherhood was considered to be so important that it superseded the tribal bond.

3. He drew a covenant with the other groups in Madinah, namely the Jews and the Arab unbelievers, making them all citizens of the new state that he established in the city. This was a detailed document specifying duties and commitments of each group. This was arguably the first written constitution in human history, establishing a pluralist society based on citizenship. The Prophet himself conducted a census in Madinah which indicated a population of around ten thousand of which only 15% were Muslims, 40% Jews and 45% pagans.

4. The Prophet's first sermon to the people of Madinah was simple, short yet had a profound message of nation building. He said:

"Praise belongs to God whom I praise and whose praise I implore. We take refuge in God from our own sins and from the evil of our acts. He whom God guides none can lead astray; and whom He leads astray none can guide. I testify that there is no God but He alone, and He is without comparison.... Love what God loves. Love God with your hearts, and weary not of the word of God and its mention. Harden not your hearts from it.... Love one another in the spirit of God. Verily God is angry when His covenant is broken. Spread peace on each other, Feed the poor and the hungry, build loving relations with your kith and kin, Pray to your one true Lord in the nights and you shall surely be of those who enter the Gardens of Paradise."

If the Miraj was a journey of spiritual and divine significance for the Prophet the Hijrah was a journey of earthly toil and struggle. Yet they both had a defining significance in the life of the Prophet and the course of Islam. Under the threat of assassination and pursuit the Prophet and Abu Bakr planned their escape wisely and it took them a total of two weeks to finally reach Madinah- a journey that should normally take 3-4 days. They actually spent around two weeks in Quba just outside Madinah before finally entering the city. They forethought, prepared, planned, were decisive, patient, steadfast and most of all placed their trust in Allah. Whilst in Quba, the Prophet foresaw the building of the first mosque and planned for a symbolic entry in to Madinah to assert the presence of the new order, unity and faith. When he left to Madinah a short distance away over 50 of the Madinites joined him from Quba as a show of symbolic significance in the history of the city.

During the journey many miracles took place like the spider weaving its web at the entrance of the cave in Thawr and the desert pigeons building a nest near it, the sinking of the horse of the lone pursuer and bounty hunter who promised not to disclose their presence or location to the Makkans and the filling of the udders with milk of a flock of goats belonging to a desert Bedouin family where the Prophet stopped to take a brief rest. However the most momentous and defining moment during their flight were the reassuring words of Muhammad to AbuBakr in the cave where they were hiding and the enemy was all around them, "Do not grieve, indeed God is with us". These words underscore the essence of God's closeness and intimacy with His servants and the proactive nature of God's actions that reaches out to us through His care and love for humanity.

The Hijrah is in many ways a powerful metaphor for the believers who struggle in the path of God, to show that the help of their Lord is always near. In an authentic hadith God states, 'when my servant draws close to me by taking a step I shall speed towards him…'. The Prophet undertook a journey of around 350 kilometers to establish Islam and in the Prophet's own lifetime God opened up the whole of Arabia to Islam and after his death over 22 terrestrial empires and as promised by God Himself to Ishmail, made a great nation from his seed.

Five

Building a Righteous City, Community and Identity

Muhammad (ﷺ), the Final Messenger and Prophet of God had persuaded a place seeking an identity to connect with an identity in search of a place. Yathrib, which was the name of the place to which the Prophet migrated to, found its eternal identity in the name Madinah or the city of the Prophet which became the early model for a righteous city based on the principles of Monotheism, justice and submission to the one true God. These same principles are the very basis of the identity that was searching for a place to nurture its seed through the overarching force that provided the cement for this coalescence through the concept of the Ummah or community of believers or the brotherhood of humanity.

"O mankind, indeed We have created you from male and female and made you peoples and tribes that you may know one another. Indeed, the most noble of you in the sight of Allah is the most righteous of you. Indeed, Allah is Knowing and Acquainted." Quran 49:13

It is the legacy of God that He does not change the condition of a people until they change themselves first... (Quran 13:11). And the transformation in Madinah was made possible by the people of the tribes of Aws and Khawraj deciding to put behind them the tribal wars that had gone on for over 100 years and seek out a Prophet they had heard was preaching in Makkah and invite him to Madinah to change their ways and beliefs for they truly desired change.

At the time of Muhammad's migration, Madinah consisted of the tribes of Aws and Khazraj who were mainly Arabs and the Jews who were made up of three major tribes and many other smaller groups and of course the 'Muharijeen' or the 'migrants'. The Aws and Khajraj accepted Islam but there were still some pagan Arabs who did not become Muslims until after the battle of Badr. The constitution of Madinah drawn up by the Prophet included all of them and named all the tribes who were signatories to the pact. The pact itself had two vital sections, the first part were terms and conditions that forged a mutual defence pact that protected Madinah against outside or foreign attacks and the second part related to inter-relationships among themselves and the concept of citizenry as equals and to be governed by their own local law and customs so long as it did not conflict with God's law. The idea was to preserve justice and equality whilst allowing the Jews in particular to practice the laws of the Torah. In case of any dispute between them, Muhammad (ﷺ) will be the final arbitrator.

The Revelations that God sent to the Prophet (ﷺ) in Madinah reflected the guidance needed and the elements of building a God fearing and righteous community. Chapters or Suras such as 'Jumma', (62:2) declare:

"It is He who has sent among the unlettered a Messenger from themselves reciting to them His verses and purifying them and teaching them the Book and wisdom - although they were before in clear error." (Quran 62:2)

Here God refers to a Messenger from among themselves rehearsing to them His signs, purifying them with the spirit of the faith, teaching them the law and showing them wisdom. The four aspects of true faith are spelt out here by God first proving His Majesty through His signs, then purifying their souls through His faith as the Holy God, then giving them the law or commands to live by through His Authority before finally endowing them with wisdom from His all-knowing Wisdom. This beautiful sequence of instruction is something that the Prophet persevered to preach right through his life in Madinah for the benefit of those who were living at that time and for those who will enter the faith in the future as indicated in the verse 62:3 *"And [to] others of them who have not yet joined them. And He is the Exalted in Might, the Wise."*

The Madinah Constitution (The Kitab)

(The following excerpt is reproduced from the article "The Constitution of Madinah-Translation, commentary and meaning today", published by the Yaqeen Institute-2021 and written by Ovamir Anjum.)

Why and how has the Kitāb of Medina become significant today? One influential and typical modern Muslim deployment of the Kitāb is by the leader of Tunisia's Ennahda party, Rachid al-Ghannouchi. He suggests that it included both a political and confessional conception of the ummah and uses this reading "to argue that non-Muslims had always enjoyed 'citizenship rights' in Islam" and that "Medina was a city of multiple religious communities in which citizenship was based on a shared possession of a territory, and not shared creed." Before the fateful 2011 uprisings, al-Ghannouchi had tried to reconcile Islam with instruments of secular-liberal democracy arguing on the basis of "the nature that God has created us with"—thus sidestepping the logical conflict that would arise if (or perhaps, when) the democratic process demanded contravention of even the unanimously agreed-upon Qur'anic norms (such as inheritance laws, as has indeed occurred in Tunisia.

This secularist reading may have been driven by political expediency rather than any evidence-based reasoning, but it must be evaluated nonetheless on scholarly grounds. Not only does this reading bear no resemblance to fact, it flies in the face of the entirety of normative Islamic legal theory (uṣūl al-fiqh). We have provided here the text which needs little commentary to preclude the fanciful interpretation offered by al-Ghannouchi and his likes. The Prophet's authority was based primarily on his mission from God and not on the secular basis of "a pluralistic political order." Those who denied his mission were offered protection and allowed to practice their religion; this tolerance is astounding for a prophet, founder, and lawgiver as absolutely committed to his mission as he was. Yet, the Jews and the polytheists included in the Kitāb did not elect or want him as their leader, nor could they vote him out, change his mission, or even side with their own co-religionists against him.

All the while, the divine revelation both invited them to join and threatened them with punishment in both worlds for failing to do so. Furthermore, the Madinan polity was never meant to be territorially constrained: by giving him protection as their leader and ultimate guide, the Madinan Believers had invited the inevitable ire of the Makkans, and this singular fact dictated all policy (including the writing of this Kitāb); concerning all this, the non-believing Madinans had no choice. If the Kitāb is to be taken as a coherent document, the community (ummah) on which the Madinan order is built must mean the community of the Believers. Furthermore, the divine laws pertaining to sociality, tribe, family, and commerce that added to or modified the norms in the Kitāb were beginning to be revealed about the same time it was written. This means that if the Kitāb were the "essentially pluralist" constitution in any usual sense and all Madinans were its participating citizens (as part of its ummah), then every new public law of the Qur'an that was subsequently revealed should be deemed an amendment or violation of this "constitution." If it is argued that those laws applied to only the Believers, this would create a hypothetical situation in which some of the presumably equal "citizens" of this "constitution" were accepting or creating new norms and policies pertaining to war and peace and fundamentals of economic and social life based on an authority (the divine revelation) that the other "equal" citizens simply did not accept.

Wary of the liberal and secular undertones of such labels, some more careful readers of the Kitāb have argued effectively that, while not a pluralist constitution, the Kitāb founded a kind of confederation or commonwealth of the Madinan tribes that were separate religio-political communities (ummahs) in cooperation against a common enemy. Although far more plausible, this interpretation too is open to objections. The Makkans were simply not the common enemy; they were the enemies of Islam. No secular interpretation that ignores the Prophet's divine mission can make sense of the Kitāb and how it was understood and subsequently applied.

The interpretation we have offered here also explains the fact that, apart from a few occasional historical references discussed in certain jurisprudential and historical debates, we find little subsequent mention of the Kitāb in Islamic normative tradition. Modern interpreters often imply that the classical tradition has been deficient in its approach to the Qur'an and the Sunnah, having left out such a major document— the very "constitution" of Medina—from its legal and political thinking. "Constitutions," after all, are a big deal. How could the Prophet's "constitution" have been so neglected that there is not a single sound isnād of it, nor any notable mention in the tradition of law and governance? Aren't constitutions preserved with the greatest care and made available to all affected by them? Why was it not passed down to every ruler, and memorized by heart by every scholar? Did Muslims really neglect the political teachings of their final Prophet? Since, as we have shown, even the Companions who preserved this Kitāb, such as 'Alī b. Abī Ṭālib and 'Umar b. al-Khaṭṭāb and their families, did not make it a cornerstone of their teachings let alone "the constitution" of their governance, nor did the classical jurists consider this Prophetic "constitution" to be the foundation of all law, we are compelled to choose between two irreconcilable options. Its proponents insinuate, perhaps unwittingly, that we set aside the rich Islamic heritage, including a holistic engagement with the Qur'an and the Prophetic Sunnah, in favor of a convenient image provided by a single, decontextualized document, open to wildly contradicting interpretations.

We have shown that this relative non-centrality of the Kitāb did not owe itself to neglect by the Companions and the subsequent scholarship, but because its parts became abrogated, updated, or incorporated piecemeal in the final form of the revealed law. Even if an argument for a particular norm may be based on this Kitāb, any potentially contradictory norm that is better attested in the sources or is shown to have been revealed at a later stage may trump it.

Even though this misreading of the Kitāb as "the first written constitution of the world" seems at first blush to bolster Muslim's tottering self-confidence in a world of nation-states and democratic constitutions, understood in the way it is currently by many influential contemporary trends, it has the potential to inflict profound long-term damage. Apologists from all wounded civilizations trying to recover after the Western onslaught—the Chinese, the Indians, even the Mongols— have tried to take credit for all kinds of modern Western inventions and progress. Like all myths, as the foundation of our edifice of faith or civilization, this one makes us not only vulnerable to scholarly objection and ridicule but also antagonizes us to fact and rigorous scholarship. It belongs to a family of apologist myths whereby the worth of God's ultimate truth and its ultimate manifestation is judged by its utility for our immediate psychological or political needs: Islam is good and worthwhile because it gave us science, technology, democracy, constitutions, law and order, civilization, and all other things that we earnestly desire. By anchoring our sense of what is truly valuable in this or that human invention, it not only makes us undervalue what God deemed the most valuable truths to teach humankind in His final revelation, but also shuts our minds to how God has guided humans before and outside of Islam to all kinds of valuable things and experiences that we can evaluate, accept, reject, and learn from. This mythification of fact sets us up for disappointment or obfuscation and deprives us of the opportunity to value the truth properly. Rather than confronting the challenge of drastic innovations in world history such as the rise of the nation-state, democracy, capitalism, constitutionalism, secularism, liberalism, and so on, such myths invite us to be intellectually lazy by accepting all seemingly impressive innovations as good—so good that God's Prophet himself had taught them. This forecloses the possibility of critique: Good luck to any scholars now actually trying to evaluate whether an innovation is good and worthy. To what extent might it be called "the first ever written constitution in the world"? Proving such universal historical claims is rarely possible, for a single counterexample can falsify it. But we may reflect here on whether the Kitāb can even be called a "constitution."

Proving such universal historical claims is rarely possible, for a single counterexample can falsify it. But we may reflect here on whether the Kitāb can even be called a "constitution." One hadith tradition (mentioned earlier) describes the document (saḥīfah) as that to which they will turn in dispute (ma yantahū ilayh) and that which will unite the matters of the people (jāmiʿ amr al-nās); both of these attributes suggest that, at least in some respects, the document resembled a constitution or a charter. Constitutions, however, typically restrain the sovereign's authority. Clearly, this was not the intention of this document. Nor should we see it as a "step toward constitutionalism," for that falls into the trap of progressivist historical fallacy or "trajectory hermeneutics," perspectives that see contemporary norms as universal, as the "end of history," and perfected forms of institutions to which all earlier societies and moral authorities had aspired. Instead, we must see the perfection and completion of the Kitāb as materializing in the law that was elaborated over the following seven years by the Prophet, as God declared in the Qur'an on the occasion of the Final Pilgrimage, "Today I have perfected your religion, and completed My blessing…" (5:3). Furthermore, typically, the meanings of constitutional norms that often originate in messy contexts are settled through institutionalization and commentary over time, a phase that this document did not experience. From the perspective of Islamic ethico-legal theory (uṣūl al-fiqh), it is like any other hadith report that needs to be placed in the context of the entire ecology of divine imperatives that unfolded chronologically during the length of the Prophet's mission. Although most of its general clauses became eternalized in the final rendition of the divine law, it had a short life as a document. If the three main Jewish tribes had been party to it, all of them had violated it by 5 AH. The Believers' Pact (Part I) remained in force a little longer until inheritance and other laws qualified many of its terms. Despite its significance, therefore, this document can be accepted neither as a constitution nor a self-standing font of Islamic political norms outside of the context in which it was written.

The Kitāb continues to be significant, however, from conceptual, histor-ical, and aspirational perspectives. It shows the willingness and eager-ness of the Messenger of Allah to secure peace and order by making and honoring treaties. As evident in the Treaty of al-Ḥudaybīyah (6 AH) that he concluded with the Makkans (e.g., see 8:72), the Kitāb shows that the Prophet, preferred diplomacy to war whenever he could, and used force only to bring the opponents to negotiate and deter them from inflicting harm upon his community, his mission, and ultimately themselves. The Kitāb most certainly imagines a multi-religious Islamic polity and protects numerous rights for the non-Believers including the Jews and the polytheists. It also shows respect for graduality in dealing with the existing cultural structures. Not only were the non-Muslims free to maintain their communities, the Believers too were initially allowed to maintain their internal pre-Islamic communal norms and organization. Nor is it the case that the teachings of the Qur'an and the Sunnah concerning the tolerance of the Jews, Christians, and even polytheists outside of Arabia outside the Kitāb are any less generous. Quite the contrary. The Qur'an and the authentic Sunnah contain far more specific commands pertaining to dhimmah, jizyah, and legal and religious protection of non-Muslim communities. They are given rights not only as individuals but—in a fashion that a modern nation-state cannot imagine—as communities with their own norms. Nor is the Kitāb the only source of our knowledge about the Prophet's cordial relations with the Jews as neighbors throughout his life, of which the Qur'an and Sunnah provide ample instances. The Prophet declared on several occasions the inviolability of the life, property, and honor of the protected people, declaring on one occasion that "Whoever wrongs a mu'āhad (non-Muslim with dhimmah or other protected status), harms him, burdens him beyond his capacity, or forcefully takes his property, I will litigate against him on the Day of Resurrection." He exhorted about this frequently in the strongest terms, once declaring, "Whoever kills a mu'āhad shall not smell the scent of Paradise and its scent spreads to a distance of forty years".

He engaged in business with them, treated them graciously as neighbors, visited them when one of them fell ill, and honored their dead. Once he stood in deference when a Jew's funeral passed by, saying to those who seemed surprised, "Is he not a person (alaysat nafsan)"? When a rabbi Zayd b. Saʿnah insulted the Prophet when asking for repayment of his loan, ʿUmar sought to discipline the man, upon which the Prophet stopped him saying, "We both deserved better from you. You should have advised me to repay more promptly, and him to ask more gently." His Companions followed in his footsteps. When a fancy meal was presented to ʿAbd Allāh b. ʿAmr, he would inquire, "Has some been sent to our Jewish neighbor?" citing the Prophet's own teaching about kindness to neighbors. When he died, his shield was mortgaged to a Jew for thirty bags (ṣāʿ) of barley. Perhaps the most important instance is found in the Qurʾan itself. An Arab, Ṭaʿma b. Ubayriq, who had at least nominally embraced Islam, stole a shield from his neighbor, and when he feared getting caught, he implicated his Jewish friend. Basing his judgment on the available evidence, the Prophet sided with the Muslim, but Allah sent several verses recorded in Sūrat al-Nisāʾ (4:105-113) declaring the innocence of the accused Jew and denouncing the Muslim, who as a result fled Medina and renounced Islam. The Madinan polity was a prophetic one, in some ways sui generis: one in which a prophet of God called all humankind to the true religion by all means necessary, but without physical coercion; prioritizing the interests of that mission over all else, yet constrained by his treaties, which were nevertheless carefully crafted to facilitate the mission. Of course, this Kitāb does not contain any clause for constraining the ruler's power or holding him accountable; he spoke for God, and no Muslim ruler after him could ever make that claim. The first act of the Prophet's rightly guided successors (caliphs) was precisely the acknowledgment that the ruler could no longer claim to be infallible.

Yet the community as a whole must continue the mission of the Prophet. In this respect, the Kitāb imagines an uncompromisingly perfectionist polity, one that exists for a collective moral purpose that is balanced by individuals' duty to God. The potential tensions between collective and individual duties to God are resolved through the norms embodied in Islamic law. This is the model of a polity we are familiar with in the classical Islamic ideal, with the obvious exception that the classical Sunni tradition does not take any ruler after the Blessed Prophet to be an infallible voice of God. The most central concern of the Kitāb is the community of the Believers, the ummah, its mission, and its political, religious, and social unity, and its peaceful coexistence with its non-Muslim neighbors.

Building of the Prophet's Mosque

When the Prophet entered the city of Yathrib he let the reins of his camel loose and it meandered through the streets and came to rest beside the property which was an open courtyard that belonged to two orphans. The Prophet bought the land from the guardian of the orphans and in order to build his mosque there and also promised to look after the orphans well. While the mosque was being erected, he stayed in the house of Abu Ayyub Khalid ibn Zayd al Ansari. In the construction of the mosque, Muhammad worked with his own hands as did the Muslims, whether Muhajirun or Ansar. When the mosque was completed, they built on one side of it living quarters for the Prophet. These operations did not over-tax anyone, for the two structures were utterly simple and economical. The mosque consisted of a vast courtyard whose four walls were built out of bricks and mud. The full extent of the mosque was about 40 meters square. A part of it was covered with a ceiling made from date trunks and leaves. Another part was devoted to shelter the poor who had no home at all. The mosque was not lit during the night except for an hour at the time of the night prayer. At that time some straw was burned for light. Thus it continued to be for nine years, after which lamps were attached to the tree trunks on which stood the ceiling. The living quarters of the Prophet were no more luxurious than the mosque although they had to be more closed in order to give a measure of privacy.

The mosque was later expanded after the Khyber expedition by another 20 meters or so on either side to accommodate the growing Muslim population and visitors who came to visit the Prophet's mosque. After the Prophet, the mosque continued to be expanded and rebuilt through time and in the 1980s king Fahad undertook the largest expansion to date when it was extended to cover an area of about 60,000 sq. meters.

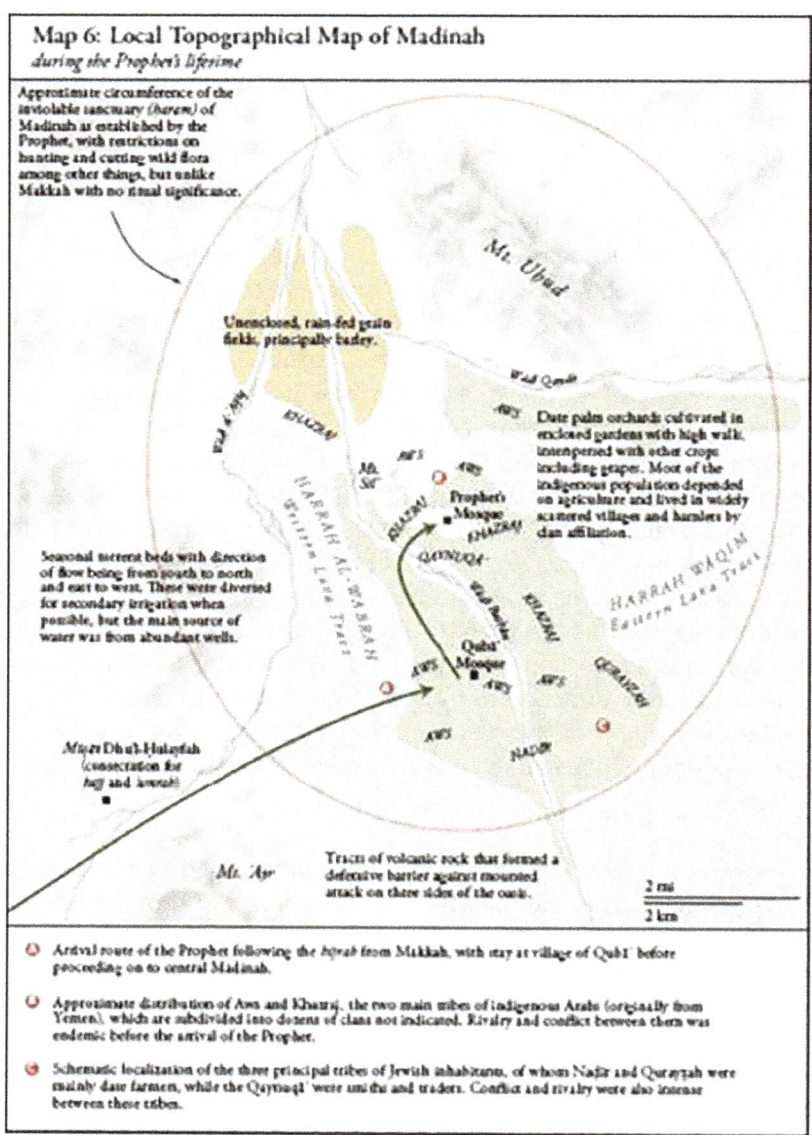

Map 6: Local Topographical Map of Madinah
during the Prophet's lifetime

Approximate circumference of the inviolable sanctuary (*ḥaram*) of Madinah as established by the Prophet, with restrictions on hunting and cutting wild flora among other things, but unlike Makkah with no ritual significance.

Mt. Uḥud

Unenclosed, rain-fed grain fields, principally barley.

Wādī Qanāh

Date palm orchards cultivated in enclosed gardens with high walls, interspersed with other crops including grapes. Most of the indigenous population depended on agriculture and lived in widely scattered villages and hamlets by clan affiliation.

Seasonal torrent beds with direction of flow being from south to north and east to west. These were diverted for secondary irrigation when possible, but the main source of water was from abundant wells.

Prophet's Mosque

HARRAH AL-WABRAH (Western Lava Tract)

HARRAH WĀQIM (Eastern Lava Tract)

Qubāʾ Mosque

Mīqāt Dhuʾl-Ḥulayfah (consecration for *ḥajj* and *ʿumrah*)

Mt. ʿAyr

Tracts of volcanic rock that formed a defensive barrier against mounted attack on three sides of the oasis.

2 mi

2 km

○ Arrival route of the Prophet following the *hijrah* from Makkah, with stay at village of Qubāʾ before proceeding on to central Madinah.

○ Approximate distribution of Aws and Khazraj, the two main tribes of indigenous Arabs (originally from Yemen), which are subdivided into dozens of clans not indicated. Rivalry and conflict between them was endemic before the arrival of the Prophet.

● Schematic localization of the three principal tribes of Jewish inhabitants, of whom Naḍīr and Qurayẓah were mainly date farmers, while the Qaynuqāʿ were smiths and traders. Conflict and rivalry were also intense between these tribes.

Source: The Study Quran

ANALYSIS OF FIRST SERMON OF THE PROPHET (ﷺ) IN MADINAH AND THE PROPHETIC MODEL OF HIERARCHY OF DEEDS

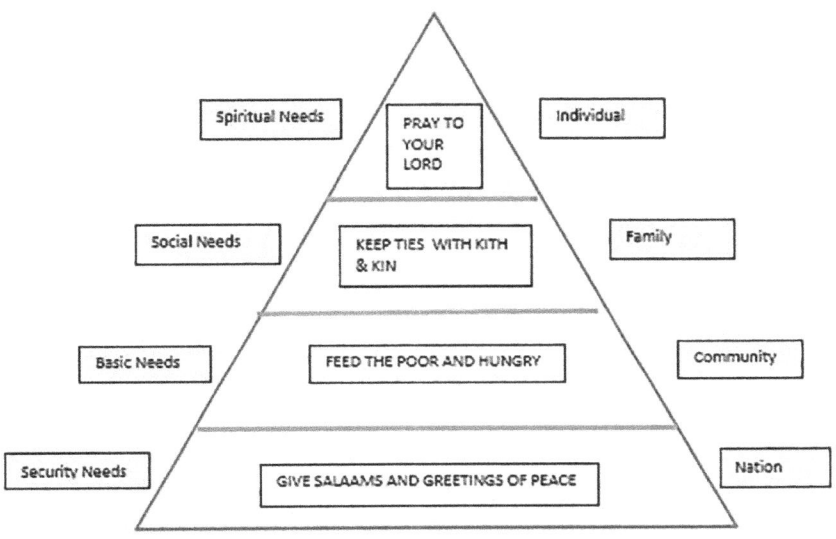

Adapted from the presentation of Shaikh Hamza Yusuf at the Knowledge Retreat 2016, Toronto

The above graphic captures the overarching wisdom and conciseness of speech of the Messenger of God in laying down the simple building blocks for a righteous community in Madinah. He made it simple so that all may understand and follow yet as shown in the illustration above it addressed the basic fundamental values and needs of a community for nation building. In fact this model echoes a more familiar theory propounded by the social scientist Maslow in the 20th century in explaining the 'Hierarchy of Motivation' in people working in communities in which the 'needs' of people have to be fulfilled starting from their most basic need for security and safety before they are motivated to seek a higher need. The difference in the two is the integration of the 'spiritual need' in people in the Prophetic model which establishes the concept of balance between the corporeal and the spiritual which nurtures both the body and the soul.

These simple yet profound instructions also covered every segment of humanity in all its elements from the level of the individual to the nation as a whole culminating in the salvation for all of humanity by entering Paradise and over the next decade of his life on earth the Prophet through his living example and Quranic revelation brought about the greatest transformative change in the world for all times and the Quran confirmed this: *"Thus, have We made of you a community justly balanced, that ye might be witnesses over the nations, and the Messenger a witness over yourselves." (Quran 2:143)*

Pause for reflection

The task of community building let alone nation building is fraught with conflict and difficulty and the Prophet was inspired and guided by God and the wisdom endowed upon him. At the centre of it all was the Revelation and the impeccable character and personality of the Prophet which held together the umbrella of faith over the city. Although the 'Ansars' and the 'Muhajirs' dedicated their lives and wealth to the cause of Islam, the nascent community of Muslims and the Prophet had to contend with the latent and later overt hostility of the Jews and the hypocrites. The hypocrites conspired to bring back civil unrest by rousing the old rivalry between the tribes of 'Aws' and Khazraj'. The external threat from outside Madinah from the various tribes allied to the Quraysh was also a formidable danger as they planned to attack the Muslims at any time.

Amidst all this, the Prophet placed his trust in God and went about the task of transforming the lives, minds and hearts of the people physically, spiritually, psychologically, socially and economically. One of his landmark achievements of administrative and political wisdom was the 'Constitution of Madinah', which is one of the first historical documents of pluralism to be ever signed by a multi-faith, multi-ethnic community to bring about civil and religious tolerance and co-existence.

In his first Friday sermon in Madinah, Muhammad emphasized the essence of the Muslim heart and the foundational values of Islam:

"Love all that God loves, and love God from the very depths of your hearts," as well as "Love one another through the tender mercy of God amongst you."

∞

The Jewish tribes in Madinah or Yathrib, as it was referred to before the arrival of the Prophet were descendants of Jews who had settled in Arabia after their exodus from the temple destruction in 70CE by the Romans and then the Jewish uprising around 200 CE in Palestine. They had travelled down as far as Yemen and had a mini kingdom there under the patronage of the Persian Empire for some time before the Christians from Abyssinia pushed them out of Yemen. They could trace their ancestry through the lineage of Prophet David and Aaron and moved to Yathrib because according to their scripture they expected a Prophet to come to Yathrib who will be empowered by God to fight the pagans and establish His law firmly on earth for all nations. In fact the Jews used to boast and taunt the pagan Arabs saying "when our Prophet comes, he will lead us Jews to victory over all of you and establish the supremacy of the children of Israel."

When the Prophet did arrive in Madinah the Jews responded in strangely different ways. The chief Rabbi of Madinah accepted the Prophet (ﷺ) as soon as he met him, stating, "I do not see the face of a liar in Muhammad", others tested him with questions and observed his actions before embracing Islam. Still others after testing the Prophet with questions realized that he was the promised Prophet but couldn't accept the fact that he came from the seed of Ishmael and not Isaac and hence swore to show him enmity whilst others vowed not to leave the Torah and the religion of Moses despite their scriptures foretelling the coming of the Prophet with a new law. In one bizarre incident when the Quraysh pagans asked the Jews whether the religion taught by the Prophet was superior to their pagan beliefs, the Jews blatantly lied and assured the pagans that their faith was superior and incited them to fight against the Muslims in Madinah. This outright lie of the Jews that went against the very spirit of the greatest commandment in the Torah was exposed by God in the Quran:

"Have you not seen those who were given a portion of the Scriptures, and yet they believe in sorcery and digression, and assure the unbelievers that they are better guided than the believers. It is those indeed whom

God has rejected. Whomever God has rejected shall have help from no one." (4:51-52)

This attitude reflected in their actions and despite signing the constitution of Madinah the three big Jewish tribes who lived in fortress type settlements around Madinah conspired to break the constitution by acts of treachery and treason including an attempt to assassinate the Prophet. Two of the tribes were exiled out of Madinah together with their belongings and the treason of the Bani Quraizah tribe was so heinous that it called for a sterner sentence and the Prophet allowed the Bani Quraizah Jews to select a Muslim convert from their former pagan allies to judge and sentence them. They got no sympathy from their former ally and friend who decided that their male fighters be put to death and the women and children taken as captives. In the oldest biography of the Prophet by Ibn Ishaq (720 CE) states that all the males were executed but historical verification and facts show otherwise and a later biography by Waqidi in 850 CE lists the names of the Jews who were executed which numbered twenty four of them. The rest of them were probably exiled with the women and children to the north of Arabia. Scholars of history point out that Ibn Ishaq could have got his misinformation from the Jews in northern Arabia who were keen to paint a different picture to gain historical sympathy and portray as the subject of victimization. Allah refers to this incident in the Quran:

"And He brought down those who supported them among the People of the Scripture from their fortresses and cast terror into their hearts [so that] a party you killed, and you took captive a party." (Quran 33:26)

The gravity of the treason committed by the Bani Quraizah was so treacherous that all the Muslim women and children who were in their homes would have been massacred by the Bani Quraizah who in violation of the treaty of Madinah colluded with the ten thousand strong confederate army headed by the Quraysh who laid siege on Madinah from the north and decided to break the pact with the Muslims and attack them from the south so that they could benefit from the spoils of war especially the lands of the Muslims.(see battle of the Trench in chapter 18) God Himself revealed in the Quran;

"Behold! They came on you from above you and from below you and behold the eyes became dim and the hearts gaped up to the throats and ye imagined various (vain) thoughts about Allah! In that situation were the Believers tried: they were shaken as by a tremendous shaking." (33:10-11)

Most if not all of the Jewish tribes exiled from Madinah settled in Khaybar some one hundred odd kilometres to the north of Madinah where a large community of Jewish tribes lived and thrived with their cultivation and posed a threat to the city of Madinah through their treachery and collusion with the northern tribes who lived near the present day Jordan border then known as Sham. These northern tribes were hostile to the Muslims and came under the influence of the Byzantine or Persian rule and had already shown their intentions through their confederation with the Quraysh via the instigation of the Jews during the battle of the Trench or Confederates in the year 627 CE. In the year 628 CE soon after the treaty of Hudaibiyah was signed which secured the southern flank, especially from Quraysh, the Prophet (ﷺ) realized the enormity of the risk of the Jewish political influence in the Arabian Peninsula to the north. On the other hand, it was not possible to reconcile them with a peace treaty like that of Hudaybiyah since the covenant of Madinah had been violated by them much to their own detriment. Were help to come to them from the side of Byzantium, their natural inclination to rise again against Muhammad could not be contained. Hence, it was thought necessary to put a final end to their influence in the Arabian Peninsula, and to do so quickly without giving them the time to forge any new alliances with any tribe hostile to the Muslims. Muhammad marched well prepared with one thousand six hundred troops loyal to the cause who were not seeking any booty or material gain and confronted the Jews of Khaybar and after a valiant effort by his closest and sincere companions over a prolonged duration that lasted over a month were able to defeat and subjugate the entire Jewish community. The terms of their surrender were for them to hand over to the Muslims half of their crops and in return they could continue to live in Khaybar but not engage in any political or hostile activity. This effectively marked the end of Jewish influence and control in Arabia and was neutralized as a force for good. They even visited Madinah on trade visits. The seventeen other Jewish tribes of Madinah remained in the oasis, living on friendly terms with the Muslim for many years, and the Quran continued to insist that Muslims remember their spiritual kinship with the People of the Book.

The hypocrites in Madinah was a group headed by Abdullah ibn Ubay who was a senior pagan Arab leader who lost his position to rule over the city when the Prophet(ﷺ) came on the invitation of the two biggest tribes in Madinah. When the Prophet invited them to Islam they pretended to be Muslims but connived and plotted with the Jews to defeat the Muslims and revert back to pagan ways. They were eventually identified and shunned and neutralized by the Muslims of Madinah and when their leader died they soon dissipated. The Quran refers to them as:

"Among the Bedouin who dwell around you, there are hypocrites; and among the people of Madinah there are such as have grown insolent in their hypocrisy. You do not always know them, but We do know them. We shall cause them to suffer doubly in this world and then they will be given over to awesome suffering in the life to come." (9:101)

God revealed to the Prophet (ﷺ) all the names of the hypocrites so that the Prophet would be aware of their machinations and he in turn disclosed the names to only one of his most confidential companions whom the Prophet knew would not make public the names and would use it only to advise the others if he left this world. The Prophet himself is reported to have said, "I have not been commanded to search in the hearts of men or to open them up." The Prophet dealt with people according to their external professions of faith even when he knew they were apostates or unbelievers in their hearts. Even when God had given the Prophet direct knowledge of someone's hidden apostasy, that person's external adherence to Islam made their life and property inviolable.

The care and empathy the Prophet had for people was amply demonstrated when the son of the chief of the hypocrites in Madinah came rushing to the Prophet to tell him about his father's death and that he had requested as a dying wish, the shirt of the Prophet be used as a shroud. The Prophet without any hesitation felt the grief of the son and gave him his shirt and in fact prayed at the burial. This again highlights the kind human nature of the Prophet vs. the divine wisdom of God, when the following verse was revealed.

"And do not pray [the funeral prayer, O Muhammad], over any of them who has died - ever - or stand at his grave. Indeed, they disbelieved in Allah and His Messenger and died while they were defiantly disobedient." (9:84)

Although the hypocrites at the time of the Prophet covertly plotted against Islam whilst showing outward signs of following Islam, present day hypocrisy which manifests in insincere actions and deeds is more latent but equally destructive both at the individual and community level. In Islam, as stated by the Prophet,

"All actions are but by their intent and every man shall have only that which he intended ...",(sahih Bukhari 1) and hence any deed that is done with the intent of boosting ones ego, gaining material power or seeking political leverage and position in the eyes of people and not to please Allah is tainted with hypocrisy if the outward purpose of the action is to make a show of piety and righteousness. Allah refers to such people in the Quran:

"Say, [O Muhammad], "Shall we inform you of the greatest losers as to [their] deeds? [They are] those whose effort is lost in worldly life, while they think that they are doing well in work."
(18:103-104)

Of the many forms in which insincerity can manifest itself is Riyaa'. At a basic level, this involves performing acts which are pleasing to Allah, with the intention of pleasing other than Allah. Riyaa' is subtle yet devastating. Many a time we may be unwittingly guilty of Riyaa' and it becomes a cause of rejection of our actions.

Six

Striving in God's Way, Just War, Prophetic Vision

When the Muslims migrated to Madinah from Makkah they literally left behind all their possessions as the Quraysh pagans did not allow them to travel peacefully. Their property and belongings were all confiscated by the Quraysh and some of the early migrants simply left with nothing more than what they were wearing. Others were persecuted or hounded and brought back while travelling over the 3-4 day journey. At times families were split as pagan and Muslim families and in-laws fought over the children. It was the overwhelming generosity and kindness of the 'Ansars' or the 'helpers' in Madinah who shared half of what they had that enabled the immigrants to settle in and start their lives anew. Throughout the twelve years of persecution and tribulation in Makkah the Muslims were commanded by God to show patience and fortitude and bear the burden with faith in God and now that God had brought them to a new land of promise, the world was about to witness the balance of God's Mercy and Justice, His Holy wrath and deliverance. And the Prophet, who had practiced a strict pacifism in Makkah for thirteen years and disliked the use of force, was now given permission by God to defend against any attacks by his enemies. The Quran asserted;

"Permission [to fight] is given to those against whom war is being wrongfully waged—and, verily, God has indeed the power to succor them—those who have been driven from their homelands against all right for no other reason than their saying "Our Sustainer is God!" For if God had not enabled people to defend themselves against one another, [all] monasteries and churches and synagogues

and mosques—in [all of] which God's name is abundantly extolled— would surely have been destroyed." (22:36-40)

Muhammad, (ﷺ) said:
"Never desire to meet your enemies, rather ask God for peace and well-being; but should you be forced to meet them, and then act courageously".

Madinah was surrounded by hostile desert pagan tribes who had their allegiances with the Quraysh in Makkah and the Muslims were wary of their intention to attack the new faith in Madinah which threatened their pagan way of life. The Prophet sent numerous expeditions to these tribes to preach the new faith and also to establish treaties or pacts with them and some of them resorted to outright treachery and betrayal when they requested the Prophet to send people to teach them the faith and then attacked them which resulted in over 80 Muslims being martyred. On another front the Prophet was painfully aware of the economic and social injustice brought upon the immigrants by the Makkan Quraysh and with a view to redress this injustice and take back what was rightfully their property, he sent a number of expeditions to intercept the Quraysh caravans that went to Syria to take back some of the wealth the immigrants had lost. This also served to disrupt the economic lifeline of the Quraysh and forced them to come to terms with the Muslims. It was during one of these expeditions that a group of Muslims attacked a Quraysh caravan in Nakhla and killed one of the Quraysh on the first day of the beginning of the sacred month of Rajab in which fighting is prohibited. Muhammad was concerned about the consequences and refused to accept the booty that the Muslims brought back when God revealed a profound declaration of the balance of justice:

"They ask you about fighting in the sacred month. Say: "Fighting in it is a grave offence; but to turn people away from the path of God, to disbelieve in Him and in the Sacred Mosque and to expel its people from it – all this is a much graver offence in God's view. Indeed, religious persecution is worse than killing." They will not cease to fight

against you until they force you to renounce your faith, if they can. But he who renounces his faith and dies a non-believer, his works shall come to nothing in this world and in the world to come. It is such people who are destined for the Fire, therein to abide forever." (2:217)

If the Quraysh could be made to realize that their precious trade and wealth were exposed to danger by their own sons who had migrated to Madinah, perhaps they might be inclined to reach an understanding with the Muslims in order to grant them the freedom to preach their faith, visit Makkah, and perform the pilgrimage, which was all they really sought. Such an understanding was not possible, however, unless the Quraysh were brought to realize that their emigrant sons were capable of impeding that trade and inflicting some material harm.

In the period before the battle at Badr in 623 CE, Muhammad(ﷺ) sent out eight 'raids' or expeditions of a mainly offensive nature predominantly against the Quraysh caravans and these raiding expeditions continued even after Badr but were more of a defensive and pre-emptive nature. In seventh-century Arabia raids among tribal communities were highly esteemed and socially expected activities in which manly qualities such as combat skill, courage, cunning, stealth, resourcefulness and hardiness were developed, demonstrated and then publicly recognized and eulogized. It drew upon every noble value and virtue of the Arabs and provided a means of distribution of wealth and resources in the harshness of the Arabian landscape. Although modern writers of the 'Seerah' or the prophetic biography have ascribed the motives behind such raids as a justified means of redressing the plight of the emigrants, the time honoured tradition of raiding among the Arabs could have been a compelling and natural reason. (see text box below "Muhammad(ﷺ) the Warrior Prophet-Historical context)

After a period of time, when the Muslims had accepted the new situation – moving away, in the process, from the rest of the Arabs – they were taught to regard the Kaaba in a different light. They were told to face it in their prayers instead of in the direction of Jerusalem because it was built by the two Prophets, Abraham and Ishmael, as a place wholly devoted to the worship of Allah alone. Thus it becomes part of the heritage of the Islamic nation, which has come into existence by way of answering Abraham's prayers to raise among his seed a Prophet who would teach them the true religion. Symbolically this change in the 'Qiblah' or direction of prayer provided a powerful centripetal spiritual force in re-establishing and aligning the identity of the Muslims with their own Abrahamic roots and as a distinctly different orientation away from the practice of the Jews.

Pause for reflection

Allah`s final revelation to mankind is not a pacifist manifesto and the concept of balance of mercy and justice comes into play. When the Prophet migrated and formed the new community in Madinah, they were the target for the numerous hostile pagan tribes around the city and in the Arabian Peninsula. The Prophet was not given a magic wand to repel and protect themselves but the new Muslim community had to defend themselves proactively and judiciously pre-empt any hostile intentions through their own effort and perseverance. The balance in Islam at times needed the exercise of God`s holy wrath against those who waged war against the truth. However only those imbued with true faith can sacrifice their lives for the sake of God and the nascent community of Muslims in Madinah will soon be tested.

The change in the direction of prayer from Jerusalem towards Makkah had a deep symbolic significance both geo-politically and spiritually. It marked in a physical sense the re-birth of the ritual orientation of the Muslim prayer towards its Abrahamic roots as the Kaaba was the first place of worship that Abraham and Ishmail erected for the worship of the one true God. It also differentiated the Muslim prayer from those of the people of the book who faced towards Jerusalem and thus signified a new covenantal identity. The Muslims as a nation of true believers now had their own direction of prayer symbolizing the pure monotheistic axis of worship in fulfilling their covenant. However Allah makes it clear that the 'Qiblah' or direction of prayer is only a physical manifestation of the unity and focus of worship and that true righteousness lies elsewhere:

"Righteousness is not that you turn your faces toward the east or the west, but [true] righteousness is [in] one who believes in Allah , the Last Day, the angels, the Book, and the prophets and gives wealth, in spite of love for it, to relatives, orphans, the needy, the traveler, those who ask [for help], and for freeing slaves; [and who] establishes prayer and gives zakah; [those who] fulfill their promise when they promise; and [those who] are patient in poverty and hardship and during battle. Those are the ones who have been true, and it is those who are the righteous."(2:177)

∞

Intelligence was brought to Madinah that a large trade caravan, in which almost every household in the Quraysh had a share, was returning to Makkah after completing a successful business trip to Syria. The caravan was led by Abu Sufiyan, a prominent figure in Makkah and the chief of the Umayyah clan. It should be remembered that when the Makkan Muslims emigrated to Madinah they left almost all their belongings behind, and the Quraysh lost no time in confiscating their property. The caravan, therefore, seemed to offer a good opportunity of getting some compensation for the Muslims' losses. It is clear that the Prophet did not issue an order to the Muslims to mobilize for a direct confrontation with a Makkan fighting force otherwise everyone would have taken part. In the event, a force of 313 men marched with the Prophet. Besides, they were not fully equipped for a major clash with the enemy. The Prophet had in mind another aim in addition to the compensation of former losses. He wanted to demonstrate the inability of the Quraysh to protect its own trade routes. This would shake the Quraysh and weaken their reputation as the master tribe in Arabia. However, through their scouts the Makkans got wind of the intentions of the Muslims and diverted their usual route and sent a messenger to Makkah to alert them of the situation. In all probability this message would have been sent by Abu Sufyan to Makkah well before their return from Syria as he would have anticipated a possible raid by the Muslims in Madinah. The Makkan Quraysh mobilized a force of one thousand men with over six hundred camels and one hundred horses and marched towards Madinah to confront the Muslims initially with the intent of protecting and safeguarding their caravan but later in battle despite the fact that their caravan had safely evaded the Muslims.

Muhammad marched at the head of his 313-man strong expedition towards Badr where they expected to intercept the Quraysh caravan and soon realized that the caravan had slipped away and they were now facing the formidable task of meeting a strong Quraysh force in battle. They had only seventy camels and two horses to ride and had to take turns in riding their camels. The two armies arrived at the plains of Badr and after two days of stand-off and staring at each other across the alley, they engaged. The Quraysh began to advance slowly over the sand dunes which had turned muddy by an overnight storm which made it difficult for the horses and camels to move. Muhammad (ﷺ) realizing the need for divine intervention if they were to win the battle spent the entire night and right upto the final moments before battle in fervent prayer beseeching Allah, "O my Lord fulfill your promise to me of victory and make us defeat Your enemies for if this small group of believers are left at the mercy of the unbelievers, ther will be no one to declare your Oneness and Glory", until Abu Bakr reminded Muhammad to leave his prayers and engage his troops assuring him that his Lord has surely heard his supplication and victory will be our's, God Willing. At that moment the Prophet received the glad tidings from Allah that they will be victorious and with a radiant face he urged the Muslims to fight the enemy as God would certainly give them victory. The actual conflict commenced when as was customary in battles at that time for both sides to send their best fighters to a one on one duel and three men from the Quraysh from the same family came forward to meet the three picked by Muhammad, his cousin Ali ibn Abu Talib, his uncle Hamza Abu Muttalib and Ubaydah ibn al Harith, a distant relative. Whilst both Ali and Hamza made short work of their opponents Ubaydah was fatally wounded and so was his opponent before Ali and Hamza came to his aid and after slaying the Quraysh opponent carried Ubaydah back to the Prophet where he passed away after being given the glad tidings of Heaven. In the fierce skirmish that followed, the Quraysh soon found that they were getting the worst of it. They fought with careless bravado, as though this was a knightly tournament, and had no concerted strategy. But the Muslims did have a disciplined plan. They began by bombarding the enemy with arrows, drawing their swords for hand-to-hand combat only at the last minute whilst maintaining their rows and ranks in formation. By midday, the Quraysh had fled in disarray, leaving some seventy of their leading men, including Abu Jahl himself, dead on the field and around seventy more captured as prisoners of war. There were only fourteen Muslim casualties in all.

Allah reminded the believers of His help at Badr in the following verses:

"And Allah had already helped you at Badr when you were weak. So take Allah for your Protector that you may be grateful."

"When thou didst say to the believers, 'Will it not suffice you that your Lord should help you with three thousand angels sent down from on high?" (3:124-125)

The Quran also reassured the Believers that this campaign was divinely ordained;

" You did not kill them but rather God killed them, and you did not cast your weapon, but rather God cast it, rendering to the Believers a great favour." (8:17)

The two earliest extant biographies of the Prophet, Ibn Hisham's (833CE) al Sira al -Nabawiya and al-Waqidi's (823CE) kitab al-Maghazi, reveal that before almost every major event in his life especially the battles, Muhammad (ﷺ) consulted with his trusted companions and Badr was no exception. On this occasion he was advised on the place-ment and positioning of the Muslim forces to gain a strategic advantage and he followed that advice to good effect.

The Quran places Shura or consultation alongside prayer and charity as essential human behaviour and sura al Shura (42:38) states:

"And those who obey their Lord and establish Prayer; who conduct their affairs by consultation, and spend out of what We have bestowed upon them;(for them is a great reward)." (42:38)

This verse encapsulates the highly consultative leadership style that Muhammad employed throughout his 23 years of prophethood.

Muhammad (ﷺ) was not a pacifist. He believed that warfare was sometimes inevitable, even necessary. After the battle of Badr, the Muslims knew that it was only a matter of time before Makkah took her revenge and they dedicated themselves to a long, gruelling struggle or Jihad. But the primary meaning of that word, which we hear so often today, is not "holy war" but the "effort" or "struggle" necessary to put the will of God into practice. Muslims are exhorted to strive in this endeavor on all fronts: intellectual, social, economic, spiritual, and domestic. Sometimes they would have to fight, but this was not their chief duty. On their way home from Badr, Muhammad uttered an important and oft-quoted maxim: "We are returning from the Lesser Jihad (the battle) and going to the Greater Jihad,"—the immeasurably more important and difficult struggle to reform their own society and their own hearts.

Pause for reflection

Here in Badr the Muslims saw the direct help from God descend upon them which made them rout the Quraysh who had an army three times larger than the Muslims and far better equipped. If we reflect on the situation and condition of the Muslims just before they engaged the enemy, many things become clear for one to expect the help from God.

They placed their trust completely in God and were in total obedience to the Prophet (their commander in chief) and were never afraid of sacrificing their lives in the cause of God. This state of mind was epitomized by the leader of the tribes from Madinah, S'ad Ibn Muadh who reassured the Prophet by stating, "Today we will not be like the Jews who told Moses to go and fight the people in the city with his Lord and they will not follow him". The psychological impact of what happened at Badr had a profound influence on the Quraysh and the pagan Arab tribes in the region. They had witnessed or heard first hand Allah's divine help descend from the heavens to aid the Muslims and although their hearts were hardened to not accept the divine message, secretly they feared the Muslims and whenever they tried to mount an attack against them and heard that the Muslims were coming out to meet them, they fled often leaving their possessions behind.

Following the battle, the Muslims took captives who were later ransomed back to the Quraysh. The Prophet ordered that save two of the prisoners who were executed because of their heinous crimes against the Muslims whilst they were in Makkah, the rest of the prisoners be treated humanely and he even let some of them free without a ransom. However the compassion of the Prophet was checked by the divine wisdom of God when it was revealed in the Quran;

"It is not fitting for a prophet that he should have prisoners of war until he hath thoroughly subdued the land. You look for the temporal goods of this world; but Allah looks to the Hereafter: And Allah is exalted in might, Wise."(8:67)

Perhaps God's wisdom became evident when in the following year the very same captives who were release formed part of a larger contingent who attacked the believers near Madinah slaying around seventy of the Muslims at the battle of Uhud.

∞

In the following year 625 CE, once the winter rains were over, three thousand Quraysh men with three thousand camels and over a hundred horses left Makkah in March and began their journey northward. After a journey of a little over a week, they camped to the northwest of Madinah on the plain in front of Mount Uhud about eight km. from the city center. Their intent was clear –to wipe out the Muslims once and for all and avenge the defeat at Badr. On hearing the news of the enemies at the gates of Madinah the Prophet mobilized an army of around one thousand men and consulted with different prominent individuals and groups about the best strategy to adapt in confronting the enemy. The younger Madinites were keen to go out and meet the enemy outside the city whereas the older generation were more cautious and suggested that they fortify themselves inside the city and repel the attack from inside the city. After listening to the different points of view the Prophet decided to go out and meet the enemy in Uhud but realized the importance of proper strategy to defeat an enemy that outnumbered them 3 to 1. These odds were made worse when the leader of the hypocrites decided not to join the Muslims because his opinion was not acted upon by the Prophet. This reduced the numbers to seven hundred and yet the Muslims were not daunted by the disparity in strength. The Jewish tribes decided from the outset to not join the Muslims despite the constitution of Madinah which required them to defend the city in the event of an outside threat.

In deploying his men the Prophet stationed around fifty of his best archers above a pass in the mountain range to prevent the enemy from charging their cavalry into the plains where the fighting would take place and advised them to not leave their positions even if the Muslims were losing or facing defeat. Unfortunately when the battle commenced and the initial onslaught by the Muslims pushed the Makkans back and they began to retreat leaving behind their weapons , the archers left their positions and came down to collect their war booty which resulted in a complete reversal in the fortunes of the Muslims as the enemy rein-forcements came through the pass and attacked the Muslims from both flanks causing complete disarray among the Muslims who had to retreat up the mountain and defend themselves furiously. It was very plausible that not only the archers but the Muslims fighting down in the valley were also after the allure of booty and this would have prompted the archers to join in. The Prophet was hurt in the process and it was the heroic bravery of his closest companions that saved the day. The Makkans sensing they had scored a victory began to retreat and the Muslim survivors were thus able to retreat in fairly good order. Twenty-two Makkans and around seventy Muslims had been killed, including Muhammad's uncle Hamzah, a renowned fighter who strengthened the Muslims during their persecution in Makkah and dearly loved by the Prophet. The pagan cruelty and debauched mind reached the lowest level of human depravity when they mutilated the slain bodies of the Muslims and their women garlanded themselves with the organs of the dead. On witnessing this terrible sight the Prophet was so saddened and overcome with grief that he explicitly forbade the mutilation of bodies in war.

The following verse was revealed soon after placing in perspective the plight of the Muslims.

"God did indeed fulfil His promise to you when ye with His permission were about to annihilate your enemy,-until ye flinched and fell to disputing about the order, and disobeyed it after He brought you in sight (of the booty) which ye covet. Among you are some that hanker after this world and some that desire the Hereafter. Then did He divert you from your foes in order to test you but He forgave you: For God is full of grace to those who believe." (2:152)

The Prophet on his part was patient and understanding of human weakness and in fact was able to remobilize the very same people to march out two days later towards the Makkans to ensure that they would not return back to attack what they would have thought a very vulnerable city. Allah revealed the following regarding Uhud:

"So by mercy from Allah, [O Muhammad], you were lenient with them. And if you had been rude [in speech] and harsh in heart, they would have abandoned you. So pardon them and ask forgiveness for them and consult them in the matter. And when you have decided, then rely upon Allah. Indeed, Allah loves those who rely [upon Him]." (3:159)

108

Pause for reflection

Although this battle was marked by the desertion of the hypocrites even before the battle commenced, and the disobedience of the Prophets instructions by a section of the Muslims, it brought out the best of bravery and sacrifice by some of the Prophet's companions that prevented a total collapse of the Muslim forces.

When the Quraysh forces counter attacked after their initial setback and following the desertion of their post by the Muslim archers, the Muslims dropped the booty they carried, drew their swords and defended themselves. But their victory was lost. Their ranks were disorderly and their unity was in shreds. Quraysh took a heavy toll of Muslim lives. Earlier, the Muslims were fighting by the command of God and out of their faith in Him and in victory; now they fought in order to save their own lives from certain death and humiliation. Earlier, the Muslims were fighting in a united and orderly manner, under a strong and resolute leadership; now they fought without order or leadership. So great was the disorder that some may have struck their own fellows. Finally, when somebody raised the cry that Muhammad was killed, chaos reigned supreme, Muslim morale plunged to the bottom and Muslim soldiers fought sporadically and purposelessly.

As for the messenger of God, he said when his tooth was broken and his face was struck and bloodied: 'Lord, guide my people, for they do not know.' Not even their actions prevented him from intending good on them.

"If the battle of Badr was a sign from God proving the veracity of Muhammad's prophethood, what was the sign of the battle of Uhud?" Detractors of Islam sometimes forward the argument that if Islam's movement in history is God willed and God incepted-such as Islam holds-leads in case of frustration, loss or defeat, to the absurdity either that God's will is being frustrated or that the movement in question is not God-willed. They omit here to consider that the unfolding of God's will in history is, in Islam, not the working of blind necessity but that of free men whose responsible decisions are the very stuff of divine will, so that defeat or victory are attributable to them by the Will of God. It was this moralism of the Muslims that saved them after their defeat at Uhud and at the hands of Crusaders and Tatars in the Middle Ages.

In March 627, a massive army of ten thousand men—the Quraysh and their confederates—were on the march toward Madinah. The Prophet could raise only a paltry three thousand warriors from Madinah and his Bedouin allies.

This time there was no bravado; the Muslims barricaded themselves into the "city" in the center of the oasis. Surrounded on three sides by cliffs and plains of volcanic rock, Madinah was not difficult to defend. It was most vulnerable from the north, but the Prophet adopted a stratagem suggested to him by Salman al-Farsi, a Persian convert. The Quraysh were in no hurry, making their way grandly and confidently in easy stages, so the Muslims had plenty of time. They gathered in the crops from the outlying fields, so that this time the Makkans would find no fodder, and then the entire community set to work digging a huge trench around the northern part of the oasis. This was nothing short of astonishing—even shocking—to Arab sensibilities. No self-respecting warrior would dream of putting a barrier between himself and the enemy. He would consider it degrading to shovel earth like a slave. But the Prophet worked alongside his companions, laughing, joking, and singing with his men. Morale was high. When the Quraysh arrived with their army, they stared blankly at the trench. The earth from the ditch had been used to build a high escarpment, which effectively shielded the Madinites in their camp and gave them a superior vantage point from which to hurl missiles. The Quraysh were bewildered. They had never seen anything so unconventional in their life.

Their cavalry, which was their pride and joy, was useless. From time to time, one of their horsemen would try to lead a dashing charge towards the enemy lines, only to screech absurdly to a halt when he arrived at the dugout. The siege lasted only a month, but it seemed endless. Feeding and supplying the allies of Madinah as well as their own people put a great strain on the city's resources.

The Jews of Khaybar had contributed a large contingent to the Makkan army, which included many of the exiled tribe of Nadir. Before the arrival of the Makkan army, the chief of the exiled Jewish tribe of Nadir, had tried to persuade Qurayzah either to attack the Muslims from the rear or to smuggle two thousand Nadiri's into the oasis to slaughter the women and children in the fortresses. Initially Qurayzah were hesitant, but when they saw the vast Makkan army filling the plain in front of the city as far as the eye could see, their chief agreed to help the confederacy and provide the Quraysh with weapons and supplies.

When the Prophet heard of this treachery, he was visibly distressed. He sent one of his companions, who had been Qurayzah's chief Arab ally before the hijrah, to negotiate, but to no avail. At one point the Qurayzah actually started to attack the fortresses on the southeast of the settlement, but the effort petered out. For about three weeks, it was quite unclear which way they would go. Throughout the Battle of the Trench, as the siege became known, the Muslims were terrified. Faced with the prospect of extermination, some came close to despair. At this critical juncture one of the leaders of the confederate enemy groups belonging to the Ghatafan tribe named Nuai'm had a change of heart and witnessing the resilience and courage of the outnumbered Muslims found his way into the Muslim camp and declared to the Prophet that he wanted to embrace Islam and asked the Prophet how he could help. When an opportunity arises the Prophet is not one who does not seize it and he requested him to break the pact between the Quraizah Jews and the Quraysh as the Prophet knew that the enemies did not know that this person of interest had become a Muslim and thus would treat him as an ally. Nua'im who was skilled in the art of negotiation and guile was able to sow distrust and suspicion of each other motives between the Quraysh and the Jews which resulted in the latter reneging on their part of the deal and removing the threat to the families inside Madinah.

But even as those inside the city trembled, on the other side of the trench, the Quraysh were becoming exhausted. They had inadequate provisions and their inexperience in military affairs meant that they were easily demoralized by a sudden reversal. Their resolve finally snapped when a violent rainstorm devastated their camp. Abu Sufiyan recognized defeat. Horses and camels were dying, the Qurayzah had failed to deliver, and his troops had no tents, fires, or utensils.

"Be off," he announced to his men, "for I am going." When the Muslims peered over the escarpment the next morning, the plain was completely deserted.

Thus ended the battle of the Trench, the enemies of the Muslims defeated and thwarted by the patience and resilience of the Muslims on one side and the forces of nature sent by God on the other. It was a tremendous victory for the Muslims whose faith had been tested to its limit and were rewarded by God with victory as referred to in the Quran:

"O you, who have believed, remember the favor of Allah upon you when armies came to [attack] you and We sent upon them a wind and armies [of angels] you did not see. And ever is Allah, of what you do, Seeing." (33:9)

Concept of Jihad

Jihad means-literally-`striving`, and applies to everything human beings can do to resist temptation within themselves or the society around them on one hand and on the other to promote the good and attempt to reform themselves and their surroundings. The effort is twofold: one of resistance and one of reform. A person can wage a spiritual jihad against egoism and arrogance, against poverty, racism or corruption, just as that person can wage jihad for education, social justice, equality and peace. Of the some eighty accepted definitions of the term Jihad, only one applies to war (qital) and involves strict conditions: war is legitimate only in self defence against aggression or colonization. War can never be justified to exploit or to colonize, seize territory or natural resources, and even less to force conversion upon anyone. The term jihad appears in the Quran for the first time when the Prophet is called upon to wage a `jihad of the mind`: when he was confronted with the mockery and aggression of the Makkans, who rejected his message. And his mission, divine revelation enjoined him `do not defer to the desires of those who deny the truth, but strive hard against them, by means of this (Quran), with utmost striving' (25:52). The life of the Way is a life of striving, of commitment and of resistance. It begins with the self and permeates every aspect of social, scientific, cultural, political, economic and even artistic life. In many ways, jihad is the visible countenance of the spiritual elevation not only of the individual but also o society as a whole when, in search for good, people collectively decide to resist the worst.

Extracted from, Islam: the Essentials by Dr. Tariq Ramadan, Penguin Random House UK, 2017

It is unfortunate that some writers of the 'Seerah' or life of the Prophet have unwittingly or otherwise used the term 'Jihad' instead of 'Qitaal' when referring to the Quranic verses in relation to fighting. The Quran itself is very clear when it states ..."Qitaal fi Sabbelillah...", fight in the path of Allah and not ...'Jihaad fi Sabeelillah.."

The Inscription on the Sword of the Prophet (ﷺ)

Soon after the demise of the Prophet, when Ali ibn Abu Talib his cousin and son in law and closest relative alive at that time took hold of the few personal belongings of Muhammad which included his shield and sword, he noticed an inscription on the sword. This inscription as recoded in an authentic narration read;

"Forgive the one who wrongs you, reconcile with the one who cuts you off, show excellence to the one who shows evil, and speak the truth even if it is against yourself."

Words that did not echo the heroic inspirational or motivational cry from a commander in chief who was in the midst of many battles against the enemies of God but the words of a Prophet, a Messenger of God who came to this world as a mercy to Mankind. Muhammad could have inscribed on his sword words about strength and courage and not fleeing from the battle field which is found in the Quran but instead he chooses to inscribe on the avatar that directed and defended righteousness and justice, words that underscored the principles of mercy, forbearance, compassion and justice; values that echo repeatedly in the Quranic verses.

Interestingly and remarkably so, it is well recorded in tradition that Muhammad did not directly kill anyone with his sword although he was in the heart of the battles he participated in, fending off enemy forces and disarming enemy combatants with his shield and sword and rallying the Muslims around him to fight with courage which he showed by example. The only instance in which he slayed an enemy was when he was injured and fallen down in the battle of Uhud and an enemy who had sworn to kill Muhammad from his early days in Makkah charged towards him on his horse, and Muhammad picked up a spear and hurled it at the attacker wounding him on his neck leading to his ultimate death. The Prophet mentioned that the worst punishment in the hereafter awaits those who kill a prophet of God or one who is killed by a Prophet and hence his restraint until it became inevitable.

Muhammad (ﷺ) , The Warrior Prophet- Historical context

During the period spanning 622CE to 632 CE, Muhammad living in Madinah ordered or undertook twenty-seven raids occurring under his own leadership, (Ghazwat) and at least fifty others led by commanders whom he appointed and sent out (Saraya). In the years after Badr, Muhammad fought mainly defensive and pre-emptive battles against non-muslims primarily for existential reasons, as well as certain offensive campaigns for demonstrable societally beneficial reasons. This begs the question whether the Prophet of Islam was a war monger for whatever reason or was he attempting to redress the plight of the emigrant Muslims who came to Madinah with virtually nothing or was he even trying to force religious compliance or was he simply practicing an embedded and accepted cultural tradition of the Arabs that was seen as 'fair play' and demonstrated courage, honour, esteem and drew upon every noble value and virtue of the Arabs and provided tangible benefits for the community. However, to place matters in perspective it should be noted that the time Muhammad spent on campaigns and battles were only 7% or just over one and a half years (which included the travel time to and back from the location) out of his 23 years of prophethood.

Prof. Joel Hayward, a contemporary Muslim historian and scholar of both war and prophetic biography, in his book "The Warrior Prophet Muhammad and War", has written an evidence-based objective, neutral and strategically insightful work on the warfare of the Prophet. In response to the question posed above, he states in his book;

"The answer seems to lie in the acceptability, indeed esteem attached to raiding throughout Arabian society. Far from being seen as an extraordinary activity much less as an acceptable act of aggression and violence as we would now see it, raiding was very much an ordinary part of the fabric of society. It was a widespread tribal activity -a recognized means of redistributing wealth and resources-with the potential for great prestige and honour attached to it.

Muhammad (ﷺ) , The Warrior Prophet- Historical context

The problem for the twenty -first century reader of the early Arabic sources is that particularly since the emergence of the Westphalian state system, we have come to see issues of war and peace differently to how they were seen throughout much of human history. Within the modern Islamic historiography of seventh-century Arabia, there is a widespread anachronistic depiction that warfare was then, like now was considered unethical. This was certainly not the case in sixth and seventh-century Arabia, the cradle of Islam."

Joel Hayward goes on to state;

"A challenge for historians and scholars seeking to understand causality is that it is often difficult to escape present-centeredness, which denotes the way that people base their understanding of processes, experiences, norms and values in the unobservable past upon their understanding of similar seeming processes, experiences, norms and values in the observable present. For example, because even competitive countries or peoples nowadays ordinarily act towards each other as though a general state of peace exists, except when there is a particular grievance between them, it is easy to today to believe that this was always the case. Yet in seventh century tribal Arabia the opposite situation existed. A state of war was understood to exist between one's own tribe and all others around it, except when a pact or treaty had been established. Similarly, if a certain type of behavior-for example raiding the territory of other communities in order to loot from their herds or their trade shipments- is morally indefensible today, then, it is natural to believe that it must have been indefensible in the past."

He also cites from other historical sources that in the context of seventh century Arabia;
"Raids were highly esteemed and socially expected activities in which manly qualities such as combat skill, courage, cunning, stealth, resourcefulness and hardiness were developed, demonstrated and then publicly recognized and eulogized".
However, Hayward hastens to emphasize the unwritten norms and traditional rules of engagement during these raids which were adhered to as far as possible by the raiding tribes.

Hence it was prohibited to kill or harm non-combatants, women and children. Minimal or no loss of human lives was the norm and in the event that the able men fled the scene sensing a rout, the raiders were to leave behind sufficient provision and transport for the others to join the rest. It is also important to make a distinction between raiding by established clans or tribes against other established tribes or clans and any type of brigandry undertaken by groups who attack innocent travellers or pilgrims and were more like vagrant bandits who were detested by even the most committed tribal raiders.

Hayward also notes that, "If the large pitched battles or campaigns such as Badr, Uhud, Azhab (Confederates), Muta, conquest of Makkah, Hunayn, Taif and expedition to Tabuk are excluded the number of warriors in the other raids that Muhammad sent out were ordinarily small with an average of less than 100 raiders and were generally fairly bloodless affairs. Also like any other tribal leader Muhammad was formally entitled to one-fifth (khums) of all income generated by campaigns. The Quran affirms this in sura 8 verse 41:

"And know that whatsoever you take as spoils, a fifth is for God and the Messenger, and for kinsfolk, orphans, the indigent, and the traveler, if you believe in God and what We sent down upon Our servant on the Day of Discrimination, the day the two hosts met—and God is Powerful over all things"-(8:41)

Here we see that Muhammad was to take one -fifth of the one-fifth portion and the other four-fifth to go as he saw fit to his relations, orphans, the needy and the travellers.

Muhammad, for his part even gave away from the portion that was rightly his after keeping the bare sustenance needed for him and his family. His needs were frugal if not sparse and he desired earnestly for the well-being of his community and was like the fierce Arabian wind when it came to giving and ensuring that anyone who came to him with an appeal or grievance was comforted both in kind and in means.

Muhammad (ﷺ) , The Warrior Prophet- Historical context

Hayward goes on to state:

"Clearly the ever reflective Muhammad did not send out all these early raids without some sense of strategic purpose, and as a pattern the raids served to restrict severely the Quraysh's trade, limit its supplies of food, acquire wealth for the Islamic community, increase prestige, strengthen Islamic tribal alliances with Bedouins and other tribes, and weaken Quraysh alliances. In the years after Badr, Muhammad fought mainly defensive and pre-emptive battles against non-muslims primarily for existential reasons as well as certain offensive campaigns for demonstrable societally beneficial reasons."

"For modern readers of Islamic origins, especially for Muslims the moral quandary remains. In today's world raiding caravans and herds for looting would be theft, in the same way that piracy or burglary is seen as theft. The logical approach to this quandary would be simply to acknowledge that moral norms and expec- tations are society specific, contextual and repeatedly reinterpreted- and re-evaluated. They are not therefore universal. Indeed many moral philosophers reason that there is no universal morality that is applicable to and binding upon everyone everywhere with the same understanding for all time regardless of context.........Seventh century inter-tribal raiding, including Muhammad's should be seen in this light. It was then unmistakably part of Arabia's moral landscape, with personal and communal honour and esteem attached to its successful conduct even though that landscape has changed so much that we no longer recognize it. Today's readers need to understand the raids as they were then understood. Raiding for booty was neither banditry nor theft. The legitimate authority-the tribal leaders-not only allowed it, but repeatedly initiated it. Just as in today's world, the legitimate authority's initiation of an action created a moral legitimacy different to an action initiated by all other individuals. Thus one cannot attribute the slightest immorality to the Muslim raids or to consider them theft. Within the raid's moral framework of course, was a firm and non-negotiable position that made an individual's taking part of the booty without authority a clear case of theft.

Muhammad (ﷺ) , The Warrior Prophet- Historical context

Muslims should see the raids as part of a contextual, time bound set of circumstances that no longer exist, socially sanctioned by customary law that has long been superseded, initiated by a type of leadership that has given way to governments and undertaken according to values that have changed considerably. Muhammad undertook them it is true, and gained the same esteem and benefit as others who successfully did so in his era, and for Muslims that might seem a problem given that they want to follow his example. Yet they could only follow it anyway if there was a return to the very same set of circumstances. In that regard, this is the same as the impossibility of Muslims today following the Quranic or prophetic direction on how Muslims should deal with polytheists performing pagan rituals at the Kaaba. The situation no longer exists; so therefore, that direction is no longer part of a sunna that 1.8 billion Muslims today can follow."

Muslims believe that everything happens by the Will of God and God wills causality for a thing to happen or not through the epistemology of that time which includes the traditions, customs, values and norms of that time unless He wills a miracle to happen. Just as slavery was the norm in 7th Century Arabia and even prior to Muhammad's time, its practice gradually and eventually disappeared never to be part of the sunna and was antithetical to the moral framework of the Quran. Dr. Khaled Abu Fadl in his groundbreaking book 'Reasoning with God' states;

"There is a serious problem with arguing that God intended to lock the epistemology of the 7th Century into the immutable text of the Quran, and then intended to hold Muslims hostage to this epistemological framework for all ages to come. Among other things, this would limit the dynamism and effectiveness of divine text because the Quran would be forever locked within a knowledge paradigm that is very difficult to retrieve or re-create."

The same principle could apply to the Sunna of the Prophet and based on the evolving knowledge and norms of the times, certain practices become redundant or abolished subject to the eternal and absolute laws of the Quran.

∞

In the year 628 CE, after years of conflict between the Quraysh and the Muslims, Muhammad had a revelation that he should visit the sacred mosque. In the eighth year after his migration to Madinah the Prophet, set out for Makkah with 1400 followers and carrying no arms and with the pure intent of performing the pilgrimage but his adversaries refused to allow him in. The Quraysh were in a dilemma, according to Arab custom they could not prevent anyone from performing the pilgrimage peacefully but at the same time they would have lost face among their own tribes if they allowed the Muslims to enter Makkah. The Muslims had in the meantime worn their pilgrimage garb and camped just outside Makkah but within its holy sanctuary in a place called Hudaibiyah, in fact the Prophet's camel had stopped at Hudaibiyah and refused to proceed towards Makkah which the Prophet recognized as a sign from God, stating *"the one who prevented the elephants from entering Makkah has prevented my camel from doing so"*. After several attempts by the Quraysh to intimidate and dissuade the Muslims from entering Makkah including sending negotiators to talk to the Prophet they realized that the Muslims were sincerely there to perform pilgrimage but their pride and status made them adamant in preventing the Muslims from entering the precincts of the sacred mosque that year. To reach an amicable solution the Prophet sent his son-in-law Uthman ibn Affan who had close family connections with the leaders of the Quraysh inside Makkah to negotiate with them. The Prophet also instructed him to visit the many Muslims in Makkah who were not permitted to migrate to Madinah and was virtually imprisoned or prevented from practicing their faith. Uthman visited them and heard their plea to negotiate a way out for them and he assured them that the prophet had indicated 'God will find a way out for them soon'. Uthman had to stay over in Makkah during the prolonged talks on permitting Muhammad and his followers to perform the pilgrimage peacefully which made the Muslims anxious about his safety and life and imagined the worst. The Muslims individually and collectively pledged to the Prophet that they would avenge the death of Uthman if it did happen, and also stand by the command of the Prophet in fighting the Makkans if needed.

This pledge given to the Prophet was called the 'Baya tul Ridwan' or the covenant of pleasure as Allah's revelation soon after confirmed:

"Certainly was Allah pleased with the believers when they pledged allegiance to you, [O Muhammad], under the tree, and He knew what was in their hearts, so He sent down tranquillity upon them and rewarded them with an imminent conquest." (48:18)

Amidst heightened emotions and tempers they saw Uthman returning back with the news that the Quraysh were eager to find a way out of the impasse without permanently damaging their reputation and prestige in the Arabian Peninsula. They sent out their most articulate and eloquent orator and negotiator Suhail ibn Amr as an arbitrator to strike an agreement that would bring the almost two week stand-off to an end. The Prophet for his part personally negotiated and made Ali his cousin to be the scribe to write down the conditions of the agreement.

Muhammad began by proposing that they start the treaty by stating in writing "In the name of Allah the most merciful, the compassionate" and Suhail retorts that the term "merciful' or 'compassionate" or "Rahman wa Raheem" is unfamiliar to the Makkans and they use the phrase "In the name of Allah" only. The Prophet agrees and at the end of the treaty when it came to signing the agreement, Suhail again objects to the title of the Prophet to be stated as 'Messenger of Allah', and states "If we knew or acknowledge you as the messenger of God then why should we object to you entering Makkah?", and again the Prophet agrees to the humble title of Muhammad ibn Abdullah. It was clear to the wise and sublime that as the negotiations proceeded Suhail was satisfied to extract short term advantages and scoring prestige points over the Prophet whilst Muhammad was focused on the longer term strategic intent of the treaty.

And so the Prophet apparently compromised his own position and that of the Muslim community in pursuit of peace much to the dismay of his companions and followers. This treaty was signed and was referred to as the "Treaty of Hudaibiyah" and its main points were:

- Both have agreed to a complete truce for a period of ten years, during which all people will enjoy peace and security and will not attack one another.
- Moreover, if anyone from the Quraysh joins Muhammad without permission from his guardian or chief, he shall be returned to the Quraysh.
- If anyone from those in the camp of Muhammad joins the Quraysh, they are not required to return him.
- Both sides agree that they harbour good intentions towards each other.
- No theft or treachery shall be condoned.
- Whoever wishes to enter into an alliance with Muhammad may do so, and whoever wants to enter into an alliance with the Quraysh may do so.
- It is further agreed that you, Muhammad, shall return home this year without entering Makkah. At the end of one year, we shall evacuate Makkah for you so that you may enter it with your followers to stay for three days only. You shall carry only the armament necessary for a traveller – namely, your swords in their sheaths. You shall not carry any other arms.

Some of the conditions smacked of inequity against the Muslims and the companions of the prophet were visibly upset and frustrated to say the least. The fact that a Quraysh who converts to a Muslim and leaves Makkah has to be repatriated back whereas a Muslim who apostatises and returns to Makkah or elsewhere is allowed to remain there. The implication of this condition was that the life of a pagan was worth more than that of a Muslim. However the Prophet's reasoning in agreeing to this condition underscores the Quranic principle of "no coercion of conscience and compulsion in religion" and the Quran declares emphatically;

"Say, 'Now the truth has come from your Lord: let those who wish to believe in it do so, and let those who wish to reject it do so." *(19:29)*

"Let there be no compulsion in religion: Truth stands out clear from Error: whoever rejects evil and believes in Allah hath grasped the most trustworthy hand-hold, that never breaks. And Allah heareth and knoweth all things." (2:256)

Orientalists and contemporary anti-Muslim elements disingenuously conflate apostasy with treason and used weak or even fabricated late antiquity hadiths or sayings of the prophet and asserted falsely that Islam prescribes capital punishment for those who leave the faith. Here in the early part of Islamic jurisprudence both the Quran and the Prophet establish the principle of "no coercion of conscience" in the most emphatic way.

After the treaty was signed and witnessed, the Prophet asked the Muslims to sacrifice the animals they had brought and shave their heads to mark the ritual completion of the pilgrimage. Though reluctant initially as they had been deprived from entering the sacred mosque and performing the rites of pilgrimage, they soon followed the Prophet when he sacrificed his animal and shaved his hair. Soon after a breeze blew across the plains of Hudaibiyah and the shaven locks of hair lying on the desert sands blew away towards Makkah and the Muslims took this as a sign that their sacrifice and pilgrimage was accepted by God. On the journey back to Madinah some of the companions were still deeply troubled by what had just taken place and disappointed that they were thwarted from visiting the holy sanctuary. When asked to explain, the Prophet, replied, "Did I say it was going to be this year?" And then God revealed the following verses which the Prophet described as more precious to him than anything else in the world at that time.

"We have given you a manifest victory, that God may forgive you your sins, past and future, and may perfect His favour to you, and may guide you on a right path. God may also grant you a strong victory." (48:1-3)

There was hence no reason to doubt that the Hudaybiyah Treaty was a victory for the Muslims. History has shown that this pact was the product of profound political wisdom and farsightedness and that it brought about consequences of great advantage to Islam and indeed to Arabia as a whole. It was the first time that Quraysh acknowledged that Muhammad was an equal rather than a mere rebel and runaway tribesman. It was the first time that Makkah acknowledged the Islamic state that was rising in Arabia. Makkan acquiescence in the right of the Muslims to visit the sanctuary and to perform the pilgrimage was equally recognition on her part that Islam was an established and approved religion in the Peninsula. Furthermore, the peace of the following two or ten years gave the Muslims the peace and security they needed on their southern flank without fear of an invasion from Quraysh. The peace also contributed to the spread of Islam. Even Quraysh, the most determined enemy of Islam and its greatest antagonist, had by this pact come to recognize Islam and its community, and to acquiesce in that in which it had never acquiesced before. Indeed, Islam spread after this treaty more widely and quickly than it had ever spread before. While those who accompanied Muhammad to Hudaybiyah counted one thousand and four hundred, those who accompanied him on his conquest of Makkah two years later counted well over ten thousand.

A remarkable and ironic twist of fate decreed by God was that following the conquest of Makkah two years later, Suhail the main pagan architect behind the treaty of Hudaybiyah accepted Islam and became a devout Muslim engaging in profuse acts of worship and benevolence. When the Prophet passed away and some of the people of Makkah were entertaining the thought of going back to paganism, Suhail made a stirring speech admonishing the Makkans in which he said," "Oh people of Makkah, do not be the last group to convert, and the first to renegade and apostasies", which brought the Makkans to their senses.

It is evident from this that there could be some goodness deep within every soul though their bad actions and beliefs may be what are apparent at a point in time. The Prophet strived to give every soul the opportunity to live to their best and noble potential and to convince them and coax them to turn to God in complete submission.

The wisdom and strategic significance of the treaty at Hudaybiyah was initially known only to God and His Messenger. Eventually the Muslims realized the import of this treaty as their lives become normalized without the hostile threat from the south and they began to engage and interact with their folks in Makkah. As the message of Islam spread into Makkah many hearts tuned to the new faith and many dared to leave and seek a new life outside Makkah along the Red sea coast as the treaty prevented the Muslims from accepting them into Madinah. The circumstances and events surrounding the treaty established basic principles of sacrificing pride and position for the sake of longer term more important goals as the Prophet gave into many of the pagan requests in order to secure the treaty and ensure a peaceful pilgrimage to Makkah the following year.

The treaty of Hudaibiyah and modern game theory analysis

A more profound analysis of the wisdom behind this treaty framed against the prevailing circumstances at that time reveals a more insightful and strategic move on the part of the Prophet in line with modern game theory logic. The Makkans were cornered into a position where they had to sign a treaty to save face and the concessions given by the Prophet to secure the treaty were merely short term in nature whereas the Makkans did not realize that they were in a long term losing position based on the condition that Islam will continue to grow and spread in the short and long term and eventually erode any advantage that accrued to the Makkans. In fact even before the treaty was violated by a tribe affiliated to the Quraysh, certain clauses in the treaty became moot points as new converts to Islam joined together to thwart the commercial freedom of the Quraysh which the treaty afforded them. It could be argued that even if the treaty was not violated- which led to the conquest of Makkah- it would have been a matter of time before the Quraysh would have had to concede victory to the Muslims due to the growing power and influence of Islam that was sweeping the hearts of people all over the Arabian Peninsula.

Seven

The Return, Forgiveness and Restoration

I n March 629 CE, it was time for Muhammad to lead another pilgrimage to the Kaabah as agreed in the treaty of Hudaibiyah. This time 2,600 pilgrims accompanied him, and as they approached the sanctuary, the Quraysh evacuated the city, as they had agreed. The Quraysh elders watched the arrival of Muhammad from the top of a nearby mountain. The sound of the Muslims loudly announcing their presence with the traditional cry: "Here I am, O Allah! Here I am!" must have echoed through the valleys and empty streets of the city like a cruel taunt. But they must also have been impressed by the discipline of the Muslims. There were no scenes of unbridled joy or unseemly celebrations; no jeering at the Quraysh. Instead, the huge crowd of pilgrims filed slowly and solemnly into the city, led by Muhammad, who as usual was mounted on Qiswa, the white she camel. When he reached the Kaaba, he dismounted and kissed the Black Stone, embracing it, and then proceeded to make the circumambulations, followed by the entire pilgrim body. It was a strange home- coming. The emigrants must have felt highly emotional about their return, and yet, although the city was a ghost town, they were not free to do as they pleased. It had been settled at Hudaybiyyah that this year the Muslims could only make the lesser Pilgrimage, the Umrah, which did not include a visit to mount 'Arafat and the valley of Mina. In temporary exile from their city, the Quraysh had to watch—no doubt appalled—as Bilal, a former slave, climbed onto the roof of the Kaabah and summoned the Muslims to prayer. Five times a day, his huge voice reverberated through the valley, urging all within earshot to come to prayer with the cry "Allahu Akbar," reminding them that Allah was "greater" than all the idols in the Haram, who could do nothing to prevent this ritual humiliation.

In accordance with the treaty the Prophet and the Muslims left after their allotted three days but not before leaving behind a permanent and deep emotion of admiration and opening of hearts of many Makkans towards the new faith. One notable and significant incident was the conversion of Khalid bin Waleed who later on became one of the greatest Muslim generals and commanded the Muslim army against the Byzantines and other foreign forces. After witnessing the behaviour and worship of the Muslims in Makkah he declared; "It has become absolutely clear to any person with the least intelligence that Muhammad is neither a poet possessed nor a magician inspired. His words are truly the words of God, of the Lord of the Universe. It follows then that every man with common sense ought to follow him." Soon after he declared his intention to convert to the Prophet and left for Madinah which opened the doors despite the treaty for any other notable members of the Quraysh to follow him. Slowly but surely the conquest of Makkah was becoming a certainty through winning the hearts and minds of the people.

∞

In the 8th year of Hijra (630 CE), a pagan tribe who were in alliance with the Quraysh violated the treaty, raiding and massacring members of another tribe Banu Kuda who were in alliance with the Muslims and had converted to Islam and hence protected by the treaty. This blatant act of treachery and violence killing several even in the sacred precinct was in clear violation of the pact. Compounding the situation further and adding to its grievous nature was the fact that the Quraysh had knowingly aided the pagan tribe by supplying weapons. Realizing the gravity of this violation and its consequences, Abu Sufiyan, the head of the Quraysh in Makkah attempted to restore the treaty by travelling to Madinah but it was not to be as the Prophet of God and the Muslims deliberated on the most judicious response to take and Abu Sufyan had to return to Makkah with a sense of foreboding and despondency. News of the massacre enraged the believers and the Prophet, summoned all of the Muslims capable of bearing arms to march on Makkah in the year 630CE. This operation was conducted with great stealth and secrecy and the Muslims knew for certain they were heading towards Makkah only the night before. The Prophet had indicated earlier that they were going on an expedition and possible battle to some place and as a diversion even sent a group of Muslims up north to scout the area for strategic deployment whereas Makkah lay to the south of Madinah. When the nearly ten thousand Muslims arrived on the outskirts of the city, the Quraysh realized they did not stand a chance and people either fled to the surrounding hills or stayed in their homes. Abu Sufiyan himself the leader of the Quraysh on hearing the march of the Muslims towards Makkah rode out to meet the Prophet (ﷺ) who called upon him one final time to declare that there is no God but Allah and Muhammad was the Messenger. On witnessing the sheer numbers and commitment of the Muslims and the manner in which they prayed in unison, the pagan chieftain embraced Islam and then rushed toward Makkah calling to his people at the top of his voice: "O men of Quraysh, here comes Muhammad with an army such as you have never seen before. Put up no resistance. Whoever enters into my house shall be secure; whoever remains in his own house shall be secure; and whoever enters the Mosque shall be secure." This assurance was given to him by the Prophet.

And so it was, after years of persecution, the Prophet (ﷺ), marched triumphant into the city of his birth at the head of the largest army ever assembled in Arabian history. Riding on his white she camel with his head bowed in humility he declared a general amnesty and granted war criminals and his arch enemies' refuge and forgave them. His only act of defiance was to topple the hundreds of idols around the Kaaba declaring:

"Say, the truth is now manifest. Falsehood is truly confuted. And it is right that it should be." (Quran 17:81)

He then recited the Quranic verse:

"Mankind, We have created you all from one male and one female so that you may know one another. The most honourable among you is the most God-fearing." (49:13)

Addressing the Quraysh he asked them:
"What sort of judgement do you think I am going to pass against you?" They replied: "A benevolent one. You are an honourable brother and the son of an honourable brother of ours."
He said: "You may go free. You are all pardoned."
The maxim on which the Prophet's attitude as based is best expressed by the Quranic verse:

"A good deed and a bad one can never be alike. Repel the latter with the one which is best and you will find that the person with whom you have a long hostility behaving to you as an intimate friend." (41:34)

The following verse of the Quran captured the spirit of reconciliation;

"This is the tradition of God, as ever before, and you will find no change in His tradition. He it is who withheld their hands from you and your hands from them in the heart of Makkah after He made you ascendant over them. God sees the things you do." (Quran 48:23-24)

His overwhelming magnanimity of character led to a mass conversion among the citizens of Makkah. Knowing that Makkah was steeped in slavery the Prophet also declared:

"O people, in God's eyes you are all created from dust and there are only those who believe and humble themselves to God and those who are rebellious and disbelieve. Your slaves are your brothers and sisters whom God has entrusted you with, so treat them with kindness, give them of what you eat and if a task is burdensome for them help them with it. Freeing a slave is like saving the life of someone and if you physically hurt a slave the only way to recompense for it is to set him or her free".

For a nation where slavery was ingrained into their customs and way of life these words of the Prophet imploded in their minds as faith steadily crept into their hearts. It is a testament to the Prophetic words designed to eradicate slavery in Arabia that the majority of the new generation of Arabs that made up the future dynasties in Arabia and the greater Islamic empire were from the children of freed slaves. During the two weeks which Muhammad spent in Makkah, he wiped out all the traces of paganism in the city. All the offices attached to the holy House were abolished except two, the Sidanah (provision of shelter to pilgrims) which the Prophet assigned to `Uthman ibn Talhah, his children, and progeny after him till the end of days, and the Siqayah, (provision of water to pilgrims) which he assigned to his uncle al `Abbas. Thus Umm al Qura [i.e. translation of Makkah] embraced Islam and raised high the torch of genuine monotheism, illuminating the whole world for generations and centuries to come.

Despite the conquest of Makkah, there were some whose hearts were not won over easily. Fadala bin Umayr was one of those seething with hatred and desperate for revenge. He vowed to kill Muhammad

(ﷺ), despite proclaiming to have accepted Islam. One day, as the Prophet was circling the Kaaba, Fadala tucked his sword under his clothing and followed him closely, gradually coming within attacking range, thinking to himself about the dastardly deed he was about to commit. Suddenly, the Prophet turned around and found himself face to face with Fadala. "What is it that you were saying to yourself?" the Prophet asked. "Nothing—I was just praising Allah," Fadala retorted visibly startled. The Prophet simply smiled and said, "Ask Allah to forgive you," and placing his hand on Fadala's chest, pressed upon it. Fadala would say, "By Allah, from the moment he lifted his hand from my chest, there remained nothing of Allah's creation except that he was more beloved to me than it." This is an assassin in the most sacred place, fully under the Prophet's control, being met with the loving supplication of the Prophet rather than the punishment he deserved.

The Prophet stayed in Makkah for around 19 days after the triumphant and peaceful march and during this time he ordered the destruction of all idols both in the public space and in the homes of people and forbade the Makkans from making and selling idols to pilgrims who treasured idols from Makkah as having special significance. The removal and destruction of all idols was both a physical cleansing and symbolic gesture of spiritual purification foreshadowing the eventual de-paganization of Arabia.

One of the most significant effects of the conquest of Makkah was the resulting unification of Arabia through Makkah acting as a central hub. Arabia was disunited at this time and tribe had its own mini city and province. The conquest of Makkah was taken as a symbolic conquest of the central nerve centre of both the spiritual and traditional realms of Arabia. The other tribes who stayed aloof in the conflict between the Quraysh and the Prophet were waiting to see who would take Makkah. If the Muslims eventually conquer Makkah, this is an indication nothing will stand in their way and they must inevitably embrace the new faith. A common sentiment and belief spread among the Arabs that, "Allah had protected Makkah from the people of the elephants; and if Allah allows this man Muhammad to conquer it, it must show he is a Prophet". The people in central, south, far north, the entire Arabian Peninsula paid homage to the city of Makkah when it comes to sacredness. Every Arab at that time considers Makkah to be the apex of their race and religion. Due to this common heritage they all shared with Makkah - the conquest of the holy city or 'Haram' translated for them as the victory of Islam. Neutral tribes began sending delegations right up until the death of the prophet, affirming to him they have converted to Islam. Allah says in the Quran:

"When the victory of Allah has come and the conquest, And you see the people entering into the religion of Allah in multitudes. Then exalt [Him] with praise of your Lord and ask forgiveness of Him. Indeed, He is ever accepting of repentance." (110:1-3)

∞

Soon after the triumphant march into Makkah and the capitulation of the Quraysh, two dominant pagan tribes who lived in the hill city of Taif and its surroundings the Thaqif and the Hawazin decided to mount an attack on Makkah and the Muslims. The prophet on hearing this mobilized a fighting force of around twelve thousand men made up of the Muslims who came from Madinah and the new Muslims from the Quraysh which included Abu Sufyan the leader of the Quraysh now fighting alongside the prophet on the Muslim side! The pagan tribes of Hawazin who lived in the environs of Taif were so confident about overcoming the Muslims because they had the advantage of the hilly terrain and a confederate pagan army of twenty thousand, they brought their entire herd of camels and goats and their families along with them making up the rear. This move was to motivate them to fight courageously because they had to protect their animals and families behind them. This move seriously backfired on the pagans as after an initial surprise attack on the Muslims which threw the large Muslim army into disarray, the prophet regrouped the Muslims and mounted a counter attack that routed the enemies at the well of Hunayn.

The Quran refers to the battle of Hunayn in chapter nine:

"On the day of Ḥunayn, when you were pleased at your numerical power, you found out that it was of no avail to you. The vast expanse of the earth seemed to you very narrow and you began to flee. Then God sent down His reassurance and tranquillity on His Messenger and on the believers, and He dispatched soldiers whom you did not see and inflicted suffering on the unbelievers. That is the rightful reward for those who reject the faith." (9:25-26)

These two verses convey an important message: numerical strength is of little importance if the other elements necessary for victory are overlooked or neglected. It is important for Muslims to be on their guard against any complacency in their attitude

At the end of the day the entire livestock and families of the Hawazin became 'spoils of war' and the Muslims had thousands of head of livestock as booty and all the women and children as their captives. The tribe of Thaqif for their part retreated back into their well-fortified citadel fortress in Taif. The Muslim army pursued them into Taif and laid siege to their fortress city for over a week with very little success of breaking in despite using large catapults to hurl boulders at the fortress. Muhammad, realizing that it would be a battle of attrition decided to return back to Makkah to deal with the enormous war booty that they captured from the Hawazin. The entire tribe of Hawazin eventually embraced Islam when the Prophet released all their women and children who were prisoners of war and according to Arab custom could have been ransomed or taken in to slavery. This act of the Prophet literally signalled the end of slavery for even prisoners of war as all other ways of acquiring slaves had been prohibited.

The Thaqif tribal leaders seeing the spread and influence of Islam eventually decided to visit the Prophet and negotiate the acceptance of Islam with concessions they are permitted to drink wine, fornicate and not pray amidst other outrageous conditions.

The Prophet would have nothing of it and refused to compromise on any law or principle of the faith and ultimately they agreed to accept Islam unconditionally and in its entirety. Their only request was that the Prophet sends someone to Taif to destroy the Idol they had which was considered the most powerful after the one in Makkah. To this the Prophet agreed and sent some of his companions to do the needful. With the destruction of the last major idol in Taif the de-paganization of Arabia was complete with no more public idols and idol worship.

After the battle of Hunayn and the return from the siege of Taif they were about to witness one of the most generous and magnanimous acts of the Prophet and listen to one of his most emotional and heart rendering talks. He gave a hundred camels each to Abu Sufyan and his son Muawiya the chieftain of Makkah and his son and fifty camels each to the heads of the different tribes who were allied with the Muslims and who had entered into Islam after the conquest of Makkah. After giving generously to the new Muslims and the leaders of the Quraysh and other tribes, the prophet distributed a smaller amount among the immigrants or the 'muhajiroon' who left all and migrated to Madinah before the conquest. The 'Ansars' or the 'helpers' which was what the Madinites who hosted the prophet and the immigrants were called, received nothing as a reward for their effort in the battle. It is only in human nature that you feel a sense of inequity when you are not recognized or rewarded for your effort in a common experience or venture. The prophet sensing the mood of the Madinites immediately called them exclusively to a large tent and addressed them;

"If all of mankind were to go in one direction and the Ansar in another, I would go with the Ansar". And he said "were it not for the Hijrah, I would be from the Ansar. And he said "I give to some people because I fear for their greed and desires, and I don't give to others because I trust what Allah has given in their hearts, that fortune is more than what I can give them", and continued "the Quraysh is still new to Islam and I wish to comfort them by bringing them close to me". And he said "Oh Allah have mercy of the Ansar, and their children and their children." And finally he looks slowly and intently at their faces and says in a tone that echoed paternal love that moved them to their core and made their eyes swell with tears; "Are you not happy that people go back with sheep and camels and goats, but you go back with the Messenger of God?" The Ansars responded in unison their voices quivering with joy and their hearts filled with love for the Prophet, "We are content with Islam and you O Messenger of God". And thus the prophet consoled them with these words of solace and affection.

Pause for reflection

Unlike any other conquest, the Muslim conquest of Makkah conferred upon it the greatest sanctity ever enjoyed by any city. The symbolism that marked the conquest of Makkah signalled one of the finest moments in history which was tempered by both victory and humility. As the Prophet marched into the holy sanctuary head bowed mounted on his she camel, he was simply grateful to God for bringing this victory to the Muslims. Though he had a force of over ten thousand men fully armed and ready for combat, he declared that this was a time for forgiveness and mercy. Imagine the emotions of the Prophet and his followers who had to emigrate from this city their home where they were persecuted and tortured and boycotted to hunger and deprivation. They were now returning by God's will victorious and triumphant and yet humbled and grateful to Allah who fulfilled His promise to the Prophet and the Muslims. It was now their turn to show mercy and love to its inhabitants and soften their hearts so that they may in turn receives God's faith.

This is one of the reasons Muhammad disposes of all the spoils of war for a larger cause. The wisdom behind not giving a share to the Ansars is best known to God and His prophet but one can infer that if they had shared in this bounty they would have lost out on a much larger eternal reward that awaits them in the hereafter. This is the tradition or sunna of God or to echo a Christian sentiment "Blessed are the poor for they shall be the richest in the kingdom of Heaven"

*This victorious march into Makkah also fulfilled the prophecy in the Old Testament, Deuteronomy 33/1-2, **"And this is the blessing, wherewith Moses the man of God blessed the children of Israel before his death. And he said, 'The Lord came from Sinai, and rose up from Seir unto them; he shined forth from mount Paran, and he came with ten thousands of saints. From his right hand went a fiery law for them."***

The Unconditional Forgiveness and Mercy of God

When it became clear that Makkah was going to be conquered, some people left the city and went away. They were "severe criminals", who did not know Muhammad (ﷺ) and who believed that no power of compassion and pardoning could forgive them. One of them was Wahshi, the murderer of the uncle of the Prophet. He sent for Wahshi and asked him to become a Muslim. Wahshi was timid. He wrote the following in his letter:

"O Muhammad! You said, 'The torture of a person who kills somebody or attributes partners with Allah is increased on the Day of Judgment; he remains in torture in a despicable state.' I did all of them. Can there still be a way of salvation for me?" Upon this answer, the 71st verse of the chapter Al Furqan was sent. Muhammad got the verse written and sent it to Wahshi.

"Unless he repents, believes, and works righteous deeds, for Allah will change the evil of such persons into good and Allah is Oft-Forgiving, Most Merciful. And whoever repents and does good has truly turned to Allah with an (acceptable) conversion."

Wahshi did not regard it sufficient. He said, "O Muhammad! Repentance, belief and righteous deeds are heavy conditions. I might not be able to do them." The 48th verse of the chapter an-Nisa answered Wahshi:

"Allah forgives not that partners should be set up with him; but He forgives anything, else to whom He pleases."

Wahshi had not been convinced yet. He wrote another letter: "O Muhammad! It means 'Allah will do so if he wishes'. I do not know whether Allah will wish something like that for me."

Thereupon, the 53rd verse of the chapter Az-Zumar was sent down:

Say: "O my Servants who have transgressed against their souls! Despair not of the Mercy of Allah: for Allah forgives all sins: for He is Oft-Forgiving, Most Merciful."

Wahshi said, "Now, it is all right." Then, he went to Makkah and became a Muslim. People asked, "O Messenger of Allah! Are those glad tidings for Wahshi only or for all of us?" He answered: "For all of you!"

∞

The expedition of Tabuk is the name Muslim historians give to that campaign which mobilized the largest contingent of Muslims numbering over thirty thousand and led by the Prophet (ﷺ) himself in August in the 9th year of Hijra (630 CE). This took place about 6 months after the conquest of Makkah and the battle of Hunayn near Taif.

History reveals that the reasons for this expedition could have well been profound and multifaceted. Although the Prophet indicated well ahead of time the intent of a campaign to the north towards the border with the Byzantine territories and to the land of the Ghassanids who were Christian tribes in alliance with the Roman Empire ruled by Heraclius at that time, there is no clear indication of a battle or war that was to ensue. An alternate name given to the expedition is 'Jayshal Usra' - the army of great difficulty. This is the more common name amongst the sahaba or companions of the prophet. Although there was no actual battle and clash of swords, the difficulties of Tabuk were much more than any other 'battle'. So it was called the difficult gazwa or expedition even though there was no bloodshed. But the experience was extreme and the Muslims faced intense heat, thirst, hunger and physical hardship. At the apex of their tribulation the prophet at the urging of his companions performed two miracles when he caused a dried up well in Tabuk to gush forth with water that quenched the thirst of the entire contingent of Muslims and their camels and at another instance prayed for rain when the Muslims began to sacrifice their camels in order to get to the water that was stored in their humps. Once again the skies opened up even before the prophet had lowered his hands from prayer and the rains came down copiously to quench their thirst and collect enough water for their journey back.

Although late antiquity Muslim historians cited the reason for the Tabuk expedition as a response to a potential threat by the Roman army from the northern border together with their clients the Ghassanids, this theory on closer scrutiny does not hold much credibility. No army or empire in their right mind would electively go to war in the middle of the torrid Arabian summer heat and the most logical reason for the Tabuk expedition was a command from God that tested the Muslims to their core and exposed them to the harshest elements during a time of the year when the date and agricultural harvests come forth. So it was a double test on both their wealth and lives.

"O you who have believed, fight those adjacent to you of the disbelievers and let them find in you harshness. And know that Allah is with the righteous." (9:123)

"O you who have believed, what is [the matter] with you that, when you are told to go forth in the cause of Allah, you adhere heavily to the earth? Are you satisfied with the life of this world rather than the Hereafter? But what is the enjoyment of worldly life compared to the Hereafter except a [very] little." (9:38)

God is literally ordering and coaxing the Muslims to go on this expedition and in the same surah reveals: *"Go forth, whether you have something, lots or nothing."*

The expedition of Tabuk was full of invaluable lessons for the advocates of Islam in all generations and societies. It posed a very hard test which could have been passed only by a person whose faith was his prime motivator. Anyone who harboured doubts about the truth of Islam was certain to fail that test. That expedition showed clearly who were the true believers who could be relied upon in times of difficulty. Their response was highly gratifying to the Prophet. The army left Madinah in the height of summer. The excessive desert heat, added to the great distance of over a thousand kilometers the army was supposed to traverse, combined to make its march exceedingly difficult. Yet the believers did not hesitate to join the army. There were an estimated thirty thousand of them, which made that army the largest ever during the Prophet's time. However there were some including the hypocrites who did not join and gave flimsy excuses to the Prophet.

Earlier in 627 CE the Muslims had engaged in a battle near the south eastern part of the Dead Sea when the Prophet sent an army of three thousand Muslims to meet a combined Ghassanid/Byzantine force of around ten thousand. This campaign was undertaken as a consequence of the tribe of Ghassanid in the northern border of Arabia who were allies of the Roman Empire, assassinating an emissary of the Prophet who was sent with a message to the governor of Bosra in Syria. The Muslims retreated back into Arabian territory after inflicting considerable deaths and casualties among the confederate Arab tribes in the north and a smaller contingent of Roman soldiers for the loss of fifteen of their men which included Zaid bin Haritha and Jaafar Ibn Abu Talib, the adopted son and the cousin of the Prophet who were appointed as leaders of the campaign. Although this engagement was technically a defeat for the Muslims the Prophet considered it an honourable withdrawal to regroup and retreat rather than lose more Muslim lives. Just as the Treaty of Hudaybiyah was the forerunner of the pilgrimage, and this in turn of the conquest of Makkah, so was the campaign against Mutah an introduction to Tabuk, and this, in turn, to the conquest of Al Sham (Syria) which took place shortly after the Prophet's death.

The Tabuk expedition was the last one which the Prophet led and was a military exercise that prepared the Muslims to mobilize and defend themselves on a larger scale and builds the nucleus of discipline and mental resilience that is required in marching over long distances to carry the message of God to all distant nations and people. With the campaign of Tabuk the word of God was fulfilled throughout the Arabian Peninsula. Muhammad had firmly secured it against all attacks. In fact, as soon as he returned to Madinah from Tabuk, the tribes of Arabia began to ponder their fate. And so it was. The tenth year of the Hijrah was indeed the "Year of Deputations," in which men entered into the religion of God en-masse. The Campaign of Tabuk amply demonstrated to the rest of the Arabian Peninsula the mental and physical strength and fortitude of the Muslims to mobilize and move in large numbers in the most trying conditions if the need arose and this would have had a profound impact on the other tribes and nations in the region.

One significant side incident during the Tabuk expedition was the issue related to Kaab ibn Malik. Kaab ibn Malik was one of the early Madinite converts to Islam when a small group of them met the Prophet in Makkah before the Hijra and was a close and sincere companion of the prophet. When the call came to go to Tabuk, Kaab procrastinated in getting ready and eventually missed the expedition. On the return of the prophet from Tabuk, Kaab confessed to the prophet that he had no excuses for not joining and it was his own lethargy and lack of effort that made him miss the expedition and he was truly filled with contrition. The prophet whilst acknowledging the fact that Kaab was speaking the truth instructed the Muslim community to boycott Kaab until he was forgiven by God. This action by the prophet presupposes the fact that Kaab though sincere in his faith was a victim of his own weakness and hence had to endure some form of trial before he could be forgiven. There were two other companions of the prophet who had also fallen into the same predicament as Kaab and they too had confessed to the prophet and faced the same consequences as Kaab.

Kaab says the command came down that "nobody was to interact with us or speak with us until Allah allowed. So we kept away, and the people's attitude towards us changed so much, that it appeared to me I am a stranger in my own land. And the world, despite its vastness, became a constricted place for me" Shunned by the community Kaab confined himself to his house and turned to God in sincere repentance and wept for over 60 days before God revealed his forgiveness through revelation. This episode of Kaab once again emphasizes the Islamic principle that trial and tribulation on earth has a redemptive value and it was necessary for Kaab and the other two Muslims to go through this trial of incarceration before they were forgiven and blessed as all the other Muslims who took part in the expedition.

Although there were only three sincere Muslims who did not join the prophet in going to Tabuk, there were over eighty hypocrites who did not join. When the prophet returned, they gave all kinds of false excuses and reasons for not joining to which the prophet simply listened and remained silent. God even gently rebukes the prophet for tacitly accepting their excuses hence giving them the impression that the prophet can be fooled. As for the hypocrites who did join the expedition, they resorted to everything from attempting to assassinate the prophet to spreading false rumours and even mocking and jesting about God and His messenger. The chapter of the Quran "Repentance" or surah Tawbah was largely revealed during the Tabuk expedition and it severely warns the hypocrites and exposes their machinations which ultimately resulted in the destroying of a false mosque they had built in

Quba for the purpose of deviant propagation of Islam. This happened soon after the prophet returned from Tabuk. This is yet another sign of God's plan in eliminating every attempt by the Satan and his followers to distort and corrupt the message of the Quran in its early stages.

With the conquest of Makkah, the acquiescence of Taif, the conversion of Yemen and the expedition to Tabuk, Muhammad had virtually secured the heart and frontiers of the Arabian topography and ensured that the message of Islam found a stable footing for propagation. The restoration back to purity of the sanctuary city of Makkah devoid of idolatry and the appointment of his trusted companions as governors to the furthest regions of the Arabian peninsula provided the backdrop for the Islamic creed of monotheism, justice, peace compassion and human welfare to weave itself into the fabric of the Arabian tapestry and what remained was for the final message of God to be heard by neighbouring lands so that all nations may hear the call.

In the course of a few years, Muhammad (ﷺ) brings about a transformation unparalleled in the history of the world. Not only is the debasing superstition of the country-idolatry-eradicated, but the entire social fabric is reclaimed and released from long-standing and deep-rooted corruption and debauchery. The single greatest act of human forgiveness was witnessed by the Makkans when upon its conquest, Muhammad's bitterest enemies were forgiven. The restoration was almost complete and what remained was for Muhammad to perform the final pillar in Islam, the Haj and to provide the physical and spiritual blueprint of the rites and rituals that the faithful will follow for all time to come.

Pause for reflection

Success or victory from God comes in the wake of human effort and sacrifice and so it was in the case of the Tabuk expedition. Critics of Islam and other polemics are quick to point out that this was an act of aggression on the part of the Muslims. However the facts speak for themselves and although the Prophet marched to Tabuk there was no aggression on the part of the Muslims or any real conflict. Only God and His prophet will know the true purpose of this expedition but it is quite evident that God intended to test the Muslims in a crucible of mental and physical tribulation and to equip them with the fortitude of true faith that brings redemption in this earthly domain and eternal felicity in the hereafter. It was almost as if God wanted to reward the early Muslims who stood by the prophet and the Quranic message by cleansing them of their sins through the 'trial of Tabuk' and preparing them for the momentous task ahead that was soon to come after the death of Muhammad (ﷺ).

The incident of Kaab ibn Malik once again underscores the path of salvation and forgiveness in Islam through faith, sincere repentance and good deeds embellished with patience and sincerity of intention. Hence for Muslims in all ages, tribulations and trials in life is to be embraced with patience and with the conviction that it has redemptive value in the life to come .The Quran echoes this sentiment poignantly:

"And We will surely test you with something of fear and hunger and a loss of wealth and lives and fruits, but give good tidings to the patient"-(2:155)

The entire campaign of Tabuk took about three months from departure to return and during the journey numerous positive outcomes and lessons were learnt by the Muslims. Tribes living in the northern border lands in Sham or present day Syria witnessed the strength and resolve of the Muslims and entered into alliances with Madinah and heard the final message of God to Mankind as preached by the prophet himself. Some agreed to pay the Jizya or tax to remain as Christians in Arabia which was soon to see the spread of Islam sweep across the region in a spirit of tolerance and peaceful acquiescence never before witnessed in history. It could also be argued that the pro-active leadership of Muhammad and his strategic intent in not being cornered as a prisoner of the strategic geo-political environment motivated him to undertake the Tabuk expedition.

Eight

From Darkness to Light and the Call to all Nations

History books which report the events that took place during the lifetime of Muhammad (ﷺ), call the tenth year after the migration (632 CE) of the Prophet to Madinah the 'year of delegations', to denote the fact that numerous delegations arrived from all over Arabia pledging loyalty to Islam and the Prophet. The lessons that can be learnt from those delegations and their conversations with the Prophet are many and varied. Some came to try to find out what was going on in Madinah and what the true nature of the new faith was. Some represented tribes who were already Muslims. The overwhelming majority of those delegations went back after declaring that they had accepted Islam. It was not to be expected that their type of life and their old habits would change overnight. When the Prophet passed away, many of those tribes had not learnt enough about Islam to continue to honour their commitment to it. The Quran does allude to their belief thus:

"The desert Arabs say, "We believe." Say, "Ye have no faith; but ye (only) say, 'We have submitted our wills to God,' for not yet has Faith entered your hearts. But if ye obey God and His Apostle, He will not belittle aught of your deeds: for God is Oft-Forgiving, Most Merciful." (49:14)

This explains why some of them went back on their pledges after the Prophet's death. There was no question of coercing or pressurizing any group of people, or indeed any individual, to accept Islam. It was sufficient from the Islamic point of view for any tribe or community to declare its willingness to live in peace with Islam, not impeding its progress or scheming against it, to maintain the friendliest of relations with the Muslim community.

The Prophet was generous to all those delegations, whether they eventually accepted Islam or not. He ordered gifts to be given to them to the extent that every member of every delegation was given a personal gift.

The Prophet's hospitality was extended to all. Those delegations who accepted Islam were assured that they were part of the Muslim community, enjoying all the rights of Muslims. With each such delegation, the Prophet sent one or more of his companions to teach them the essentials of their new faith and to help them lead an Islamic life.

Some of these delegations behaved in the manner to be expected only from uncultured Bedouins. The Prophet overlooked their rough manners and rudeness and did not allow these to interfere with his relations with them. They were people whom he loved dearly to win over to Islam, just as he loved dearly to win every person to his faith. Some delegations tried to exact concessions, or to make compromises over certain aspects of the faith of Islam. The Prophet would have none of that. He viewed his task as that of an honest messenger who had to convey his message full, complete and intact. It was not for him to change any of its principles, or indeed any of its details. Those delegations continued to arrive, one after another, throughout the tenth year of the Prophet's settlement in Madinah. Hence, that year was generally a year of peace which the Muslim society in Madinah had not experienced before. At the same time it was a year full of activity. The work of consolidation continued throughout. One must remember that the majority of Muslims now were new converts who had not had enough training or education in their new faith. They had not lived through its 22 years of struggle and were not called upon to give the sacrifices that early Muslims had to give. Hence, they needed to learn more about Islam and they needed help in remoulding their lives in an Islamic fashion.

In the south of Arabia, and a short distance to the north of Yemen, lies the city of Najran. At the time of the Prophet, Najran and its surrounding area was a Christian valley. It had a Bishop from the tribe of Bakr ibn Wa'il. He was considered an authority on the Christian faith.

He was in touch with Byzantine emperors who respected him, sent him financial aid and helped build a number of churches in the area. When the conflict in Arabia moved strongly in favour of the Muslims the Prophet sent a letter to the Bishop of Najran which read;

"In the name of the God worshipped by Abraham, Isaac and Jacob. I call on you to worship God alone and not to worship anyone alongside Him, and I call on you to give your loyalty only to God rather than to any of His servants. Should you refuse, you have to pay jizyah" [A tax denoting loyalty and entitling the people who pay it to be protected by the Muslim state.]

When the Bishop read that letter from Muhammad, he felt that the matter was very serious indeed and read out the letter to all the heads of the seventy odd villages in Najran and asked them for their opinion. They agreed to send a delegation of 60 people to Madinah, headed by the three men first consulted and including leading figures that held official positions, in order to get first-hand information about the Prophet. Their discussion with the Prophet in the mosque took quite a long time. When it was time for their evening prayer, they prepared to pray and the Prophet (ﷺ) requested the Najran people to offer their normal prayer in the mosque. The discussion was resumed afterwards and over the following two days. They eventually asked the Prophet: "What do you say about Jesus? Since we are Christians, we would love to know your opinion so that we may be able to tell our people." The Prophet recited the following verses from the Quran which was revealed to him:

"Jesus, in God's view, is the same as Adam, whom He had created from dust and said to him: 'Be' and he was there. This is the truth from your Lord. Be not, therefore, one of the doubters. Should anyone argue with you about him after what has been given to you of true knowledge, say to them: let us call in our children and your children, our women and your women, and ourselves and yourselves. Let us then all pray God and ask that God's wrath overwhelm the liars." (3:59-61)

The Najran delegation on hearing this about Jesus, refused to accept it and the Prophet then offered them the challenge which was outlined in the Quranic verses quoted above. It was a serious challenge.

It meant for the Najran people that they risked being cursed by a Prophet and a Messenger of God. Such a prospect was not to be trifled with. The Christian delegation refused to go through with the challenge and when the Prophet asked them for their response, the Bishop answered, "Whatever you judge in our case is acceptable to us." Najran's offer to accept the Prophet's judgement without question, giving him twenty-four hours to make it known to them, meant that they wanted a peace treaty with the Prophet, and left it to him to specify the terms of that treaty, promising to accept those terms whatever they were. They relied on what they knew of his absolute fairness.

The following day they went to the Prophet, who caused the terms of the peace agreement to be written down for in exchange for a specified amount of two thousand ounces of silver every year they would in return be entitled the protection of God and the pledges of Muhammad, the Prophet, to protect their lives, faith, land, property, those who are absent and those who are present, and their clan and allies. They need not change anything of their past customs. No right of theirs or their religion shall be altered. No bishop, monk or church guard shall be removed from his position. Whatever they have is theirs, no matter how big or small. They are not held in suspicion and they shall suffer no vengeance killing. They are not required to be mobilized and no army shall trespass on their land. If any of them requests that any right of his should be given to him, justice shall be administered among them.

He who takes usury on past loans is not under my protection. No person in Najrān is answerable for an injustice committed by another. When the delegation from Najran returned home and reported what had transpired between them and the Prophet, some of the village leaders decided to visit the Prophet and embrace Islam and in the years following some of the Najran tribes converted to Islam and eventually they would have either all come into the fold of the new faith or migrated to Abyssinia or Syria as the whole of Arabia embraced Islam. A group of Christians from Najran opted to keep their faith and not to follow the example of Banu al Harith, the majority of whom had joined Islam. To these the Prophet sent Khalid ibn al Waleed to preach to them the faith and to bring them into the pax Islamica that had just covered the Peninsula end to end. They responded favourably to his call and entered Islam. Khalid then arranged for a delegation of them to visit Madinah where the Prophet met them with friendly welcome.

Pause for reflection

"Invite (all) to the Way of thy Lord with wisdom and beautiful preaching; and argue with them in ways that are best and most gracious: for thy Lord knows best, who have strayed from His Path, and who receive guidance." - (Quran 16:125)

This Quranic verse lays down the fundamental principle of 'Dawah' or inviting people to truth and both the content of the message, its delivery and the actions of the individual are important in undertaking this task. There is no room for arrogance, self-righteousness or ridicule. The challenge thrown to the Christians of Najran was a special case that was commanded by God and the Prophet never desired to or curse any one or community of people as he constantly responded when requested to do so to his enemies, "I have come as a mercy to Mankind"

In relation to the Christians, the Quran states:

"Surely you will find strongest (of) the people (in) enmity to those who believe, the Jews and those who (are) polytheists; and surely you will find nearest of them (in) affection to those who believe, those who say, "We (are) Christians." That (is) because among them (are) priests and monks, and that they (are) not arrogant." (5:82)

To this day the lack of desire for material wealth and power among many sincere Christians and their humble attitude makes their hearts softer to the truth and they follow some of the true traditions of Prophet Jesus, may peace be upon him.

This peaceful conduct by the Christians was also witnessed after the Siege of Jerusalem in 637 CE by the Muslims. Patriach Sophronius refused to surrender except to the Caliph Omar (579-644 CE) himself. Omar travelled to Jerusalem and accepted the surrender. He then visited the Church of the Resurrection (today better known as the Church of the Holy Sepulchre) where Sophronius invited him to pray inside the church, but Omar declined so as not to set a precedent and thereby endanger the church's status as a Christian site. Instead he prayed outside, on the steps east of the church. The Christians would have heard about the just and peaceful ways of the Prophet and decided to invite the Muslims as their rulers.

∞

As the divine light gradually dispelled the darkness in Arabia Muhammad was ready to make the call on the universal nature of the Islamic faith. He always stated to his people that his message was "to all mankind." At no stage of his life is any special importance given to the Arabs as a nation or a race, despite the fact that the Prophet grew up in a tribal society where narrow pride in one's lineage or tribal ancestry was common to all people. At no time did the Prophet think of himself as an Arab reformer whose task was to put his nation on the right footing. He always emphasized that the message he conveyed to people was meant for everyone and for all ages. If the message of Islam had not until then gone beyond the borders of Arabia, it was because Islam was still fighting to consolidate its base in Madinah and to win supremacy in Arabia. It was not likely that the Prophet should expand his call beyond Arabia, when his position in it was not yet secure.

In the early months of the seventh year (629 CE) of the Prophet's settlement in Madinah, the Arabian scene changed radically. First there was the peace treaty of al-Hudaybiyah, which was signed in the last month of the preceding year and which, in effect, neutralized the Quraysh, the major Arabian power opposing Islam. Then Khaybar fell to the Muslims, thus ending the Jewish threat to the new call of Islam. Shrewd and practical head of state that he was, the Prophet moved quickly to widen the horizon before his followers. He picked a number of his companions who combined pleasing personality with intelligence and ability to handle difficult situations, and he sent them as envoys that carried his messages to the rulers of neighbouring countries, some of which were the superpowers of the day: Byzantium and Persia. It is important to follow the fortunes of those ambassadors in order to gauge the likely response to Islam worldwide. The Prophet sent his emissaries with letters of invitation to God's final message to:

- Heraclius- the emperor and military commander of the Byzantine empire to the north of Arabia

- Khusru II - the emperor of the Persian Sassanid empire to the east of Arabia
- Al Muqawqis- the Governor and ruler of Egypt and head of the Coptic Church in Alexandria to the west of Arabia.
- King Negus – the ruler of Abyssinia to the south west of Arabia.
- Mundir Al Abdi- the ruler of Bahrain to the east of Arabia.
- Harith ibn Shammar- ruler of Damascus of the Arab tribes of Ghassan appointed by the Byzantines to the North
- King Badhan – ruler of Yemen, a vassal state of the Persian Empire to the south of Arabia.

The responses the Prophet received from the different heads of state reflected the conflict between their personal beliefs and the demands placed on them as leaders of their people and their cultural and historical legacies. For some their conviction of faith overcame their desire for kingship and continuity of earthly rule and for others positions of power and kingship were too seductive to let go although they recognized the truth and yet for still others their arrogance and desire for power blinded them and their hearts from the truth. King Negus of Abyssinia and the ruler of Bahrain accepted the Prophet and the message of Islam as the truth whereas Heraclius and Muqawqis recognized the truth of the message and the mission of the Prophet but officially and politely declined accepting the new faith due to their powerful positions and status among their people. Others such as Khusru and the ruler of Damascus were outright hostile and rejected the message and the Prophet at the outset. Little would they have known that very soon within a span of ten years after the death of the Prophet, the message of God will sweep through their lands and conquer the hearts and minds of its people.

The letters of invitation to Islam followed the principle of 'no coercion of conscience' though in some he warned of the consequences of rejecting the true message. Brevity was Muhammad's forte and some of the letters are recorded in history. To the King of Abyssinia Najashi or Negus he wrote:

"Peace be upon him who follows true guidance. Salutations:

I entertain Allah's praise; there is no god but He, the Sovereign, the Holy, the Source of peace, the Giver of peace, the Guardian of faith, the Preserver of safety. I bear witness that Jesus, the son of Mary, is the spirit of Allah and His Word which He cast into Mary, the virgin, the good, the pure, so that she conceived Jesus. Allah created him from His spirit and His breathing as He created Adam by His Hand. I call you to Allah Alone with no associate and to His obedience and to follow me and to believe in that which came to me, for I am the Messenger of Allah. I invite you and your men to Allah, the Glorious, and the All-Mighty. I hereby bear witness that I have communicated my message and advice. I invite you to listen and accept my advice. Peace be upon him who follows true guidance."

It is a well recorded fact in history that Najashi embraced Islam formally and conveyed his conversion to the Prophet in Madinah and upon hearing about the death of Najashi a short time later the Prophet prayed the funeral prayer in absentia of the body in Madinah.

To Heraclius, Muhammad wrote as reported by the Muslim historian Tabari:

In the name of God the Beneficent, the Merciful: From Muhammad son of Abdullah, the Messenger of God to Heraclius the Great of the Romans. Peace be upon him, he who follows the right path. Furthermore I invite you to submit your will to God; submit your will to God and you will be safe, and God will double your reward, and if you reject, you bear the sins of persecuting Greeks. 'And people of the scripture! Come to a word common to you and us that we worship none but God and that we associate nothing in worship with Him, and that none of us shall take others as Lords beside God. Then, if they turn away, say: Bear witness that we are Muslims.'"

The response and reaction of Heraclius on receiving the letter from Muhammad portrays the soul of one who was torn between his temporal kingdom and the acceptance of the possibility of God reaching out to humanity after Jesus through Muhammad. Heraclius in his time was not only the emperor or Caesar of the Holy Roman Empire but also an accomplished theologian and had tried to bridge the 'theological chasm'

153

between the Chalcedonian creed and the Miaphysite doctrine of Arius but it did not take root and the former prevailed. Could Heraclius have believed that God had sent a final prophet to clarify and make clear the true nature of Jesus and fulfil His Word to humanity? Was Muhammad the 'Paracletos' (the 'advocate' though erroneously translated from Greek as 'comforter') that was prophesized in the gospel of John? (John 14:16)

Heraclius happened to be in Jerusalem when the Prophet's letter reached him and he immediately ordered his officers to bring to his court any Arab who had interacted with Muhammad and was from the same city. Abu Sufyan the leader of the Quraysh happened to be in Bosra to the south of Jerusalem at that time leading a trade caravan from Makkah and he was summoned to the court of Heraclius together with his fellow travellers. Abu Sufyan was brought right in front of Heraclius and his fellowmen were asked to stay behind Abu Sufyan and Heraclius then addressed and warned him, "You say that you know Muhammad very well and I will ask you several questions about Muhammad and his claims to be a prophet, and you shall answer truthfully. Your fellowmen behind you will nod their heads in agreement if you say the truth and will also indicate if you state anything untrue and you will face dire consequences if you lie." Abu Sufyan realized that he was in the presence of the Roman Caesar who had just defeated the mighty Persians and had restored the Holy Cross back in Jerusalem from whence it was taken by the Sassanid emperor Chosroes. He had no intention of lying and facing the wrath of the Caesar. Heraclius then proceeded to ask a number of questions from Abu Sufyan who replied truthfully fearing otherwise for his life. The questions ranged from; Is Muhammad of noble birth? What is his character? What is he known for? Who are his followers? Are they increasing in numbers? What does he command you to do? Has he been ever accused of lying? Do his followers love him and do they leave the new faith? After hearing the responses from Abu Sufyan Heraclius stated, "If what you have said is true, he will very soon occupy this place underneath my feet and I knew it (from the scriptures) that he was going to appear but I did not know that he would be from you (Arabs)".. And he continues "if I could reach him definitely, I would go immediately to meet him and if I were with him, I would certainly wash his feet.'

The spiritual conscience of Heraclius had been aroused and he was so eager to find out more about Muhammad that he sent an emissary by the name of Tanuq from an Arab tribe to meet the Prophet and pose some questions and to confirm by sight the sign of the seal of prophet hood on Muhammad's shoulder. The Prophet had apparently responded to the questions posed and showed the Tanuqi the seal of prophet hood by exposing his shoulder. On hearing the responses of Muhammad and the sign of prophet hood, Heraclius's conviction that Muhammad was a true prophet of God probably increased to the extent that he summoned his bishops and senators and asked them. "What do you all think about me accepting the faith of the new Prophet?" The court immediately broke into an uproar as they all declared that he cannot be the emperor if he did so, to which Heraclius then responded ," I was just testing you all". Heraclius was still emperor when the Muslims entered Jerusalem in 637 CE and he died in 641 amidst a coup. This report is narrated by Bukhari in the canonical traditions of the Prophet.

The letter to Chosroes the Sassanid Persian King had quite a different reaction to the Prophet's call to Islam;

In the Name of Allah, the Most Beneficent, the Most Merciful.

From Muhammad, the Messenger of Allah to Chosroes, king of Persia. Peace be upon him who follows true guidance, believes in Allah and His Messenger and testifies that there is no god but Allah Alone with no associate, and that Muhammad is His slave and Messenger. I invite you to accept the religion and call of Allah. I am the Messenger of Allah sent to all people in order that I may infuse fear of Allah in every living person, and that the charge may be proved against those who reject the Truth. Accept Islam as your religion so that you may live in security, otherwise, you will be responsible for all the sins of the Magians."

This message was sent around early 628CE about the time Heraclius's offensive battle against the Persians drove them out of the Levant and Mesopotamia back to present day Iranian borders. On receiving the letter the Sassanid king's hubris got the better of him and in his anger he tore up the letter and ordered his generals and client ruler in Yemen to reciprocate by delivering a message to Muhammad (ﷺ) ordering his arrest and capture knowing little what was transpiring in the heart of Arabia.

When the Persian emissaries reached the Prophet to deliver the 'warrant of arrest', they were given an audience after two days at which time Muhammad informs them, "Your king has been overthrown and deposed and has been imprisoned, so you can accept Islam or go back now". Visibly shocked and surprised the emissaries return back to Yemen and find out that the Prophet's words to be true. It was Gabriel who had revealed the reality to the Prophet and eventually the ruler of Yemen and its people soon embraced the new faith peacefully. In a symbolic sense the responses to these three calls to the truth echo the manner in which the hearts of people react to the message of Islam even to this day and probably till the end of time. They fully embrace it or perceive its divine truth but do not accept it because of their earthly status and finally reject it in blind arrogance and bigotry.

Within a space of a hundred years after the Prophets death, Islam had spread both to the east and west of Arabia, from Toledo in Spain to Samarqand in central Asia and eventually to the Indian subcontinent and China. Great historians have noted that this phenomenon was largely due to the simplicity of its creed rather than any form of coercion and the greatest testament to its spirit of tolerance is shown in the co-existence of different faiths in Islamic lands.

Muhammad Haykel in his book 'The life of Muhammad' captures the call to other nations;

"The fire of the new faith which illumined the soul of the Prophet and the indomitable power of his soul explain the fact of his calling the kings of the earth to Islam, the religion of truth and perfection, the religion of God-May He be revered! The great kings were called to the religion which liberated the mind to reason and the heart to see for itself. Islam was the religion which gave man, whether in the life of worship or in the ordering of society, general principles which harmonized the powers of spirit and matter and made possible the highest levels of life on earth. Where such harmony prevails, there is neither weakness nor false pride. After going through all the stages of necessary development, human society can reach the highest possible level of existence designed for it."

Edward Gibbon (1737-1794) considered the greatest British historian of his time, said: **"The greatest success of Muhammad's life was affected by sheer moral force without the stroke of a sword."** ...... **"His memory was capacious and retentive, his wit easy and social, his imagination sublime, his judgment clear, rapid and decisive. He possessed the courage of both thought and action."**

A fitting tribute to the final Messenger of God whose responsibility to convey the Message embraced the whole of humanity and transcended time and space, race and colour, language and form to reach every human on earth.

The fact that within barely thirty years of the time he sent those missions, the kingdoms of these kings were conquered by the Muslims and most of their inhabitants converted to Islam. The surprise, however, is dissipated when one remembers that the two great empires disputing the leadership of the world and dividing it between their two civilizations were really disputing only the material possessions of the world. In both of them, spiritual power had long been decaying. Persia, for its part, was divided between paganism and Zoroastrianism. The Christianity of Byzantium, on the other hand, was rife with dispute and controversy between various sects. As for the new call of Muhammad, it was purely spiritual, raising man to the highest levels of his humanity. Wherever matter contends with spirit, wherever care for the present contends with the hope for eternity, matter and concern for the present are sure to lose.

At the end of the day, the Quran turns away from the minutiae of theology, religious law, coercion of conscience and warns against the human ego and raises instead the question of how far a religious community achieves its own moral ideals and how much it helps those in need. The Quran reminds the monotheists that their ultimate charge is to do good and be charitable, and if they want to demonstrate their superiority to other faiths, they must show more kindness and philanthropy than others, not simply claim a superior doctrine or ritual exactitude.

∞

Muhammad (ﷺ) decided not to perform Haj or the major pilgrimage in the 8th year of Hijra (630 CE) after the conquest of Makkah as there were still remnants of pagans, detractors, hypocrites and insurrectionists in the region and it would not have been safe nor prudent to perform a holy pilgrimage in that environment. The 9th year of Hijra became a watershed year in the prophetic timeline as the Prophet (ﷺ) decided to 'cleanse' the sanctuary city of Makkah of all pagan customs and rituals and restore it to its Abrahamic sanctity. He took a number of measures aimed at de-paganizing Makkah and its environs and eventually the entire Arabian Peninsula. Abu Bakr was instructed to lead the Muslims to Haj in this year as it was still not befitting for a prophet of God to perform Haj whilst there was lewdness and idol worship within Makkah and pilgrims from all corners of Arabia came to perform Haj with their own pagan rituals which included performing Tawaf or the circumambulation of the Kaaba in the nude! Ali, the son in law and cousin accompanied Abu Bakr as the representative from the family of the Prophet.

Choosing the 10th day of pilgrimage in the 9th year of Hijra (631 CE), which is the grand day of sacrifice, for the announcement of the termination of all treaties previously made between the Prophet and all unbelievers was revealed by God. It was the most natural choice, since all Arabian tribes would normally be represented by their pilgrims who were certain to convey the contents of the announcement to their peoples. Thus, all Arabia was certain to know of the termination of treaties and no one could make an excuse of ignorance. On the appointed day that is on the 10thof Dhul-Hijjah, when all pilgrims were in Mina, Ali, the Prophet's son-in law made his declaration:

"This is an address to all people. Let them all know that no unbeliever may be admitted into Heaven. No unbeliever is allowed to offer the pilgrimage after this season, and no one is allowed to do the Tawaf round the Kaaba in the nude. Whoever has a treaty with the Prophet, that treaty will be honoured for its full term. Those who do not have a treaty with the Prophet are hereby given a four months' notice."

In the fifth and sixth verse of the chapter Repentance, God revealed His ultimatum to the pagans as follows:

"Then when the Sacred Months have passed, then kill the polytheists wherever you find them, and capture them and besiege them, and prepare for them each and every ambush. But if they repent and perform prayers, and give Zakat (charity), then leave their way free. Verily, Allah is Oft-Forgiving, Most Merciful."

And if anyone of the Mushrikun (polytheists, idolaters, pagans, disbelievers in the Oneness of Allah) seeks your protection then grant him protection, so that he may hear the Word of Allah (the Quran), and then escort him to where he can be secure, that is because they are men who know not." (Quran 9:5-6)

Abu Bakr despatched several people to make the same declaration at the encampments of various tribes so that everybody would hear of it on the same day. What this declaration amounted to was a determination to make Arabia a land of Islam, to which no other grouping might have a claim. This applied only to the unbelievers of Arabia. It amounted to the total elimination of idolatry from that land or the *de-paganization of Arabia.*

Islam spared no effort over a period of 22 years to make people realize what evils they brought on themselves by worshipping statues and idols. The opposition to its call was simply an opposition which served the interests of certain leaders and groups who did not care for the well-being of mankind. Now that the issues were absolutely clear, and the opposition to Islam was no longer a matter of mistaken concepts, only those who harboured no good intentions towards Muslims and Islam were expected to hold to their idolatrous beliefs. They were a source of danger which had to be stamped out. Secondly, the experience of those 22 years had shown absolutely clearly that there could be no real co-existence between Islam and polytheism. The great historian Edward Gibbons in his magnum opus `The `History of the World` noted that, 'If Christianity eventually conquered paganism, it is equally true that paganism also corrupted Christianity'. God through His law and commands to Muhammad ensured that Islam would permeate the hearts and minds of people in an environment devoid of pagan influence.

Followers of other religions, such as Christians and Jews, are treated differently. They may be citizens in the Muslim state, provided that they respect the rules and laws of that state. Any act of treachery or aggression against Islam is dealt with firmly by the Muslim state. If they maintain their peace with the Muslim state, they are given the right to be protected by the state; this protection means that they are free to live, work and worship in complete security. Islam needs no preaching about tolerance; its history shows that it has always been the most tolerant of religions. Tolerance, however, does not mean allowing a confirmed enemy to live and prosper in one's own back yard, knowing for certain that he will seize the first chance to evict his enemy. That was always the attitude of the unbelievers, as history has clearly shown.

Historians are quick to note that this declaration sometimes referred to as the 'sword verses' did not result in the execution or death of a single person as a direct consequence of that verse and only acted as an extreme deterrent eliminating polytheism in Arabia once and for all. These verses are cited by Islamophobes as symptomatic of the violent nature of Islam without understanding the context and time determined relevance of these verses. The verses reflect the legacy of God in bringing down His punishment on a people who have been given all the time and opportunity to turn away from idolatry and immorality and can only be applicable for a specific time, context and place. The Quran is explicit in its declaration of freedom of choice and tolerance.

"There is no compulsion in religion." (Quran 2:256)

"And say, "The truth is from your Lord, so whoever wills - let him believe; and whoever wills - let him disbelieve." (Quran 18:29)

"Your only task is to give warning; you are not there to control them." (88:21-22)

The Prophet never forced the religion upon anyone, but rather he only fought those who waged war against him and fought him first. As for those who made peace with him or conducted a truce, then he never fought them and he never compelled them to enter his religion, as his Lord the Almighty had commanded him as above.

Fighting is only necessary to confront war and not to confront unbelief. For this reason, women and children are not killed, neither are the elderly, the blind, or monks who do not participate in fighting. Rather, the Muslims were commanded only to fight those who waged war against them. This was the way of the Messenger of God, with the people of the earth. He would fight those who declared war on him until they accepted his religion, or they proposed a peace treaty, or they came under his control by paying tribute and in turn allowed to freely practice their faith.

Towards the end of the 9th year, the prophet sent many of his companions as either governors or teachers of Islam to various places around the Arabian peninsula, especially in the north and south; Muadh ibn Jabal was sent to Yemen and as the Prophet walked with him to the outskirts of Madinah before his departure, he gave Muadh one of the most beautiful and practical advice recorded in Islamic tradition;

"Make things easy and do not make things difficult. Give glad tidings and do not repel people. Cooperate with each other and do not become divided, and in this is bringing hearts together of those who are close to Islam and to avoid harshness with them, likewise with whoever among children near or at the age of maturity and who has repented from sin. All of them should be treated with kindness and gradually encouraged to perform acts of obedience little by little. Responsibility for the affairs of Islam should be done gradually." (Bukhari3038)

Pause for reflection

God had destroyed many nations and people throughout history when they continuously rejected the guidance He sent down through His prophets. Even the children of Israel were subjected to mass oppression and driven out from their homelands when they resorted to violating the commands or scriptures they were given and rejected the Messiah and prophets from God. Islam is God's Word and religion and to preserve His final testament every residue of paganism was removed from Arabia so that there will be no compromise, influence or contamination from pagan beliefs, practices or customs that Arabia was deeply immersed in for centuries.

Even when paganism tried to raise its ugly head soon after the Prophet's death in the guise of false prophets and apostasy by tribal factions who wanted the old ways of ignorance, they were swiftly dealt with by Abu Bakr the first caliph of Islam after the Prophet. Here again anti-muslim elements and detractors jump at the opportunity to point out the intolerance and coercion in Islam, indicating that anyone who leaves Islam is put to death, whilst in reality and in the context of the situation, what the Muslims did was to eliminate any pagan uprising that was the handiwork of the satan designed to corrupt and attack the essence of monotheism. Hence this was not a simple case of apostasy and reverting back to idolatry but an upheaval followed by treason in undermining and attacking the established faith of God.

In the post-modern world primitive paganism has been unfortunately replaced by the likes of atheism, secularism, scientism and liberalism which have become the idols of modern man. Devoid of the engagement of the body, mind and soul, once again man has fallen victim to his arrogance, pseudo-intellectualism and ego. The eventual failure of these ideologies lies in its definition of self, community and morality and the fallacy that unfettered and absolute freedom using rationality and anti-intellectualism can find moral and spiritual guidance.

Islam like all monotheistic Abrahamic faiths defines man`s freedom as a freedom of the self than freedom from the self.

Nine

Completing God's Favour and Returning
to the Presence of the Most High

n the year 632 CE (10 AH) when the time of pilgrimage drew near, the Prophet (ﷺ) caused it to be known all over Arabia that he intended to offer the pilgrimage. This would be his only full pilgrimage or Haj and his final one. It is well known that pilgrimage to the Kaaba has always been a religious ritual ever since Prophets Abraham and Ishmael raised that construction which was, according to the Quran, the first house of worship ever to be built.

Although distortion crept into the religious beliefs of the people of Arabia over the centuries to the extent that they worshipped idols and statues in place of, or in association with, God, they continued to do the pilgrimage as a religious duty, albeit in a corrupted form. Many habits were included in pilgrimage which cannot be acceptable to God, to say the least. Examples of these were the fact that the Quraysh considered themselves to be privileged over all Arabs and did not share in certain parts of pilgrimage because they were exempt from them, being the custodians of the Kaaba.

They also imposed on pilgrims from outside Makkah to do the ṭawaf either wearing garments made in Makkah or in the nude. There were other forms and traces of polytheism in the rituals offered by the Arabs in their pilgrimage before the victory of Islam. During the Haj of 631 CE, the Prophet had dispatched his companion, Abu Bakr, to put a stop to all those aspects in the preceding year. Now it was time for the Prophet to make clear to the Muslims the duties of Islamic pilgrimage as a major act of worship which earned the pilgrim forgiveness of his or her past sins. For this reason, the Prophet caused it to be known that he welcomed anyone who wished to offer the pilgrimage with him. People started to come to Madinah from all over Arabia to join in this great Islamic worship. Moreover, a pilgrimage was the one act of worship which the Muslims had not yet seen the Prophet doing. Since every act of Islamic worship serves social, national and human purposes in addition to its spiritual and personal importance, it was necessary that the Muslims should learn how to offer pilgrimage directly from the Prophet (ﷺ). Furthermore, pilgrimage is an important part of the religion of Islam. Hence, the message of Islam would not have been conveyed complete unless the Prophet himself offered and taught Muslims how to offer pilgrimage. Estimates of the number of people who joined the Prophet on his trip of pilgrimage from Madinah vary from 90,000 to 115,000. A similar number were waiting for him in Makkah to join him there.

On the 9th day of the month of Hajj which defines the pilgrimage at Arafat he delivered his major sermon, still mounting his she camel. A companion with a loud voice, stood next to the Prophet's camel, repeating every sentence the Prophet said so that all those who were with the Prophet heard everything. The Prophet's speech that day was the highlight of his pilgrimage, outlining the nature of Islamic society. As usual, his sermon began with the praise and glorification of God.

The Prophet (ﷺ) then went on to say:

"People, listen to me as I explain to you, for I do not know whether I will ever meet you again in this place after this year. People, do you know in what month, day and city you are?" They said: "We are on a sacred day, in a sacred month, in a sacred city." He said: "Know, then, that your blood, property and honour are sacred to you till you meet your Lord in the same way as the sanctity of this day of yours, in this month of yours, in this city of yours. You will certainly meet your Lord and He will certainly question you about what you do. Have I delivered my message?" They answered: "Yes." He said: My Lord, bear witness. He who holds something belonging to another for safekeeping must give it back to the person to whom it belongs. All usury transactions which have been made in the past days of ignorance are hereby abro-

gated. You may claim only your capital, neither inflicting nor suffering any injustice. God has decreed that no usury is permissible. The first usury transactions I abrogate are those of my uncle, al-Abbas ibn 'Abd al-Muṭṭalib. All cases of vengeance killings are hereby waived.

When I am gone, do not revert to disbelief, killing one another. Have I delivered my message? They answered: "You certainly have." Continuing his sermon he said: My Lord, be my witness. People, you have an obligation towards your womenfolk and they have an obligation towards you. It is their duty not to allow into your homes anyone whom you dislike without your permission, they have the right to be provided with food and clothing, in fairness. Your womenfolk are in your custody; they are helpless. You have taken them on the basis of a pledge to God, and they are lawful to you with God's word. Fear God, then, in your treatment of women, and be kind to them. Have I delivered my message? They replied: "Yes, indeed." He said: "My Lord, be my witness. People, the believers are brothers. It is illegal for anyone to take the property of his brother unless it is given without any coercion. People, your Lord is one and your father is one. All of you are the children of Adam, and Adam was created from dust. The most noble among you is the most God-fearing. No Arab enjoys any privilege over a non-Arab except through the fear of God. Have I delivered my message?" They answered: "Yes, you most certainly have." He said: "My Lord, be my witness. People, Satan has given up any hope of being worshipped in this land of yours. He is satisfied, however, to be obeyed in matters which you consider trivial. Guard yourselves against him, lest he corrupts your faith. I have left with you what should keep you safe from going astray should you hold fast to it. It is something clear and simple: God's Book and the Sunnah of His Prophet.

You will be questioned about me. What will you say?" They said: "We bear witness that you have delivered your message complete and you have discharged your mission and given good counsel."

The Prophet pointed his forefinger at the sky and lowered it to point to the people, saying all the time: "My Lord, bear witness. My Lord, bear witness." The Prophet then said: "Let those who are present communicate what I have said to those who are not with us today. It *may happen that those who come to know of it in this way may understand it better than some of those who have listened to it."*

Thus the Prophet (ﷺ) concluded his final public sermon. This memorable sermon outlines five basic principles of the Islamic programme of action. Two of this work on the level of the individual and three relate to the structure of Islamic society. Islam moulds the character of the Muslim on to the structure of Islamic society. Islam moulds the character of the Muslim on the basis of two fundamental principles.

First, Islam severs all ties which a Muslim has with Ignorance, its idols practices, financial dealings, usury transactions and so on, because the adoption of the religion of Islam means a start of a new life for a Muslim which is completely divorced from the erroneous ways of the past.

The second principle is to guard against all forms of sin. The effects of sin are far more serious than the danger presented by any enemy in battle. All catastrophes in this life are caused by our sins, which also lead us to suffer in the hereafter. The Prophet also made it clear that he did not mean by sin the sinking back into idolatrous worship. Any intelligent person who comes to know of the faith based on God's oneness will never degrade himself to the extent of willingly accepting and claiming that God has partners. Yet the Satan does not give up his attempts to seduce people into committing sins in order to lead them further astray.

The Prophet has also outlined three basic principles on which Islamic society is founded. The first is the tie of Islamic brotherhood which moulds the proper relationship between all Muslims. It is this brotherhood which makes every Muslim a patron of every other Muslim, giving him whatever help he can. The second principle is supporting the weak so that their weakness does not make the whole society vulnerable. One should note in particular how the Prophet stressed the importance of being kind to women, since they are the weaker element in society. The third principle is the cooperation between an Islamic government and the members of an Islamic society to achieve the proper implementation of Islamic law which works for the removal of all evil from society and its replacement with what is good.

The total sum of these five principles is to translate the Quran and the Sunnah into practice. Hence, the Prophet did not forget to enjoin his companions to hold fast to them and implement them in their lives. Short as it was, the Prophet's speech included all the principles which are needed for the moulding of the perfect believer in Islam and the perfect Muslim society. The principles stated above and derived from his farewell sermon should not be confused with the five principles of submitting as a Muslim which are declaring the oneness of God, establishing daily prayers, fasting in the month of Ramadan, giving charity (zakat) and performing the Haj pilgrimage for those who are able to do so. These pillars of Islam together with the six articles of faith constitute the backbone of the practice and expression of the religion that takes one from simple submission as a Muslim to firm faith or Imaan and finally to Ihsaan or the aspiration and achievement of the most excellent form of worship where one is fully cognizant of the holy presence of God although he/she sees Him not but knows in his/her heart that God is all seeing and ever present before His servant.

This in essence captures the model of salvation in Islam where God through the Prophet has shown humankind the truth, the way and the means. Humans will always fall short in their good deeds, acts of righteousness and worship in comparison to the sins they accumulate during every breathing moment of their lives on earth and it is through the adherence and perfection of these principles and articles of faith that we can achieve the grace of God and enter His kingdom of Paradise. Hence the key to eternal bliss lies within this model and eventually within us as these acts of worship and faith wash over us like incessant waves of Mercy and forgiveness cleansing and purifying our souls until we drown in the compassionate and majestic ocean of His infinite Grace. It is this balance between sincere faith, righteous works and heartfelt repentance that defines the model of salvation in Islam in its final manifestation. This model is clearly different to those followed today by the Jews and Christians for whom salvation comes either because they are the chosen people or race of God or their sins have been forgiven and they are redeemed through the blood sacrifice of Jesus.

Aisha reported: The Messenger of Allah said, **"Be deliberate in worship, draw near to Allah, and give glad tidings. Verily, none of you will enter Paradise because of his deeds alone."** They said, "Not even you, O Messenger of Allah?" The Prophet said, **"Not even me, unless Allah grants me mercy from himself. Know that the most beloved deed to Allah is that which is done regularly even if it is small."** (Saheeh al-Bukhari 6467, Saheeh Muslim 2818)

Many non-Muslims and detractors of Islam are quick to point out that based on the above hadith, that Muslims have no guarantee that they shall enter heaven and hence have no definitive assurance of salvation. This again is a classic example of not understanding the humility and reverence to Allah's power and mercy that a Muslim submits to. He does not strut upon the earth with spiritual arrogance as if his faith and actions have saved him for certain without acknowledging that only the Will and Might of God alone can save him in the final reckoning. In fact God Himself teaches us to pray in fulfilment of His promise thus:

"Our Lord, and grant us what You promised us through Your messengers and do not disgrace us on the Day of Resurrection. Indeed, You do not fail in [Your] promise." (2:99)

The Quran also mentions giving, forgiving, the love of God and the good news of paradise:

"And compete with one another for your Lord's forgiveness and a Paradise as vast as the heavens and earth prepared for the God-fearing, who give generously whether in times of plenty or in times of hardship, and hold in check their anger, and pardon their fellow human beings; Allah loves such doers of good." (3:133-134)

As long as a Muslim keeps his covenant with God and does it with sincerity and endeavours to the best of his ability to fulfill those covenants and reaches out to God every time he slips or comes short, God has assured him or her through His very scripture that He will not fail in His promise to grant salvation. God reveals to the Prophet to:

Say: "O my servants who have transgressed against their souls! Despair not of the Mercy of God: for God forgives all sins: for He is Oft forgiving, Most Merciful." (39:53)

A simple and straightforward one to one communion with God with a sincere heart of repentance is all that is required with no other soul either human or divine having to bear the burden of another. A theologically, spiritually and rationally sensible and pure formula devoid of mystery and irrational justification that resonates with the innate nature of the human soul.

The Prophet was keen to impress on his followers that he had delivered his message and discharged his mission. He repeatedly prayed to God to be his witness. If the message was duly delivered, and if that message, or the faith it represented, was complete, then the mission of the Prophet was over.

Hence, when the Prophet recited to his companions during his pilgrimage the verse which was revealed to him:

"This day I have completed your religion for you, and perfected My grace to you and chosen Islam as your religion." (5:3)

When Abu Bakr heard this verse he realized that with the completion of the divine message, the Prophet's life was soon to come to a close. Such a definitive statement of finality was never revealed to any other Prophet except the last Messenger of God, Muhammad.

Shortly after the Prophet and the Muslims had returned from the farewell pilgrimage he sensed the need to secure the northern frontier with Byzantine in order to pre-empt any hostile invasion from the Christian empire who were eyeing with growing concern the rise of Muslim power in Arabia. The Prophet appointed Usamah ibn Zayd, the commander of the army, who was then a young man hardly twenty years of age. His appointment and precedence over the elders of Islam, the early Muhajirun, and greater companions of the Prophet, would have caused quite a stir among the people had it not been for everybody's genuine faith in the Prophet's judgment and calculation. By appointing him, the Prophet sought to place him in the same command in which his father fell in the campaign of Mutah. The Prophet had wanted to give Usamah cause for pride in victory tantamount to a reward for the martyrdom of his father. Moreover, such an appointment was sure to stir within the soul of the youth the greatest resolution, determination, and bravery. It was also meant as an example for the youths of Islam to carry the burden of great responsibility. A truly symbolic passing of the baton. Usama's march was delayed by the Prophet's illness and ultimate demise a few days later, nevertheless the Muslim army did march after a day of grieving and returned after inflicting a great defeat on the Byzantine allies in Sham or present day Jordan. Fittingly even immediately after the demise of the Messenger of God the Muslims faithfully continued the Prophetic mission of carrying the message of God to all of humanity and protecting the faith from any invasion or corruption.

Once again, Muhammad's intent behind ordering the expedition to the northern frontier with the Byzantine empire was probably based upon his desire to enhance and increase the strategic degrees of freedom of the nascent Islamic nation. He apparently did not desire that the Muslims be entrapped by the geo-political forces in the neighbouring territories and the intent and mission to carry the final message of God as a mercy to all mankind was made clear beyond the Arabian borders.

Pause for reflection

The Haj is an outward enactment of an inward journey. A journey of submission of the heart to Allah and behind every ritual is a profound sense of experiencing the nearness of God who declares that he is closer to the believer than his jugular vein. In the most emphatic declaration of God's closeness to his servants, the Quran states;

"And when (O Messenger) My servants ask you about Me, then surely I am near: I answer the prayer of the suppliant when he prays to Me. So let them respond to My call (without hesitation), and believe and trust in Me (in the way required of them), so that they may be guided to spiritual and intellectual excellence and right conduct."(2:186)

During the reign of Umar the second Caliph of Islam, a prominent rabbi mentioned to Umar that (referring to verse 5:3),`Your scripture has a verse that our scriptures don't have and I envy it, for if our scriptures had such a verse we would have celebrated the day that such a verse was revealed``

God's final revelation and testament to mankind was moulded in the crucible of human trial, tribulation, sacrifice and patience and its completion was marked by thousands of companions who were witnesses to this epic divine scripture and the instructions for its practice. It is recorded in some books of history that several companions rode off to deliver the message to the world in whatever direction their horses or camels were facing after the last sermon. Whether this is a historian's hyperbole or dramatic exaggeration one fact was for certain, faith had fully entered their hearts and the generation who witnessed the Prophetic mission were the best of men and women who faithfully practiced, recorded, taught, preserved and delivered the Message to the next generation. History records that Saad ibn Waqqas, a companion of the Prophet was buried in Canton in the Ghuandong province of China in the latter part of the 7th century.

The 'baton' of faith has been handed down through generations faithfully and in its pristine purity and they paid a price for it through their sacrifice in tribulation and life. It is every generation's responsibility to carry the 'baton' however difficult the lap or relay is going to be and pass it on preserving its core message of mercy, compassion and the glad tidings of the life to come.

The Miracles of Muhammad (ﷺ)

The Prophet Muhammad was granted a range of miracles and these touched every aspect of his life. He was personally given exceptional miracles such as the Night Journey to al-Quds and the Ascent through the heavens, which while not witnessed by others, were supported by evidence they had to believe. He was given physical miracles such as the flowing of water from his fingers, the ability to make the skies open up with rain and to make dried wells and springs gush forth with water which were witnessed and reported by those present at that time. The well and mass reported incident during the battle of the Trench where Muhammad turned the invitation of one of his companions to partake a simple meal with a few other companions, into a miraculous feeding of over a thousand men. In addition, he was also granted knowledge of the unseen through Divine revelation and helped against his enemies in various ways. In fact, everything about the Prophet was unique and blessed, in his words, his prayers and his miracles themselves. The reasons for the miracles were as varied as miracles were designed to strengthen the resolve of the Muslims and to give them encouragement and support, both spiritually and physically. An example of this is the assistance that Allah gave to the Muslims at the battle of Badr. The people of Makkah had asked the Prophet Muhammad for an epic miracle and God enabled the Prophet to split the moon on a clear night sky by pointing to it with his finger. This 'moon splitting' is referred to in the Quran in chapter 54:1 and was witnessed by the pagan disbelievers who exclaimed that their eyes were bewitched although they received confirmation that it did happen from travellers coming into Makkah. Over a thousand miraculous incidents during the 23 years of his prophethood have been documented from early sources by scholars in a genre of writing called 'Evidences of Prophethood', and include how both inanimate objects and animals recognized the prophethood of Muhammad and interacted with him. It is within the power of Allah to show miracles that would make everyone believe: `*If We wished We could send down a Sign to them from heaven, before which their heads would be bowed low in subjection*` (42: 4). However, this is contrary to the free-will that Allah has given us, which enables us to reason and discern. In fact, a miracle is often a way to differentiate between those who truly believe and those who do not. The Quran refers to those who deny: `*When they see a sign they only laugh with scorn. They say, 'This is just downright magic.'*` (37: 14-15). However, the most enduring miracle, which has been witnessed by billions of people through the ages and throughout the world, is the Quran itself, a book of clear guidance with no contradictions, inconsistencies or errors.

∞

The women in Madinah were taught and instructed by the Prophet at his mosque and by the wives of the Prophet who played a defining role in being role models. The way they interacted, the way they were treated seemed nothing like what was being taught about Muslim women. They were liberated, active in their communities, having natural interactions in mixed gatherings. They had respect, authority, and value in their communities. In fact the companions of the Prophet who were from the 'Muhajireen' or immigrants from Makkah complained to the Prophet that their women after coming to Madinah were more emboldened and assertive in their relationship and were concerned that they would have a rebellion on their hands! The powerful message of the Quran on equality and justice was empowering the women to be more active and contribute to the community of believers. Once Umm Salaama, one of the wives of the Prophet queried from him as to why God in the Quran always addressed the people in the masculine gender (although in Arabic grammar the masculine plural gender is inclusive of both males and females). The Prophet acknowledged her comment and indicated he will think about it and let her know. Shortly afterwards, when the Prophet was in Umm Salaama's house she heard the Prophet reciting the following verses:

"Indeed, the Muslim men and Muslim women, the believing men and believing women, the obedient men and obedient women, the truthful men and truthful women, the patient men and patient women, the humble men and humble women, the charitable men and charitable women, the fasting men and fasting women, the men who guard their private parts and the women who do so, and the men who remember Allah often and the women who do so - for them Allah has prepared forgiveness and a great reward." (Quran 33:35)

Ayesha, who collected and narrated over two thousand traditions of the Prophet and hence was the first acknowledged woman scholar in Islam was consulted by the companions of the Prophet after his death on various religious matters and at one time Umar the 2nd. Caliph in

Islam remarked, "There is no matter that we would close that Ayesha would open it, and no matter that we decided to open that Ayesha would close it". Such was her knowledge and confidence imparted to her by the Prophet. The Prophet encouraged women who came to the mosque to learn and ask questions and admired and commended women who used to ask profound question on faith and gender relationships and equality. In one authentic hadeeth it is narrated that a woman from the 'Ansari' or the Madinites posed the following question to the Prophet, "O Messenger of God, how can we be expected to compete in righteous deeds with the men when they are at the front rows in the mosque, and can fast and pray throughout the year and fight in the path of God whereas the women are unable to do such things freely because of our chores, do women get less of a reward from God?" The Prophet was so taken up by this question that he faced the men and asked of them," Have you ever heard of a more insightful question than this?" The men responded rather bemused that they never thought that a woman can ask such profound questions! One should keep in mind that this was 7th century Arabia where women were treated like chattels and the men were not used to this kind of open forum where the women could ask from the Prophet in a mixed gathering. The Prophet replied to the woman as follows, "A woman by virtue of being a good companion and partner of men can achieve the same reward or more than the men". Some of the actions and righteous deeds of the women at that time included:

- women who observed the Fajr (dawn) and Isha (night) prayers in the mosque.
- A woman who memorized Surah Qaf from the mouth of The Prophet.
- Women who spent the last ten nights in itikaaf (staying overnight) in the mosque.
- Women who worked and even supported their husbands financially as the main breadwinner.
- Women who taught the religion and spread the Word to both men and women.

- Women who fought on the battlefield and attended to the injured combatants and were martyred.
- A woman who served men and women at her own wedding feast, even serving the Prophet himself.

Polemics and detractors have tried to quote verses from the Quran taken out of context and devoid of the moderating influence of the Prophet's actions and examples, to portray that the Quran is misogynistic. This type of thinking is absolutely without understanding the worldview of the Quran and its holistic concept of gender relationships and equality as narrated through the pages of the Quran and the twenty three years of the Prophet's life. In the economic sphere the Quran alludes to the responsibility and rights that women have in determining their affairs in an independent manner if that is appropriate:

"Men will have a share of what they earn, and women will have a share of what they earn." (Quran 4:32)

"And for women are rights over men similar to those of men over women." (Quran 2:228)

The following verse from the Quran exemplifies the gender equality and neutrality in the eyes of God and honours women in the most noblest manner:

"O People! reverence your Guardian-Lord, who created you from a single person, created, of like nature, His mate, and from them twain scattered (like seeds) countless men and women;- reverence Allah, through whom ye demand your mutual (rights), and (reverence) the wombs (That bore you): for Allah ever watches over you." (4:1)

One must first ask: was the Prophet Muhammad a feminist? Some have argued that he was, because his revelation certainly condemned female infanticide (Quran 81:8-9), forbade the ugly practice of Zihar (men declaring that their wives were like the backs of their mothers and hence shunning all intimacy with them) - Quran 58:1-4, abolished the sons' right to inherit their fathers' wives, gave women the right to inherit from their parents and husbands, gave women the right to marry outside of their tribe, enshrined certain rights for women in marriage; and he adored and honoured the women in his life.

However, this must be balanced with the fact that the Prophet Muhammad also introduced new restrictions on women that weren't there in Jahiliyya (ignorance and darkness): he forbade polyamory and free love, dissolved institutionalized prostitution, mandated the khimar (head and bosom cover), restricted abortion, and produced a dimorphic tradition that gave different rights and responsibilities to the two sexes. Although the Quran says that all things were created in pairs (51:49), it also says that males and females, like day and night, are different (92:3-4). All of this runs totally against the feminist advocacy of freedom and complete equality. The Prophet Muhammad came to a society that worshiped goddesses (53:19-22), deemed the angels as God's daughters (17:40), and had female royalty and prophetesses — and yet, he set out to restructure everything.

Islam should be viewed as a religion that had immensely improved the status of women and had granted them many rights that the modern world has recognized only this century. Islam still has so much to offer today's woman: dignity, respect, and protection in all aspects and all stages of her life from birth until death in addition to the recognition, the balance, and means for the fulfillment of all her spiritual, intellectual, physical, and emotional needs.

Yes. We are in a world full of femicide, human trafficking, gender-specific abortion, prostitution, honour killings, forced marriages, domestic violence, and sexual assault – both in Muslim and non-Muslim countries. We should seek to uplift and honour women in accordance with the prescriptions of the revelation. The Prophet Muhammad famously told us to be dutiful to "your mother, your mother, your mother, [then] your father." He said that Paradise is beneath the feet of mothers. He said that "the best of you are those who are best to your women." He was a man that helped around in the house, displayed love and patience in his marriages, and commanded the good treatment of women. One does not need to subscribe to a whimsical, fallacious, radical, selfish, and antagonistic ideology to establish the rights of women. We can fight the evils that unjustly harm women by using orthodox principles and practical ideas that aren't rooted in a juxtaposing paradigm.

Pause for reflection *- Is there a place for feminism in Islam?*

*Islam has been accused of many things. The most significant of them is that it oppresses women. In this age it is proving to be difficult, if not in-sufficient, to highlight the fact that Islam gave women inheritance rights (Q 4:11-13), self-ownership (Q 4:19), and many other social protections that they did not enjoy prior to the advent of the Prophet. As for the claim that patriarchy is foreign to the Quran, this is an even harder point to prove if this claim includes a rejection of familial patriarchy. This is be-cause the Quran is clear when it declares that **"Men are the caretakers of women"** (Q 4:34). As for this declaration and the other that **"Men have a degree over them"** (Q 2:228), both should be read in the context of the family; not as a reference to every public and private office in society, nor to individual moral superiority. In other words, men are expected to over-see the family, secure it, and to maintain it. They are to protect women from the sinister intents of other men. As far as utilizing these verses as evidence that women have no place in the public sector regardless of the occupation, this is a view that requires one to make a broader stretch of the imagination. The main assumptions of feminism, that patriarchy is inherently evil and that an egalitarian order will resolve inequality, are irreconcilable with the teachings of the Quran. Feminism, on the other hand, calls for women to rebel against social hierarchy in general and patriarchy in particular. This problematizes the relationship between hus-band and wife according to the Quranic teachings. Should a Muslim wife believe that the Quranic duty of obedience is an injunction revealed by the All-Wise Creator? Or should she simply say 'no' to the text because it encourages something that runs contrary to feminist principles?*

To quote Prof. Jonathan A.C. Brown,

"The move to assuming that scripture contains the truth but need only be understood properly to saying 'no' to scripture because it says something unacceptable or impossible is a blow that shatters the vessel of scriptural reverence. It means that some extra-scriptural source of truth has been openly acknowledged as more powerful and compelling than the words of God in scripture."

In other words, the very impulse to question the authenticity of the divine origin of the Quranic injunction is a direct affront to the divine wisdom that Muslim feminists claim to believe in.

The Prophet's seclusion from his wives

The Prophet's patience and kindness to his wives were one of the hall-marks of his domestic life and he took great care to be fair by all of them. To the best of his human ability he was empathetic to their needs and never once did he resort to physical abuse and always responded with understanding even when it was apparent they were in the wrong. However matters came to a head when their demands (for material needs), jealousy and petty conspiracies against each other was too much for the Prophet to bear and rather than confront them in argumentation he secluded himself into a small loft like room in the mosque and swore not to see them for a whole month. Scholars have listed some of the major incidents that led to this situation and among them were the demands by some of them for greater material comforts from the wealth that came to the Islamic State, accusing the Prophet of favouritism towards some wives, the lying conspiracy by some against another relating to a special type of honey that she gave the Prophet which he liked and the divulgence of a matter that the Prophet requested one of his wives to keep secret for the sake of domestic peace. This latter incident has been blown out of context by Orientalist's and Christian evangelists and apologists to impugn on the Prophet's character, nevertheless even a cursory reading of history reveals the reality and innocence of this incident for which a Quranic verse was revealed rebuking the wives concerned:

O Prophet! Say to your wives: "If you desire the life of this world, and its glitter, then come! I will make a provision for you and set you free in a handsome manner. "But if you desire Allah and His Messenger, and the Home of the Hereafter, then verily, Allah has prepared for the doers of good among you an enormous reward." (33:28-29)

One day while the Prophet was in Hafsa's quarters, Mariyah a Coptic Christian who was presented to the Prophet by the archbishop of Egypt and whom the Prophet married, came to him and stayed with him some time. Upon Hafsah's return she found the Prophet and Mariyah in her quarters and, as she waited for them to come out, her jealousy broke all bounds.

The Prophet`s seclusion from his wives

When, finally, Mariyah left the quarters and Hafsah entered, she accused the Prophet of insulting her. Sensing the deep jealousy that Hafsa harboured for Mariah which was probably shared by the other wives, the Prophet requested Hafsah not to divulge the incident among the other wives and in an attempt to please her, Muhammad promised that he would not see Mariyah. Hafsah promised to comply. However, she could not keep her promise as jealousy continued to affect her disposition. Hence, she intimated the secret to Ayshah, who in turn reported it to the Prophet. There is nothing unusual in the whole story, such gossip and petty jealousies being commonplace between man and his many wives. A man's affection belongs where he puts it within his household, and the controversy which Hafsa and Ayesha had woven around the Prophet's affection for Mariyah was utterly groundless. With the revelation (33:28-29), the whole affair was brought to a close. The wives of the Prophet, having regained their wisdom and common sense, returned to their husband repentant, pious, and confirmed in their faith. Once reconciled by their repentance, Muhammad returned to his wives and his domestic life resumed its peace-the necessary prerequisite for any man with a mission to perform.

An interesting yet profound incident related to Hafsah was when the Prophet decided that she had crossed a red line and was contemplating divorcing her, for the sake of matrimonial harmony with his other wives, when God sent Gabriel himself to inform the Prophet to desist from doing that, as Hafsa was a woman who fasted much and prayed much at night seeking the pleasure of God. The Prophet did not go ahead with the divorce and Hafsah would have repented and reformed.

Here we see the all hearing and seeing God intervening in the marital affairs of His beloved Messenger to bring about reconciliation through His grace and mercy. It might appear not altogether an unfair assumption to make that God was answering the sincere prayers of Hafsah and manifesting His closeness to the servant who calls on Him.

∞

Two weeks before Muhammad (ﷺ) drew his last mortal breath on earth in the month of Safar, eleventh year after Hijra, 632 CE, he asked his servant to accompany him in the depths of the night to the cemetery where the early martyrs, companions and those beloved to him were buried. 'I have been requested by Allah to pray for the forgiveness of the dead', he told his servant and then proceeded to greet those buried, *"Peace and blessings of Allah be upon you the people of the grave, blessed are you who passed away when the call to God was new and the hearts united, blessed are you who passed away in the difficult times when the rewards were great, blessed are you who passed away and spared from the trials the living are experiencing".* Then turning to his servant the Messenger of God says," I have been given the choice of possessing the treasures of this world and living in this world until the last day and then meet my Lord or to meet my Lord in His kingdom in heaven now". The Prophet's servant exclaims "Choose us!", but the Prophet says that he has made his choice to meet his Lord sooner in heaven. Muhammad then prays and seeks forgiveness for the departed souls and then soon after he gets back home, his illness that started with a high fever and headache overcomes him.

The Prophet passed away on a Monday afternoon and two days prior to that day he had requested his wives that he is allowed to stay in Ayesha's house as he was too weak to move. As he lay his head on Ayesha's lap he asked her if there was any wealth left in the house and she replied that there were seven coins which could buy two handfuls of dates and he asked her to go out and give it away to the poor saying that Prophet's leave this world without any worldly possessions or leaving any inheritance. As his fever got worse Muhammad requested that his body be bathed in water drawn from the wells of Madinah and for the last time went to the mosque to lead prayers and he had to be literally carried by Ali ibn Talib his cousin and another of his uncle Abbas's sons. After leading prayers whilst seated he advised and urged the congregation to safeguard their daily prayers, to uphold and protect the rights of the Ansars or the original inhabitants of Madinah who had now become a minority due to the influx of migrants to Madinah seeking the new faith. He also advised them to be compassionate to their slaves and to fear God when it came to treating the womenfolk with kindness. Surely, in this mini sermon was a message of justice to look out for the vulnerable among the people, the minorities, the slaves and the women. Too weak to go to the mosque to lead prayers he requested Abu Bakr his dearest companion during his early days and in his migration to lead the faithful in prayer. During the Morning Prayer on Monday the Prophet wanted the curtain that was between his door and the mosque to be parted so that he could watch the believers in prayer and a bright smile crossed his face belying the pain and high fever that afflicted him. The assuring voice of Abu Bakr leading prayers would have comforted and soothed him as a testament to the accomplishment of his mission. Ayesha reports that the last words he said were "to the companionship of the most High" or "Arafeequl Ala" in Arabic. That was when the final Messenger of God left this world. "Ar-rafeequl A'la" is none other than God Himself and his words "to the supreme communion with God the "Al A'la" which means "The Most High" is one of the ninety nine beautiful names of God. Ayesha says "At that time I remembered the hadith of the Prophet, that he once told me "never does the angel of death come to a prophet, except that he asks the prophet 'Can I take your soul or not?' And the prophet has to agree and then his soul is taken. So when I heard him utter "to the companionship of the most High" I knew that he had chosen God over us", and that's when it struck her that indeed the Prophet of God, a mercy to all mankind had departed. Muhammad had once said that a prophet should be buried where he had died and since he had died on the sleeping platform in Ayesha's room, this was where he was laid to rest.

It would have been difficult in any case for the followers of Muhammad to prepare them for his death, an event they referred to as the "closing of that gate of mercy." They would often recall that the Quran called Muhammad,

"A mercy to all the universes." (21:107)

In many times and places, human beings have been more affected by the tangible people of God than by the present though a transcendent God. Thus, even some of those who had been closest to Muhammad, like Umar (who would become the second successor to the Prophet), refused to believe that one such as Muhammad could have died and believed instead that Muhammad must have only gone up to be with God, as Moses had gone to be with God on Mount Sinai, and would return after forty days. It was only when Abu Bakr (the father of Muhammad's wife Ayesha, and the first successor to Muhammad went in to see the Prophet for himself that he could see that, like all mortals, Muhammad too had passed away. Abu Bakr kissed the face of the Prophet and said: "You are dearer than my father and mother. You have tasted the death which God had decreed." Then Abu Bakr gently hushed Umar and gathered the community around him. He offered praises to God and then said:

"O People! Whosoever wishes to worship Muhammad, verily Muhammad has passed away. But whosoever wishes to worship God, verily God is Living, Immortal."

Abu Bakr then recited for the people the following verse from the Quran, a verse that seems to have been intended to prepare the community for life after Muhammad:

"Muhammad is not but a messenger, many were the messengers that passed away before him. If he died or were slain, will you turn back on your heels? If any did turn back on his heels, not the least harm will he do to God; But God will swiftly reward those who are grateful." (3:144)

And yet even those close to the Prophet said that, until that very moment, they had never imagined that these verses would refer to Muhammad's actual death. Even the messengers of God have to end their earthly existence. Perhaps at times like this the best that can be done is to remind oneself of the Eternal, Ever-Living God of Muhammad, God of Abraham, God of Jesus, and God of Moses. If the sending down of each prophet is seen in Islam as an opening of a gate of mercy, then the death of each prophet is also accompanied by grief.

Muslims love the Prophet as part of their faith. God says: *"The Prophet is closer to the believers than their own souls." (33:6).* This love is not merely because of the importance of his mission. Rather, it is because the way he carried it out; because of his love for them. It is enough here to quote God's words:

Indeed there has come to you a messenger from among yourselves for whom it is grievous that you should suffer; who is full of concern for you, to the believers full of pity, merciful (9:128)

Say: "if you love God, follow me, and God will love you." (Quran 3:31)

Imagine a civilization where aspiring to Muhammadi ethics (akhlaq-Muhammadi) is considered the noblest ethical norm.

Imagine intellectual traditions charged with the task of tracing a lofty pattern of behaviour indeed, the ideal model of human conduct all the way back to Muhammad. This community and its intellectual traditions have in fact existed in the Islamic civilization as it has sought to embody The Sunna, the Way of the Prophet of Islam. Although the word Sunna today is understood to mean the way in which Muhammad conducted himself, like many other Islamic words, it originally had a more immediate and existential meaning: "the trodden path in a desert." Words and phrases like "the path" were all the more immediate in an arid context where following a trodden path in a desert could mean the difference between being led to a cool, refreshing, and life-giving oasis and getting lost among ever-shifting and treacherous sand dunes and possibly dying a miserable death from thirst. To this day, the language of "the path" has a life-giving and immediate resonance for Muslims.

Thus Muhammad (ﷺ) left this world just as he had entered, without material shackles. His only inheritance left to mankind was the religion of truth and goodness. He had paved the ground and laid the foundation for the great civilization of Islam which had covered the world in the past and would cover the world in the future. It was a civilization in which tawhid, or the unitization of God, was the cornerstone; and an order in which the word of God and His commandments are always uppermost. It was a civilization purged absolutely clean of all paganism and of all idolatrous forms and expressions, a civilization in which men were called upon to cooperate with one another for the good and moral felicity of all men, not for the benefit of any group or people.

Muhammad left to this world the Book of God, a guidance and mercy to mankind, while the memory of his own life gave the highest and noblest example for man's emulation. He elevated the low, and he lowered the elevated that they might meet in that middle place known as brotherhood. When you reflect on the fact that the benefit of religious guidance – which leads to eternal happiness and joy in Paradise and safety from eternal pain and despair in Hell – is the greatest favour and benefit to be desired. When you further reflect on the fact that on the day of judgement when no other creation of Allah can help you, the Prophet will be in prostration to Allah pleading to save his Ummah, a day in which your own mother will not give one of her good deeds to ransom you nor would you ransom her. When you reflect on his sublime character, impeccable manners, justice, mercy, and his devotion to Allah, you can only arrive at the conclusion that the only person deserving your highest love is the beloved Prophet because his benefit to humanity is the greatest and the most lasting.

In his book 'Life of Muhammad", Muhammad Haykal concludes very aptly as follows:

"Muhammad left a great spiritual legacy which enveloped the world in its light and guided human civilization throughout many centuries, a legacy which will envelop the world again and guide human civilization once more until the light of God has filled the universe.

∞

But Muhammad was more than just a great historical person, he was a father and friend, a husband, a companion and above all he was a human being. The Quran states:

"Say, O [Muhammad], "I am only a man like you to whom it has been revealed that your god is but one God; so take a straight course to Him and seek His forgiveness." And woe to those who associate others with Allah." (41:6)

The Prophet's unique physical appearance, his high character and willingness to sacrifice for others, are often at the essence of any description of him. He was once described by a contemporary in the following words:

"The Messenger of God was imposing and majestic. His face was luminous like a full moon. He was taller than medium but not excessive in height. He had wavy hair, which he parted and it never went beyond his shoulders. He was light-skinned with a high brow. He had full eyebrows and a small space between them. He had a fine, aquiline nose. His beard was full, his eyes black. His physique was supple and lithe, with a full chest and broad shoulders. When he walked, he was determined and his pace was as if he was walking downhill. When he spoke he was always brief and reflective. He spoke when he saw benefit and spent long periods in silent contemplation. His speech was comprehensive being neither wordy nor laconic. He had a mild temperament and was never harsh nor cruel, coarse nor rude. He expressed gratitude for everything given to him no matter how insignificant. When he spoke, his companions lowered their heads as if birds were perched upon them. When he was silent, they felt free to speak. He never criticized food or praised it excessively. He never swore, nor did he find fault in people. He did not flatter people but praised them when appropriate.

People entered his gatherings as seekers and left enlightened. He would ask about his companions when they were absent often making inquiries about people's needs. He never stood nor sat without mentioning the name of God. He never reserved a special place for himself in a gathering and sat where space provided. He gave each of those who sat with him such full attention that everyone felt that he was the most important person in that gathering. Voices were not raised in his presence. The aged were respected for their age and the young were shown compassion for their youth."

The Western reader, raised in a centuries-old tradition of aversion to Muhammad, will probably be surprised to learn that in all reports the quality that is particularly emphasized in the Prophet is his humility and kindness. Qadi 'Iyad, (d.544 H/1149CE) one of the best representatives of the reverent admiration of the Prophet so typical of Muslim piety, writes:

"God has elevated the dignity of His Prophet and granted him virtues, beautiful qualities and special prerogatives. He has praised his high dignity so overwhelmingly that neither tongue nor pen is sufficient to describe him. In His book He has clearly and openly demonstrated his high rank and praised him for his qualities of character and his noble habits. He asks His servants to attach themselves to him and to follow him obediently. It is God—great is His Majesty!—who grants honor and grace, who purifies and refines, He that lauds and praises and grants a perfect pense ... He places before our eyes his noble nature, perfected and sublime in every respect. He grants him perfect virtue, praiseworthy qualities, noble habits and numerous preferences. He supports his message with radiant miracles, clear proofs, and apparent signs."

Ayesha, the wife of the Prophet notes that she once asked the Prophet whether he would sleep before performing his late night prayer before dawn and he replied, "O Ayesha my eyes sleep, but my heart remains awake". In another instance she noted the Messenger crying in prostration during his night prayer and she noticed the unusual length of time he was in that state and became concerned and feared something might be wrong. She gently approached the Prophet and said, "O Messenger of Allah why do you do this when Allah has forgiven you for everything you have done in the past and everything that will follow?"

The Prophet looked at Ayesha and gave this moving response, "Shall I not be a grateful servant? Verily on this night a verse was revealed to me. Woe to the one who reads but does not ponder over it"

The verse to which the Prophet was referring to was the following;

"Indeed in the creation of the heavens and the earth; the alternation of the day and the night; the ships that sail the sea for the benefit of humanity; the rain sent down by God from the skies, reviving the earth after its death; the scattering of all kinds of creatures throughout; the shifting of the winds; and the clouds drifting between the heavens and the earth- are surely signs for people of understanding." (2:164)

The Prophet's tears and humility in prostration were a manifest evidence of the Majesty and Wisdom of God and the certitude of His existence through the signs that He makes clear for us. In numerous such instances of devout expression of his gratitude and complete submission to the Message of God, the Prophet is an embodiment of the Quran which he internalized and conveyed to the world to affirm the truth of God and His divine mercy to Mankind. Should we not then be of the people of understanding who reflect as well?

Once a companion of the Prophet asked him "Since when did you become a Prophet?" the Prophet replied, "Since before Adam was even between the state of water and clay-prior to him coming into existence". This very profound statement of the Prophet indicates the essence of his pre-existent state as a light (Noor) that was created before the creation of Adam in the image of God and gives deep spiritual depth to not only the status of the Prophet as the seal of all the prophets but also the reason for the creation of the Universe.

Prophetic Hardship-Ease time line

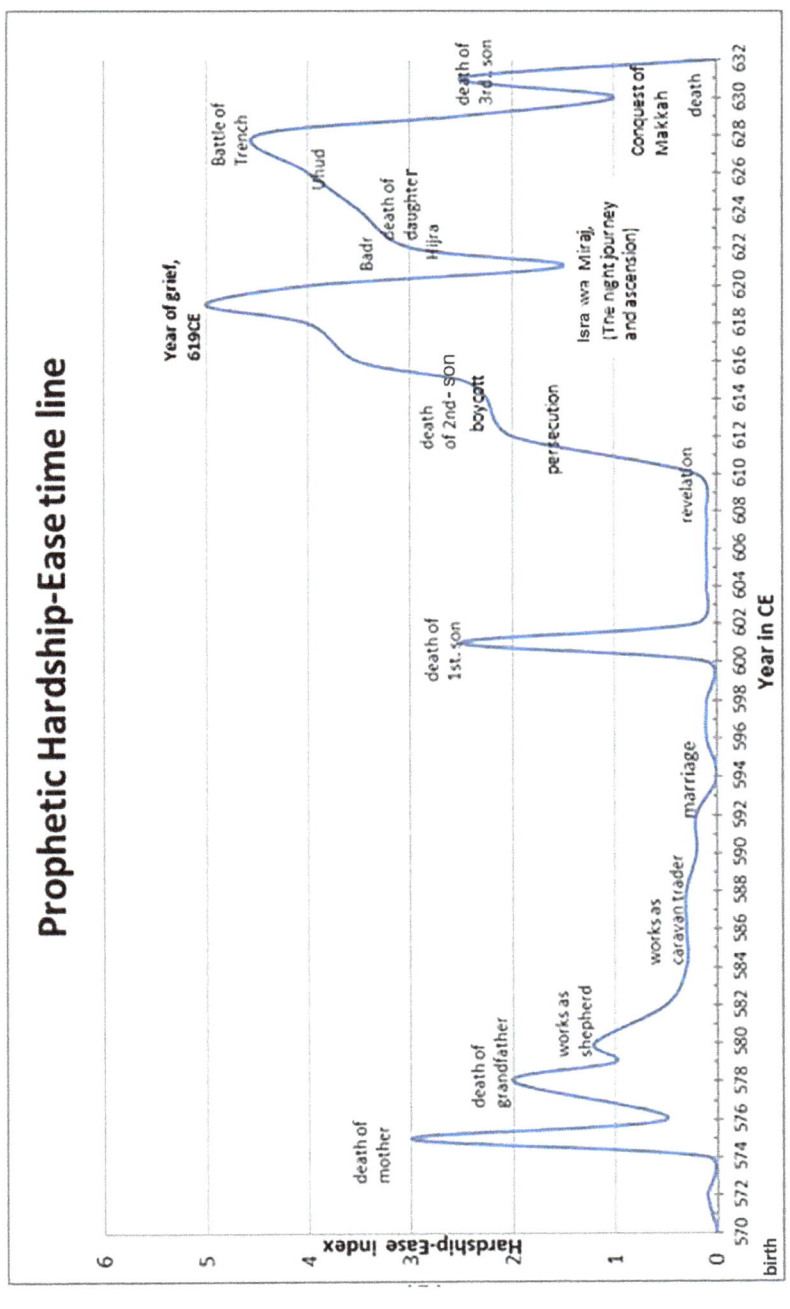

∞

A graphic portrayal of the Prophet's life as illustrated in the adjacent page brings sharply to focus the hardship and ease he faced during his life especially after prophethood. The hardship- ease index along the Y axis is a subjective yet relative and existential measure of increasing adversity or hardship with normalcy being experienced at the origin or zero point. Its vissicitudes seem to echo the oft recited and cited Quranic verses:

"Verily with every hardship there is ease,
Verily with hardship there is ease." (94:5-6)

Muhammad experienced the apex of his hardship and distress during the year of grief in 619CE following the death of his wife Khadija and his uncle Abu Talib, at the valley of Aqaba after he had been stoned and chased out of Taif, bloodied and distraught yet placing his trust in God, he made the most moving and humbling supplication to the most Merciful and Compassionate, when left stranded between a neighbouring tribe who rejected him and his own people who did not accept him. In an authentic hadith as narrated by Ayesha, the Prophet's wife; she asked him, "At which point in your life did you face the most difficult and painful moments, was it at Uhud?" to which Muhammad replied, "No Ayesha, it was that time in the valley of Aqaba".

Through rejection, insults, persecution, loss of beloved ones, boycotts, expulsion, hunger, distress, fear and physical injury, Muhammad bore all his tribulations and travails with patience, fortitude and most importantly trust in God. The question is often asked as to which prophet of God faced the most extreme hardship during his life? Was it Joseph abandoned by his brothers and spent long captivity in Egypt, or Jonah who was in the belly of the whale or was it Job who was afflicted with loss of everything in this life and an incurable disease? The Christians would make a case for Jesus (although they consider him to be God and the second person of the trinity) as depicted in the passion narratives, which is rejected in the Quran. It could be argued that no prophet witnessed and buried six of his children with his own hands, like Muhammad did and that alone could define the essence of hardship and grief.

'In the final analysis, God elevated Muhammad in dignity and status both in this life and the hereafter through his trials and tribulations so that he will be in the most exalted position on the day of resurrection and to eternity.'

Prophetic Ethics- a complete moral ecology and its relevance for all times

In this abridged and abbreviated essay Dr. Ovamir Anjum explores the nature and essence of Islamic Ethics and reflects on the wisdom (the why) and modality (the how) of the divine choice to embody His final guidance in a man, and how his mission and method, teachings and conduct and circumstances of life and community of companions together created a perfect ecosystem for the revelation and expediation of the final truth and perfect goodness.

"Because real life is bigger than words, only a living, breathing exemplar confronted by the enormity and complexity of real life—followers and detractors, ups and downs, surprises and tragedies—could express the fullness of the divine moral teachings. This is why it is the role model, the Sunnah, of a human being, who was sent as "Mercy to all the worlds," that is at the heart of Islamic teachings on right and wrong, their nature and consequences, and ways to acquire virtues and avoid vices. Islamic ethics involve three complementary elements:

(i) obedience to divine commands--this being the most distinctive dimension of Islamic ethics that orients the believer towards an afterlife and infuses moral actions with an eternal concern;

(ii) rational comprehension and reflection for the purpose of appreciating the truth, knowing appropriate ways and occasions to practice, prioritizing competing values, reconciling general principles and particular teachings, and the like; and

(ii) finally, love, the proper drive for being virtuous, which prompts one to seek God's pleasure and love.

In the following, we show how God embodied the elements of obedience, reason, and love in the person of the Prophet Muhammad (ﷺ).

It is important to differentiate at the outset between the Prophet's personal traits and the normative aspects of his role-model. As a complete human being, the Prophet Muhammad (ﷺ) had a unique combination of personal traits, such as a preference for gentleness, patterns in speech, and preferences in dress, cuisine, perfume, and appearance, etc., traits that do not have normative value. Every prophet had such personal traits that allow us to relate to them as human beings. Moses, for instance, is known to have possessed the strong, dominant character of a leader, whereas Jesus had the gentle and patient character of a sage. Both types of traits are fitting in their place.

What we shall call prophetic ethics refers to the character not only of the Prophet Muhammad (ﷺ) but all the prophets through whose example Allah Almighty taught our Prophet and us (as in 4:26: "Allah wishes to explain to you and guide you by the examples [sunan] of those who were before you"). And precisely because a number of moral exemplars are included in this Sunnah, the diversity of their personal characters enriches this guidance. Prophetic ethics, therefore, is inclusive of the virtues of all the prophets like Jesus, Moses, Noah, and Abraham, upon them be peace, whom Allah has praised as role models, as well as the virtues that the Prophet cultivated and encouraged in his disciples, the Companions, in whom we witness a great variety of human personalities. Following the prophetic character, then, is not merely a matter of imitating a single text or a single personality type on every matter, but the employment of revealed teachings and the best of our rational capacity—as Allah says in the Qur'an, "those who listen to speech and follow the best of it"—to understand and emulate the moral import of the entire ecosystem of prophetic ethics.

Consider, for instance, the remarkable Qur'anic story of Moses's harshness toward his assistant and brother prophet, Aaron, upon them both is peace, when he found upon his return from his meeting with God that the Israelites had fallen into worshiping the calf. In rage and sorrow, Moses pulled his brother's hair, until Aaron explained how he pleaded with them but due to their obstinacy decided to wait for Moses to return and strengthen his hand rather than aggravating the situation. Moses understood Aaron's wisdom and turned to Allah to seek forgiveness. In this case, the prophetic ethics does not consist merely in the imitation of any one person in the story, but understanding the priorities and complexities of action in real life. We can appreciate both Aaron's patient diplomacy and Moses's overpowering personality; Moses's rage and sorrow are prophetic ethics, as are Aaron's patience and wisdom. In this one story, we learn all three virtues of obedience, reason, and love for God.

As the site and embodiment of God's final revelation, the Prophet (ﷺ) was made to live a full, complex, and eventful life. Earlier prophets were presented to him as his role models, and he was to become the role model for all humans to come:

Surely there is in the person of Allah's messenger an excellent example (uswa) for you: for those of you who seek Allah and the Afterlife and remember Allah much.

This verse states the fundamental principle of the Islamic ethical system, which is that for all those who seek Allah and success in the eternal hereafter, Prophet Muhammad (ﷺ) must be the role model and exemplar. In turn, he himself was called to follow the role model of earlier prophets, in particular our father Abraham, upon him be peace and blessings, who had lived over 2,000 years earlier. The essence of prophetic character, we learn, is timeless. It follows that in its essence, the Prophet Muhammad's (ﷺ) example is identical to that of all the great messengers and comprises the core of all that is truly good. This also means that by role model (uswa) what is meant is not the peculiar personal traits of any given prophet, but their moral mission to respond and call to God and hence to goodness.

Yet, there is another reason why the Prophet Muhammad's (ﷺ) Sunnah is relevant for all times. He (ﷺ) lived among a people and under conditions that were closest to nature, fitted with the bare necessities of life and uncorrupted by artificial luxuries that conceal the fullness of life from human experience. Like all prophets, he was taught the bare nature of human beings as a shepherd: "Allah did not send any prophet but that he herded sheep." Although there is nothing morally wrong with power and wealth, he was given, and loved, a life of austerity, postponing extraneous pleasures to the eternal afterlife with God. This self-sacrifice was stressed by the Almighty through an angel sent down to the Prophet (ﷺ) offering him a choice between being a "prophet-king" or "servant-messenger"—he chose the latter, the servant messenger ('abdan rasūlā).To live like a servant is both physically and symbolically closer to nature than to live as a king.

Encompassed within his mission was the entire gamut of human experience. He was like Jesus in Mecca and Moses in Medina. He was like Joseph in his forgiveness in the moment of triumph, Job in his patience, and his father Abraham in his sincerity and nearness to God and in his concern for his ummah. Just as the Qur'an is encompassing (muhaymin) of all the divine scriptures sent before it, the Prophet's example encompasses the righteous examples of all the prophets before him. And in contrast to nearly all prophetic missions narrated in the Qur'an, his is the only mission that succeeded through a human struggle; rather than supernatural interventions such as parted seas, cooled fires, and great floods, God gave him success through his unrelenting struggle, beautiful character, and supporting cast of Companions. This is not to deny that Allah guided every step of the Prophet's mission, granted him miracles, and indeed aided early Muslims through angels (as in the Battle of Badr) as well as natural events (as in the Battle of the Trench), but to underscore that rather than annihilating the enemy through supernatural events named above Allah used the believers to combat the forces of unbelief. This makes the Prophet's struggle accessible as a model to believers in any time and place, a fact in which Muslim scholars and revivalists have always found inspiration.

In the rare cases that he chose anything less than beautiful, he was corrected by the Almighty Himself. Far from being a scandalous secret, these corrections were recorded in the Qur'an. Even his frowns, for instance, could become an occasion for divine attention. During his converse with Meccan leaders, with whom he stood pleading to embrace faith, a blind believer interrupted and a most understandable frown appeared on the Prophet's (ﷺ) forehead. But God chose to raise His Prophet (ﷺ) to an even higher rank. A sūrah was sent down announcing this incident:

He frowned and turned away
Because the blind man accosted him. (80:1-2)

And the believers have since recited in their prayers these divine correctives to their Prophet, feeling in their hearts the Prophet's humanity and assured of God's eyes watching over His most beloved creation. Similarly, when Muhammad was moved to pray against the unbelievers of Quraysh after the Battle of Uḥud, Allah corrected him that it was the Almighty's will whether to forgive or punish. When he vowed to give up eating honey to please his wives, Allah corrected him, for as a role model even his private choices were consequential. Far more numerous than these rare occasions are the instances when the Prophet was praised for his judgment or guided before taking an action through divine inspiration or through the Archangel Gabriel, as recorded in countless edifying anecdotes in hadith.

The character of the Prophet Muhammad, therefore, is to be emulated because, on the one hand, it is natural, practical, and feasible, and on the other, it embodies the timeless ideal of prophetic ethics, one which comprises a loftier and more comprehensive answer to the nature of the good than any alternative. Other philosophies often ground ethics in rule-following, from answering to an abstract universal imperative to maximizing 'happiness' (setting aside the question of true happiness for now) to cultivating virtuous habits. Prophetic ethics, however, is a judicious use of all of these strategies in service of the ultimate good and for the attainment of true happiness, in light of the divine revelation and the guidance of the concrete role model in the form of the Sunnah of the Prophet.

Who doesn't appreciate virtues such as truthfulness, forgiveness and justice? Yet, a preacher of peace who always forgives powerful bullies and tyrants but seeks justice from the weak and the poor is not a moral person, but a sniveling hypocrite. Someone who speaks truth about other people's flaws and weaknesses with the intent of harming them while hiding his own flaws is not a truth-teller. A loudmouth who publicly plays up sin and debauchery, others' and his own, in the name of being "real," candid, and funny, may be a comic hero in American society, but he is an immoral scoundrel in Islam. A dressed-to-a-tee religious preacher who has mastered every pleasantry and memorized every religious text and yet uses his fine manners to maintain his status and secure his fortunes, failing to speak truth to power, defend the weak, and uphold truth is an empty shell, devoid of Prophetic character. Being virtuous, it turns out, is not as easy as it might seem at first.

As the following will make clear, his example would never permit the divorce of doctrine from practice or morals from manners, nor perversions of virtuous ideals for selfish ends. Those closest to him were the most aware of this deep harmony. He was not only praised by God for his virtue and unmatched faith in God, but also given a personality that was most receptive to virtue. Even his gentleness, demeanor, and natural habits—traits in which even prophets as humans differed among themselves—set him apart and made him shine. The Prophet's beautiful manners and personality are singled out by the Almighty for consistent praise in the Qur'an:

And indeed [O Prophet] you are possessed of a great character (khuluq).

The Almighty endowed His Final Messenger with all manner of beauty: in looks, manners, feelings, wisdom, and most of all, in morals and character. Allah has given commands and prohibitions in His Noble Shariah, but has placed the secret of His special love in doing above and beyond what is required, in living as if in the presence of God, as if seeing Him and knowing that He sees us, instilling in His servants love for Him, in obedience that is so beautiful that it becomes a sign of Him, an object of art; in short, in imitating the character of the Messenger of Allah. In the words of Imam Abū Ḥāmid al-Ghazālī, one has to merge oneself with the Messenger's personality, "through the experience of an inner relationship;" in a fashion that is not merely the practice of virtue but an embodiment of its truth. "The truth of prophecy" is not merely known, but experienced, as it is further "authenticated by the moral influence it exercises on the soul."

The Almighty did not send the greatest teacher of good with a book of ethical philosophy dedicated to ethical riddles and dilemmas, solving trolley problems, and formulating categorical imperatives. Rather, Allah sent a Book along with its embodiment, the law and its fulfillment, and a role model and its explanation in the person of the Prophet (ﷺ). It is through this perfect vehicle of delivery that the greatest ethical revolution in human history was affected by the Final Revelation. The truth sent down by the All-Wise Creator deeply resonated with human nature, al-fiṭra. To use the Qur'anic image of "light upon light," the light of divine revelation shone upon the divinely bestowed nature. The men and women of the first generations came to embody the "perfected way of life," each to the extent of his or her receptivity and effort, and as more and more peoples from lands far and near entered Islam, decade after decade, century after century. Without abandoning their distinctness altogether, they all adjusted their ways of life to accord with the Prophetic example.

The transformation of the first Muslims from petty, warring dwellers on the fringes of civilization into its leaders, masters, and teachers was the greatest of the miracles of Islam. And this miracle was repeated over and over in history: in Arabia, the Levant, Persia, Africa, Central Asia, India, Southeast Asia, and now, we are witnessing it day by day in Europe and the Americas. This struggle to surrender is never over and is renewed with every generation and every new turn in history.

*This is the model of spiritual excellence and beauty (ihsan) embodied by Muhammad that is referred to in the Quran as a "lovely example" (uswatun hasana): **You have indeed in the Messenger of God a Lovely Example, for anyone whose hope is in God and the Last Day, and who engages in the frequent remembrance of God. (Quran 33:21)** Here is one of the keys for understanding the Muslims' connections to the Prophet. Muhammad does not merely drop the Quran on the front door of humanity. He lives the Quran, he embodies the Quran, and as his wife said, his nature is the Quran. Muslims do not connect to Muhammad simply to learn disembodied hadith statements; they look to him to embody the very meaning of the connection with God. This is why for Muslims the key spiritual and intellectual guide to answering every legal and ethical dilemma has always been to ask: what would Muhammad do? Yet Muhammad himself prophesied that his community would not find the answer to every new challenge spelled out in the pages of the Quran or in his sayings. Part of Muhammad's mission was to provide his community with the tools they would need to encounter every fresh challenge in situations from China to Africa, Malaysia to America. The well-commemorated episode that identifies this account is Muhammad's interaction with his companion Muadh ibn Jabal, who was being sent to lead an- other province as its new governor. In their last conversation, Muhammad asked Muadh how he would deal with the new challenges that would surely come his way. Muadh answered that he would first look into the Quran for guidance. Muhammad asked his close companion what he would do if he did not find the answer there. Muadh pondered further, and then stated that he would look at the example of the Prophet himself—he would wonder what Muhammad would do. The Prophet pressed on a bit further, asking one last time what Muadh would do if asking this question revealed no specific instruction. Reflecting one last time, Muadh offered that then he would exert his own independent reasoning to come up with a fresh solution to the new dilemma. Finally satisfied, Muhammad sent his companion forth to lead his community. This episode has been important for Muslims throughout the centuries because, as Muslims expanded from being the citizens of a small Arab community centered on Muhammad* to a cosmopolitan community living on every continent, they would perpetually be forced to deal with new cultures, challenging situations, fresh dilemmas, and exciting opportunities. The question of "what would Muhammad do?" was never intended to be a fossilized and fully codified system, but rather a way of preparing the community of Muhammad to live in a global and perpetually changing world. It is this creative reimagining of what Muhammad would do that has in part allowed Islam to expand and become indigenous in so many cultural contexts.

One of the intriguing realities of contemporary Islam is that most Muslim speakers and movements claim to be following in the footsteps of Muhammad. Every Muslim wants to embody the Sunna, the paradigm of Muhammadi behavior. The question is, which is the correct understanding of this paradigm? Or to put it differently, what would Muhammad do today?

What is the prophetic 'Sunna' or tradition?

For Muslims, the actions, behaviour and the role model set by the Prophet is collectively termed the 'Sunna' and they follow these practices to varying degrees of meticulousness through both a devotional love for the prophet and also in the belief that it has divine merit and blessing. Whilst this falls well within the normative principles of the faith and the Quranic injunctions, these prophetic actions are rooted in the epistemology of the 7th century and context and should be viewed through that optic. The paradigm and epistemology in the 21st century has to be placed in perspective against the eternal objectives of the Sharia (Maqasid-al-shariah) or God's law and hence the appropriate 'sunna' or the prophetic way interpreted in that context. The answer to the question "what will Muhammad do today"? Should take into consideration not only Quranic and prophetic guidance, consensus of scholars and reason but also customs and practices of a community. The 'Sunna' hence is not only the documented and reported traditions from the prophetic era but is also the evolving reasoned response to the question of "What would Muhammad have done?"

Prof. Khaled Abu El Fadl of UCLA captures the essence of the Sunna thus: "The Sunnah of the Prophet is there for all to follow it. But it is not about clothes or about hygiene. It is not about looks, smell or taste. It is about ethics, dignity and virtue. That is the Sunnah of the Prophet. To live in a society where you can investigate the truth , and, once convinced it is the truth, be free to speak it without fear of punishment- that is the Sunnah of the Prophet until we realize this, God will never bless us."

Where do Muslims stand today vis-à-vis Muhammad?
Muslims in the post-9/11 era often cite the verse from the Quran that identifies the Muslim community as ummatan wasatan, meaning "the middle community," or the mediating community: Thus have We made of you a middle community that ye might be witnesses over the nations and the Messenger a witness over yourselves. (Quran 2:143) This verse is nowadays taken by many Muslims to mean that Muslims should be drawn to the "middle path," avoiding an extreme that is, being moderates. Historically, many Quranic commentators have interpreted this verse to mean that the Muslim community is to be characterized by the quality of justice in its dealings with humanity—that the community of Muhammad is to be a just community. However, one leading tenth-century Quranic commentator, Imam Tabari, offers an ingenious reading: if Muslims are the "middle community," it is because they stand between the world and Muhammad. In other words, the task for Muslims is to deliver Muhammad's message to the world, as Muhammad stood between the Muslims and the Divine. If Muslims are to be worthy of the name "Muhammad's people," if the adjective "Muhammadi" is to be meaningful, then it is incumbent on Muslims to embody the qualities of mercy and justice that Muhammad so perfectly embodied.
If "Muslim" is not to be simply a historic designation or civilizational marker but a spiritual indicator of aspiring to the ethics of Muhammad, then it is vital to live by the "lovely example" that Muhammad set (Quran 33:21).

(Adapted from "Memories of Muhammad" by Omid Safi)

What does it feel like to be a Muslim?- A question of introspection

As Muslims are we intellectually and spiritually detached from our faith? Although we engage in the rituals and duties of Islam and being a Muslim, to what degree are our hearts attached to our actions and how pure are our intentions? A self-test that addresses this issue is to ask oneself the question 'What does it feel like to be a Muslim? One possible response would be:

"To be a Muslim feels like I am responsible and accountable to God first-ly for every action of mine and people feel safe from my deeds and my actions are beneficial and not harmful to humanity; whatever calamity or trial befalls me, I say 'to God do I belong and to Him is my ultimate return' and whatever goodness or blessing that visits me, 'I say praise be to God who has willed it and has power over all things'. I feel grateful in times of good fortune, patient in the face of adversity and remain content with Qaḍā (what was decreed).I feel humbled and grateful for the blessings He has conferred on me and I strive to fill my heart with faith that infuses His love, forgiveness and mercy. I feel His closeness to me and my Lord hears me when I supplicate and I feel like expressing my gratitude through prostration and remembrance of His Glory. I feel like He has given me the greatest gift in Islam and honoured me as the best of mankind for enjoining good and forbidding evil and spreading the word of truth and has made me as a witness to humanity to stand by justice and compassion. I feel compelled to do acts of kindness and righteousness and strive to please my Lord and do so with sincerity and humility. I also feel compelled to improve and perfect my character and mannerisms with the Prophet Muhammad being my role model. I feel my Lord hears my prayers and answers them in a manner that is best for me. I feel the urge to excel in my worship as if I see my Lord before me though I see Him not. I fear His judgement for the transgressions I commit but have hope in Him accepting my repentance as He is the most forgiving. Most merciful and forgives all sins. I also feel like I can rely on patience, constancy and prayer for my success in this world and the hereafter and in dying as a Muslim lies my ultimate salvation to enter Paradise through His Mercy and to eventually feel and be in His presence and the presence of the beloved Messenger of God for whom my heart yearns to meet more than any other being."

Islamic Spirituality and the Prophetic Way

In an authentic hadith where God speaks through the Prophet in the first person (hadith Qudsi), it was narrated that the Prophet Muhammad (ﷺ)said:

"My servant draws not near to Me with anything more loved by Me than the religious duties I have enjoined upon him, and My servant continues to draw near to Me with supererogatory works so that I shall love him. When I love him I am his hearing with which he hears, his seeing with which he sees, his hand with which he strikes and his foot with which he walks. Were he to ask [something] of Me, I would surely give it to him, and were he to ask Me for refuge, I would surely grant him it. ."-Al-Bukhari.

This hadith on many levels defines the essence of 'spirituality' or 'nearness to God' which in Arabic is referred to as "Tawassul" or "Tazkiya" and sometimes as "Tassawuf". All these concepts in turn capture the term "Ihsan" which is the highest expression of faith as clarified to the Prophet by the archangel Jibreel in the famous and oft quoted hadith where Gabriel visits the Prophet in his final year in the presence of his companions and questions the Messenger of God about Islam (submission), Imaan (faith) and Ihsan (excellence in worshiping God as if you were before Him though you see Him not whilst He sees you all the time). There are many phases to this state of excellence or divine nearness. The first phase is on the level of following the exoteric law or shariah. The next and deeper phase is on the level of cultivating decorum (adab) or the beauty of outward behaviour. The third and yet deeper phase is the beautification of the character by the elimination of negative traits and the establishment of positive ones with the teachings and actions of the Prophet as a model. (hasan al-khuluq). He is reported to have said "I was only sent to perfect the good manners and personality." The fourth phase is spiritual rigour in following the spiritual practices that he taught in taming the unruly soul so that once it is at rest it is capable of reflecting the Presence of God which is referred to in the Quran as 'Nafs al-mutamainna" or the soul that is at peace with God in perfect repose. To the righteous it will be said;

"O reassured soul, return to your Lord well pleased, and pleasing to Him".
[Quran 89:27-28]

Islamic Spirituality and the Prophetic Way

The meaning of the second part of the hadeeth qudsi narrated above is that when the believing slave strives to draw closer to Allah by doing obligatory acts of worship, then voluntary acts, Allah will bring him closer to Him, and will raise him from the level of Imaan (faith, belief) to the level of Ihsaan, so he will start to worship Allah as if he can see Him, and his heart will be filled with knowledge of his Lord, love and awe for Him, fear of Him, and glorification and veneration of Him. When his heart is filled in this manner, any attachment to anything other than Allah will disappear, and the person will no longer be attached to any of his whims or desires, and he will have no wish for anything except that which his Lord and Master wants. At that point the person will not speak except to remember Allah, he will not move except to obey His command. So when he speaks, he speaks for the sake of Allah; when he hears he hears for the sake of Allah; when he looks, he looks for the sake of Allah; i.e., he acts with the help and guidance of Allah and for the sake of Allah in these matters. So he only listens to that which Allah loves; he only looks at that with which Allah is pleased; he only strikes with his hands and walks with his feet for purposes with which his Lord and Master is pleased. It does not mean that Allah is his hearing and his sight, and Allah is his hand and his foot. Exalted be Allah above that, for Allah is above the Throne and He is Exalted above all His creation. Rather what is meant is that He guides him with regard to his hearing, seeing, walking and striking. Hence it was narrated in another version that Allah says: "In Me he hears, in Me he sees, in Me he strikes and in Me he walks," meaning that Allah guides him in his actions, words, hearing and seeing. At the same time Allah answers his prayers, so if he asks Him, He will give; if he seeks His help, He will help him; if he seeks refuge with Him, He will grant him refuge.-

Islamic spirituality defines the nearness of one to the transcendent God who is closer to man than his jugular vein and is not a remote abstract deity removed from the heart of the believer. The Quran captures the essence of this in chapter 2 verse 186:

"And when My servants ask you, [O Muhammad], concerning Me - indeed I am near. I respond to the invocation of the supplicant when he calls upon Me. So let them respond to Me [by obedience] and believe in Me that they may be [rightly] guided."

The Proof and the historical necessity for Prophet Hood

(The text and contents in this section has been extracted from the article/paper published by Yaqeen Institute for Islamic Research and authored by Mohammed El Shinnawy).

At the time when the Messenger of God walked upon the earth and called the people to the path of God, the disbelieving amongst them responded by asking him to perform the most absurd of miracles as proof of his prophet hood so that they can successfully silence their consciences and sedate the guilt of denying the undeniable. As the Most High said,

"And [even] if We opened to them a gate from the heaven and they continued therein to ascend, they would say, 'Our eyes have only been dazzled. Rather, we are a people affected by magic.'" [Hijr (15): 14-15]

Anyone versed in biblical scripture, and anyone who has studied the condition of the world before the prophet hood of Muhammad, would conclude that Almighty God had to send a messenger. This was for two reasons: people were waiting for the final prophesized messenger, and an all-compassionate God could not let the atrocities of the world continue much longer.

Biblical Prophecy

"And has it not been a sign to them that it is recognized by the scholars of the Children of Israel?" [ash-Shuara' (26): 197]

Though some contemporaries of the last prophet rejected him out of animosity and prejudice, and others simply hadn't yet been guided, some of the biblically versed – like 'Abdullah bin Salam – quickly accepted Islam, and that was of the proofs Allah cited against Quraysh, since most of the Arabs were illiterate, did not ascribe to any scripture, and held that the Jews were superior to them for being People of the

Book. These People of the Book knew God's promise to bless Ishmael; to make from him in particular a great nation. They did not believe that being born of a slave-woman detracted from his legitimacy, and knew that the first-born son of Abraham was most entitled to the covenant (had it been meant to be only for one of the two sons, which is not the case here, as we Muslims believe). Despite adulteration, there still remained – until today, even – clear indicators of the prophet hood of Muhammad in the Judeo-Christian tradition, of which we will mention a select few.

- **A Great Nation**

"And also of the son of the bondwoman I will make a nation, because he is thy seed. And Abraham rose up early in the morning, and took bread, and a bottle of water, and gave it unto Hagar, putting it on her shoulder, and the child, and sent her away: and she departed, and wandered in the wilderness of Beersheba. And the water was spent in the bottle, and she cast the child under one of the shrubs. And she went, and sat her down over against him a good way off, as if it were a bowshot: for she said, let me not see the death of the child. And she sat over against him, and lifts up her voice, and wept. And God heard the voice of the lad; and the angel of God called to Hagar out of heaven, and said unto her, What aileth thee, Hagar? Fear not; for God hath heard the voice of the lad where he is. Arise, lift up the lad, and hold him in thine hand; for I will make him a great nation." [Genesis: 21/13-18, KJV]

A "great nation" in biblical terminology can never be a nation of polytheists or idolaters. Therefore, when did the progeny of Ishmael become a great nation worshipping the one true God? This did not happen at anyone's hand before Muhammad. Some claim that this took place in Sinai, but this is sheer absurdity, because it was a given that the Arabs were a people who forever maintained knowledge of their lineage, which they traced back to Ishmael. Nobody ever denied this history, while on the opposite end; nobody has ever documented a great Ishmaelite nation in Sinai. It is a staggering proposition that the Ishmaelite Arabs were somehow all mistaken about their ancestry that converges at Ishmael, and that a great Ishmaelite nation rose and then vanished in Sinai without anyone ever knowing. Couple these historical facts with the biblical description of Paran – where Abraham left Ishmael – being a wilderness south of Jerusalem, making it even clearer that Paran must be Makkah. Hence, both the historical facts and biblical texts concur that the Makkans were the descendants of Ishmael, and that his mother brought him a wife from Egypt, not that his offspring took residence in Sinai, Egypt.

- **Zamzam & the Flourishing City**

"Then God opened her (Hagar's) eyes and she saw a well of water; and she went, and filled the bottle with water and gave the lad a drink. And God was with the lad; and he grew, and dwelt in the wilderness and became an archer. And he dwelt in the wilderness of Paran: his mother took him a wife out of the land of Egypt." [Genesis: 21/19-21]

In Makkah, there exists the well of Zamzam – the oldest spring of water the world has ever known. Put the two millennium before the Prophet Muhammad aside, and merely consider the multitudinous millions of pilgrims visiting for Hajj and Umrah over the past 1,500 years. They all return home with immeasurable gallons of Zamzam water. Alongside this, an endless round-the-clock supply of this water is transported to Quba' and the Prophetic Mosque in Madinah, while residents of Makkah have tanks installed in their homes for standardized Zamzam delivery. Hence, this was certainly a blessed well which Hagar and Ishmael received, and a clear first brick set by God for this city to flourish.

- **Shining from Paran**

"And this is the blessing, wherewith Moses the man of God blessed the children of Israel before his death. And he said, 'The Lord came from Sinai, and rose up from Seir unto them; he shined forth from mount Paran, and he came with ten thousands of saints. From his right hand went a fiery law for them." [Deuteronomy: 33/1-2]

Sinai (Egypt) is a clear reference to Moses and the Torah, and Seir (Palestine) is an allusion to Jesus and the Evangel. If we refuse to accept that the third reference is to Muhammad and the Quran, we will be stranded for another momentous event suitable for mention alongside Sinai and Jerusalem. At the climax of his ministry, the Prophet Muhammad returned to Parana (Makkah), marching with 10,000 of his Companions, and reinstating in that land the worship of the one true God alone. Polytheism and idolatry were ousted from around the House built by Abraham, and the glory of God shone anew.

- **Where Kedar Lives**

"Behold my servant, whom I uphold; mine elect, in whom my soul delighteth; I have put my spirit upon him: he shall bring forth judgment to the Gentiles. He shall not cry, nor lift up, nor cause his voice to be heard in the street. A bruised reed shall he not break, and the smoking flax shall he not quench: he shall bring forth judgment unto truth. He shall not fail nor be discouraged, till he have set judgment in the earth: and the isles shall wait for his law."... "Sing unto the Lord a new song and his praise from the end of the earth, ye that go down to the sea, and all that is therein; the isles, and the inhabitants therefore. Let the wilderness and the cities thereof lift up their voice, the villages that Kedar doth inhabit: let the inhabitants of the rock sing, let them shout from the top of the mountains." [Isaiah: 42/1-13]

This servant in Isaiah cannot be Jesus, when Christianity and Islam agree he rose without bringing justice to the nations, as his handful of disciples did not possess the strength required to enforce justice. This servant cannot be Moses who died in the wilderness of Sinai, exasperated by the resistance of his own people. Interestingly, the Bible identifies Kedar as the first born of Ishmael. The Bible also asserts that the first son is most entitled to the covenant. These combined truths become painfully problematic for someone wishing to conceal that where Kedar settled fits nothing but Makkah, and that Ishmael's descendant who gained enough power to enjoin "God's justice" fits nobody but Prophet Muhammad. It was because of these glaring facts that they kept hidden that Allah (the Exalted) said, **"Those to whom We gave the Scripture know him as they know their own sons. But indeed, a party of them conceal the truth while they know [it]."** [al-Baqarah (2): 146]

209

- **John & the Prophet**

"And this is the record of John, when the Jews sent priests and Levites from Jerusalem to ask him, Who art thou? And he confessed, and denied not; but confessed, I am not the Christ. And then they asked him, What then? Art though Elias? And he saith, I am not. Art thou the prophet? And he answered, No." [John 1:19-21]

Who is "that prophet" who is neither the Christ, nor is he Elijah? Who is "that prophet" whose name apparently does not even need stating, as if his identity was common knowledge and his promised coming was awaited by all? This passage insinuates – at the very least – that people were not just awaiting another prophet, but rather something unique. Indeed, they were awaiting the greatest prophet and the finality of prophet hood; one who would illuminate for humanity the path to God one last time – permanently. But where would he come from?

"I will raise them up a Prophet from among their brethren, like unto thee, and will put my words in his mouth; and he shall speak unto them all that I shall command him." [Deuteronomy: 18/18]

The prophet they asked John about was not from among them (the Israelites), but rather from among their brethren (the Ishmaelite's). The New International Version added "Israelite brethren," but this is a very recent change – as if concealing the message is a perpetual work in progress, or that a committee steps in to improvise every time they feel something is going to be correctly interpreted. Secondly, nobody from the Ishmaelite's – or from humanity, even – had a greater semblance to Moses than the Prophet Muhammad. Thirdly, only Muhammad tirelessly taught his followers that not a single word that leaves his lips should be credited back to him. **"By the star when it descends, your companion (Muhammad) has not strayed, nor has he erred, nor does he speak from [his own] inclination. It is but a revelation revealed."** [An-Najm (53): 1-4]

- **Jesus & the Comforter**

"Nevertheless I tell you the truth; It is expedient for you that I go away: for if I go not away, the Comforter will not come unto you; but if I depart, I will send him unto you?" … "I have yet many things to say unto you, but ye cannot bear them now. Howbeit when he, the Spirit of Truth, is come, he will guide you into all truth: for he shall not speak of himself, but whatsoever he shall hear, that shall he speak: and he will shew you things to come." [John 16:7-13]

Jesus could not be implying the Holy Spirit here, calling him the Comforter that cannot arrive until Jesus departs, since the Holy Spirit was always with Jesus. Jesus could not be implying Paul or the papacy, since they did away with laws instead of perfecting them, and have not shown us proof that they communicate with the heavens. Only the Prophet Muhammad revived the honor of Jesus without burying his legacy of worshipping the Creator alone. Muhammad taught his followers that he would only speak that which he would hear, and he would precisely foretell future events. He brought definitive guidance on all truths, perfecting by it the Divine code of law for humanity. In one splendid metaphor, the Prophet Muhammad describes prophet hood as a magnificent structure that people observed in awe, short of a single missing brick that needed to be placed in its structure to fill the gap and perfect its glory. He then commented, **"I am that brick; I am the seal of the prophets."**

- **Construction of the Kaaba**

Scriptures aside, simply consider the religious paradigm in Arabia. Among the Arabs, Abraham was recognized as the ultimate patriarch, and due to the esteem they held him in, all paid homage to him – by visiting the House he built in Makkah (the Kaaba). Despite the fact that they were idolaters, the polytheists affirmed that Makkah was a special sanctuary whose veneration was desired by God. They saw themselves as the heirs of that heritage, and thus they felt compelled to honor this Kaaba that Abraham had erected. Why else would God command Abraham to just leave

Hagar and his firstborn infant in a particular place, and a barren wilderness at that? For an Arab whose worldview stems from that paradigm, it is inconceivable that Allah sent Abraham to construct the Kaaba, sprung a blessed well beneath it, gave rise to a great nation because of it, and protected it from invasions – just so it would be surrounded by idols and become a venue for depravity. It is no surprise, then, why people at that time were of a certainty that something was about to happen, something momentous that would change the entire scene in that part of the world and soon far beyond.

The Sharia - the Way to the Water

Any new reader or one introduced for the first time to the biography of the Prophet Muhammad might hasten to ask the question, "What about the 'Shariah'?" and what it had to do with the Prophet's life. No modern biography of the Prophet's life would be complete without mention of at least a few words on the meaning and concept of the Shariah which directly and literally translates as 'way to the water' which could be interpreted in essence as a way of reaching towards the source of sustenance, at least on earth. Very few words in the Islamic / Arabic vocabulary have been more misunderstood and maligned than this word possibly with the exception of the word 'Jihad'. Unfortunately, for most westerners and non-Muslims, the word 'Shariah' conjures up images of injustice, cruel/harsh laws, medieval customs and even barbaric practices. Nothing could be further from the truth. For Muslims, the 'Shariah' is the essence of God's divine guidance to humanity and as demonstrated and elucidated by the traditions of the Prophet, his way, his deeds and his words. The underlying sources for the 'Shariah' are the Quranic text, the 'hadeeth' or sayings of the Prophet and the continuing and evolving interpretation of these two sources through a well-defined methodology and science of analogy, consensus of scholars and intellectual /rational reasoning.

Most if not all misconceptions about the Shariah arise from a literalistic adaptation of Quranic and prophetic sources rather than one based on the overarching worldview of the Quran and Sunnah (the traditions of the Prophet) and the central concept of Maqasid al Shariah al Kulliya (the overarching objects and purpose of Shariah). According to this doctrine, Shariah aims to protect five essential social values – life, lineage, reputation, intellect or reason and property. Many jurists have added religion as a sixth value. In other words, a critical component of what makes Shariah a path to godliness and goodness is that it is acutely engaged with social values.

In his ground breaking book "Reasoning with God"-Reclaiming the Shariah, Dr. Khaled Abou El Fadl states that, "Shariah is an ongoing discourse on how to be a good Muslim within a communal system and a metanarrative on being a good human being within human society.....

What is important is they recognize shared common standards of virtue and godliness. At a minimum the ultimate standards or objective elements are peace, repose, tranquility, justice, balance, compassion, love and care for one another. There is an interconnected symbiotic relationship between these constituent elements and the essential values or objectives of Shariah."

This should not be misconstrued as Shariah being subject to modernism and liberalistic values but on the contrary will always adhere to the eternal ethical and moral values of Islam whilst pushing the frontiers of Shariah development through contextualizing and synthesizing multiple disciplines and moving towards evaluating God's law within a relevant epistemological framework for our time and space in history.

Historically, sharia and fiqh, or law and jurisprudence have frequently been confused: almost overnight, the interpretive efforts of scholars of law and jurisprudence were elevated to the status of an absolute and sacred `divine law`. Legal opinions became indisputable edicts; despite all the counsel of the earliest great scholars to maintain a critical and selective attitude as they developed a system of law and jurisprudence, some of their followers were not able to avoid the temptation and began to treat certain opinions as sacred.

The construction of a legal system, the application of the law and the exercise of jurisprudence are not `divine law`. They are human constructs that must be assessed, criticized, viewed selectively and sometimes renewed on the principles of mercy, wisdom, social justice and human wellbeing.

Professor Jonathan Brown in his paper titled 'The issue of apostasy in Islam' published by the Yaqeen Research Institute states:

"The Sharia consists of some laws that remain the same regardless of changing circumstances and others that change with them. Most of the Sharia is up to individual Muslims to follow in their own lives. Some are for judges to implement in courts. Finally, a third set of laws is for the ruler or political authority to implement based on the best interests of society. The Sharia ruling on Muslims who decide to leave Islam belongs to this third group. Implemented in the past to protect the integrity of the Muslim community, today this important goal can

best be reached by Muslim governments using their right to set punishments for apostasy aside."

Tariq Ramadan in his book - 'Islam -the Essentials', goes on to state:

"Applying Sharia calls for a constant effort of mediation between the Texts and context between principles and their application all in the light of the higher objectives that believers must seek out and strive to attain. By no means must they destroy or reject the world for the sake of immutable 'divine laws' to be blindly applied. They must instead struggle to reform and transform the real and existing world in the name of these very values, principles, rules and higher objectives. The approach must be broad, inclusive and progressive. Everything that comes from other religious traditions or human inventiveness, all that is in accord with and does not oppose the values, the principles and objectives of Sharia naturally becomes an integral part of the Way in legal, intellectual, cultural, artistic, scientific socio-economic and political terms. The capacity to absorb and to make its own the heritage of humanity- in all its diversity had long been the hallmark of Islamic civilization. It has incorporated the founding elements of earlier religions, different cultures and philosophies, scientific discoveries and artistic expressions and tastes. Its Golden Age was precisely that of its greatest openness and dynamism."

The Preservation of the Quran

The Quran we have in our hands today is the exact same one- to the letter-that was revealed to the Prophet Muhammad (ﷺ). The process by which the Quran was preserved is well recorded and historically remarkable. During the Prophet's own lifetime, whenever new verses were revealed his companions wrote them down on parchment, skin, leaves etc. and then read them back to him. (The Prophet could not read). Around 65 of the Prophets companions functioned as scribes at various time for the revelation. The exact ordering of the verses and the chapters was personally overseen by the Prophet himself during his own lifetime. The Prophet also forbade anything but the Quran (including his own sayings) to be written down alongside the Quran-in order to avoid any confusion. So the entire Quran was available in written form during the Prophet's own lifetime. Because new revelations were being revealed until not long before the Prophets death in 632 CE, these revelations were not collected in a single book during his own lifetime. A number of his companions who had memorized the Quran in its entirety were killed in battles after the Prophet's death and they not only knew and studied the Quran but were experts in classical Arabic and there were concerns that the Quran would be lost. Therefore the first successor to the Prophet - Caliph Abu Bakr tasked one of the main scribes of the Quran during the Prophet's time, Zayd bin Thabit, who had memorized the Quran himself, to collect all the fragments into a single folio. Zayd set about gathering all the fragments that had been written down in the Prophets presence and checked by him and did not accept any that was not sworn to by two witnesses. He also imposed on himself a more stringent condition of wanting to ensure that those who knew it by memory also had a written fragment of it.

This process and compilation took place at the Prophet's mosque and led to a complete collection of the Quran in proper order into a single folio, albeit of differing 'page' sizes. This master copy was kept with the widow of the Prophet, Hafsa for safekeeping. About 15 years later during the period of the 3rd. Caliph Uthman, reports reached him that the Quran was being read in different dialects of Arabic in different places of the vast Islamic empire which had spread from West Africa to central Asia. So Uthman decided to make the Quran into an actual book (Mushaf) and keep it as it was revealed in the dialect of the Quraysh (the Prophet's own tribe).

The Preservation of the Quran

To be absolutely certain of the written text, Uthman independently re-peated the whole gathering and verification process done earlier and formed a committee of twelve knowledgeable companions including Zayd as the head of it and then checked it with the master copy with Hafsa compiled earlier. Uthman then ordered all other remaining frag-ments to be burnt or harmonized with the new compiled Book (for fear of scribal errors). A number of copies of this Mushaf were made and sent to all regions and a master copy kept in Madinah. It is very plausi-ble that the oldest fragments of the Quran discovered in the Birming-ham library in England in 2010 could have come from one of these early Uthmanic copies as it has been carbon dated to be between 600 CE to 645 CE. The words and verses in this manuscript are identical to what Muslims read today. The chronological order of revelation and the ac-tual numbering of the chapters or suras as they appear in the Quran is listed in Appendix H.

Variant readings or recitations of the Quran

The Quran was revealed to the Prophet in the dialect and language of the Quraysh Arabic which was the Arabic dialect spoken by the tribes of Quraysh who lived in the Arabian Peninsula. The Prophet however realized that Arabic is spoken in different dialects in various parts of the greater Middle East in places like North Africa, the Levant and other far flung regions. He asked God to make the recitation of the Quran easy on the tongues of people from different regions and Allah answered his request by revealing the Quran in seven different `Ahkraaf`` which resulted in ten different recitations or `Qiraat``. This word Àhkraaf` could mean letters, dialects or even limitations and in no way changed the essential meaning or message of the Quran but merely facilitated the ease of recitation by different Arabic dialects and in some instanc-es different synonyms were used in the variant recitations which still preserved the integrity of the message. The fact that the Quran was transmitted as an oral tradition meant that the Quran was recited in the seven permissible Àhraaf`. Hence the presence of early manuscripts dating back to the 7th century CE or the 1st century Hijra indicate the reality of these different readings and a thorough scriptural analysis of these show no changes to the essence and theological and moral thrust of the message of the Quran.

Strategic leadership of Prophet Muhammad

The events, activities and outcomes during the lifetime of the Prophet and the manner in which he acted, managed , planned, decided and executed them as a leader provides profound insights into a strategic model of leadership and the attributes or traits that were needed to accomplish them.

The two dimensional matrix illustrated in figure 1 below captures the parameters of time in the short and long term on one dimension and key tasks from the Prophets mission in 'Convey & Transform' and 'Build & Complete' on the other. The resulting matrix brings to focus the four critical phases of Prophet hood defined by its core mission and purpose. In addition to analysing the mission of the Prophet this framework offers an insightful perspective into the art of strategic leadership in accomplishing goals and objectives both short and long term whilst pursuing the overall vision and mission.

Both the 'Convey & Transform' and 'Build & Complete' parameters contain operational and strategic elements and echo the essence of the Prophetic mission in conveying the 'Message', transforming the faith of people through the declaration of the Oneness and unity of God, building the foundations and pillars of the faith and as asserted in the Quran 'completing' God's favour on humanity and choosing Islam as their religion. Strategic leadership requires attention to both detail and operational issues which are short term and also the ability to visualize how current actions will impact future outcomes. The Messenger of God had the innate ability to demonstrate a diverse and farsighted range of personal skills and attributes during his life time that enabled him with God's Will to fulfill his mission on earth.

The matrix in figure 1 also depicts the macro elements of the Prophetic mission and the role of strategic leadership in achieving that goal. Embedded within these macro elements are the 'micro' elements that are needed to effectively build and transform the individual, the community and the nation as a cohesive whole. These 'micro' details are found in the message of the Quran and the prophetic traditions and include but not limited to the principles of Islam, the articles of faith and the concept of Ihsan or excellence in both worship and conduct.

Ultimately the essence of these micro elements is to transform the heart of the believer towards God consciousness and worship, serving humanity, developing excellent character and acquiring knowledge.

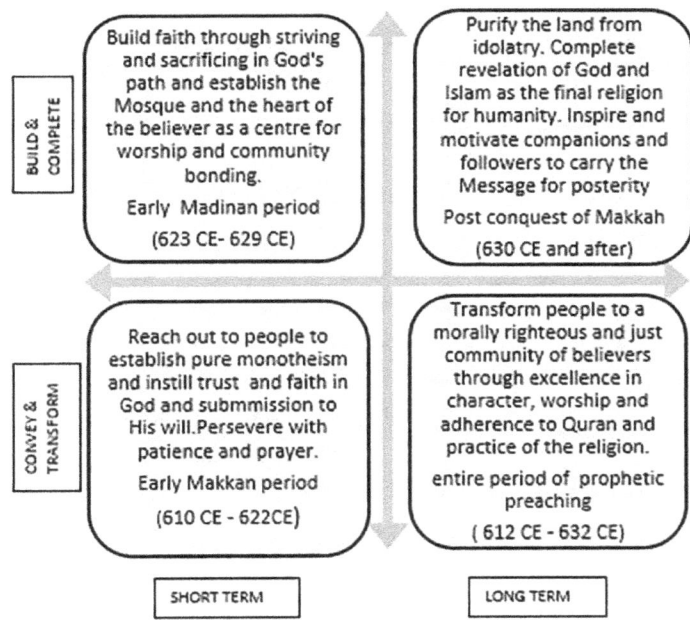

Two dimensional analysis of the Prophet's Leadership Model

Figure 1

An additional dimension to the above matrix is the judicious and appropriate choice of people to lead and execute the situational and time related strategies within each grid. The Prophet showed great skill and acumen in choosing his companions for different tasks and activities based upon their innate abilities and skill sets. A classic example was the appointment of his cousin Jaafar Ibn Abu Talib to lead the first group of emigrants to Abyssinia. Jaafar not only had an extensive knowledge of the Quran but was eloquent and courageous in the face of power. His appeal to the Abyssinian king Negus on behalf of his fellow emigrants was legendary and moved the king to treat them favourably. Likewise the Prophet appointed generals and commanders for various expeditions during his absence based not on seniority and rank but on capability, intent and the motivation to accomplish a mission.

Two outstanding examples of leadership and the manner in which the Prophet handled and dealt with his companions and followers in motivating and encouraging them was after the battle of Uhud and the expedition to Mutah. The battle of Uhud proved disastrous in terms of loss of lives for the Muslims and was a direct consequence of disobedience on the part of a group of Muslims who were stationed on a hillside as archers with express instructions from the Prophet not to leave or abandon their positions. On seeing the initial victorious advance by the Muslim army, the archers deserted their positions to collect their war booty which left the pass undefended and the Pagan cavalry charged through the pass and attacked the Muslims from the flank causing panic among the believers until the Prophet rallied them back into a position of defence. The Prophet too was badly injured in the face during this attack and matters could have been worse if not by God's Will for the heroic bravery of some companions who stood by the Prophet and repulsed the attack.

Instead of accusing those who disobeyed of not following orders and chastising them, the Prophet responded with empathy and understanding and invited them for consultations and was able to mobilize an army within a day to prepare for a possible counter attack by the Makkans. This made the guilty more remorseful about their greedy act and turned their hearts into loyal and obedient followers for the future. As a true strategic leader the Prophet showed his longer term vision for the community over short term emotional reaction.

The expedition to Mutah inside Byzantine territory was ordered by the Prophet and he appointed two who were very dear to him to lead the expedition with each one assuming command when the other was martyred. Both Zaid bin Haritha, his adopted son and his cousin Jaafar ibn Abu Talib were martyred during this battle and finally Khalid ibn Waleed the third commander in line seeing the futility of battle against a vastly outnumbered force and a well-equipped Roman army, tactically withdrew and returned to Madinah to avoid a greater number of casualties among the Muslims. Initially the Muslims in Madinah treated them as fleeing from the enemy but the Prophet quickly intervened and called their retreat honourable and wise so that they may fight another time when better prepared. Here too the Prophet demonstrates the importance of tactical withdrawal in certain situations and the value of Muslim lives and the importance of focussing on the longer term objective. Eventually during the caliphate of Umar in 640 CE, the Muslims marched into Byzantine and conquered the Romans with ease and loss of minimal lives.

The Prophet (ﷺ) stated:

"Every one of you is a shepherd and is responsible for his flock. The leader of people is a guardian and is responsible for his subjects. A man is the guardian of his family and he is responsible for them. A woman is the guardian of her husband's home and his children and she is responsible for them. The servant of a man is a guardian of the property of his master and he is responsible for it. No doubt, every one of you is a shepherd and is responsible for his flock." Ṣaḥeeḥ al-Bukhaarī 6719, Ṣaḥeeḥ Muslim 1829

This hadith has profound implications for individuals as leaders in both their personal, public and corporate lives. We play multiple roles in our daily lives as team leaders, group leaders, community leaders etc. and each role requires one to exercise responsibility to the flock they guard. This responsibility may well extend beyond the material to the psychological and spiritual wellbeing and would require attributes displayed by the Prophet as shown below.

At a more detailed level figure 2 identifies the major milestones within each phase and figure 3 highlights a listing of the critical attributes the Prophet displayed during the period of his Prophet hood.

Key events/milestones during the Prophet's lifetime. (figure 2)

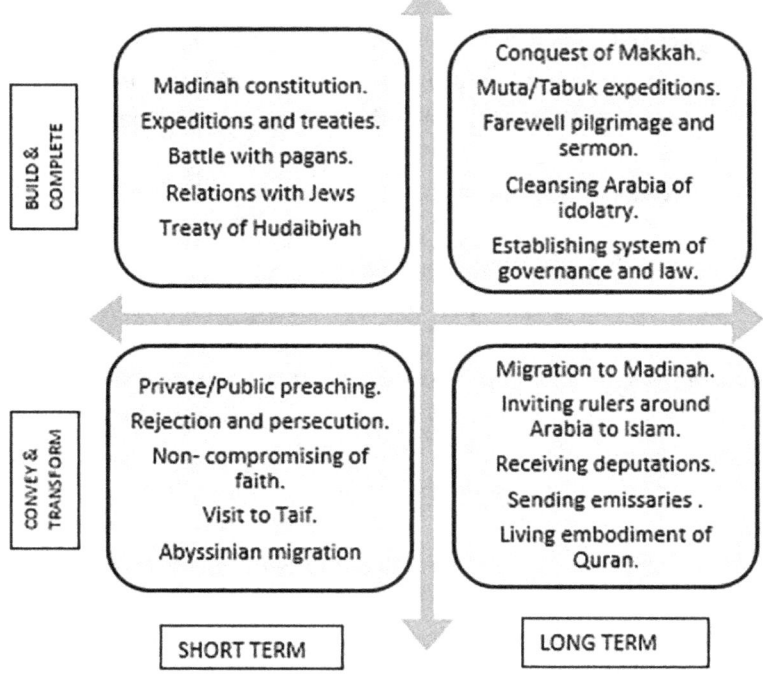

BUILD & COMPLETE

Madinah constitution.
Expeditions and treaties.
Battle with pagans.
Relations with Jews
Treaty of Hudaibiyah

Conquest of Makkah.
Muta/Tabuk expeditions.
Farewell pilgrimage and sermon.
Cleansing Arabia of idolatry.
Establishing system of governance and law.

CONVEY & TRANSFORM

Private/Public preaching.
Rejection and persecution.
Non- compromising of faith.
Visit to Taif.
Abyssinian migration

Migration to Madinah.
Inviting rulers around Arabia to Islam.
Receiving deputations.
Sending emissaries .
Living embodiment of Quran.

SHORT TERM   LONG TERM

The matrix in fig.2 depicts only some of the key events and activities of the Prophet during his lifetime to illustrate the strategic wisdom in his leadership. The reader could probably figure out a number of other events from his Seerah to add to the above. It is important to appreciate that each element described above could be further analysed into its own programmes, tasks, activities and schedules.

A common thread and defining trait of the Prophet that runs through all four quadrants is his personal humility as shown during his visit to Taif before the migration and fierce resolve on his part as epitomized during the major battles and a balanced execution of the two traits exemplified during the conquest of Makkah.

Leadership attributes of the Prophet (figure 3)

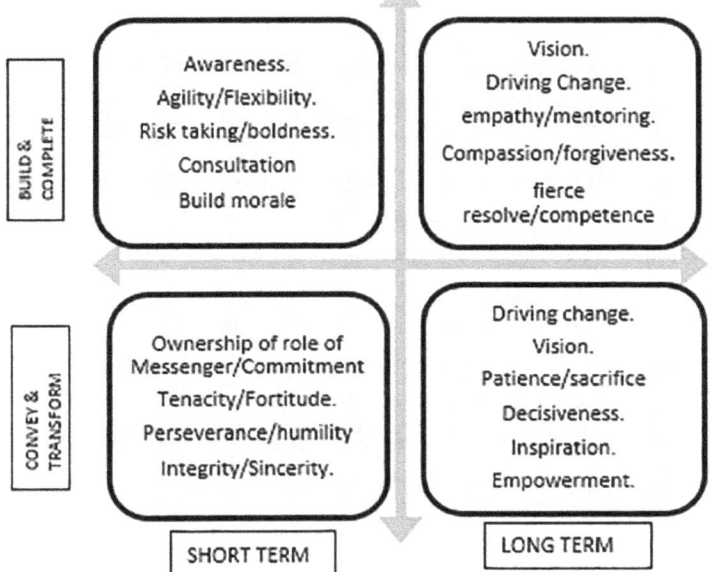

Modern leadership theory has defined this type of leadership that demonstrates both humility and fierce resolve as level five leadership that is inherent in the DNA of greatly successful leaders. His leadership style exemplified the Servant-Leader style which was far removed from the Ruler-Leader, Master-Leader or Figurehead-Leader styles of alternate leadership. At the heart of his leadership was the deep concern for the wellbeing of his followers and the Quran states:

"Now hath come unto you a Messenger from amongst yourselves: it grieves him that ye should perish: ardently anxious is he over you: to the Believers is he most kind and merciful." (9:128)

It goes without stating, that his greatest and most potent attribute was to place his trust in God in all matters big or small. These attributes and qualities of the Prophet are not meant to be exhaustive and represent the more dominant traits from a leadership perspective rather than a human role model perspective.

Strategic Positioning and Operational Effectiveness from the life of the Messenger of God- A competitive strategy perspective

The strategic leadership and fullfilment of the Prophet's mission can be illustrated through the graphic below which highlights the major or core activities (grey) of his mission and the manner in which he orchestrated and created an interlinked network of supporting activities (white) designed to effectively establish Islam in Arabia and in the region and provide a platform for global propagation of the Message of the Quran. This is an illustrative representation and not intended to be exhaustive. The ``Strategic fit`` resulting from such a clustering and positioning of activities is what created a sustainable and enduring legacy of God`s final testament.

The effective leadership of the Prophet and his success in achieving both operational excellence and strategic direction in building the Islamic nation is illustrated depicting the different diverse activities (tangible and intangible) that had to be planned and executed as clusters around the major strategic activities in an interconnected design to create synergy and 'strategic fit' so that the longer term vision could be achieved and sustained through time as the final revelation.

In a sense the Prophet was the CEO of the most responsible, demanding and challenging enterprise that was ever entrusted to a human being. He had to make it go global and build the platform for it and ensure that all the resources, i.e. knowledge, legal, moral, spiritual and temporal were established and the clear vision of the ultimate objective and mission of human life on earth was made plain through the revealed scriptures and his traditions.

Derived from the sahih hadith, the Prophet is reported to have said "Allah has prescribed excellence in whatever you do". The concept of 'Itqan' is to strive for excellence in the tasks that one undertakes and employ best practice or quality standards that reflect striving for excellence. This pursuit is not confined to matters of faith but extends to all affairs of life whether it is domestic chores, community affairs or corporate tasks. The Messenger of Allah (s) said: **Allah loves to see one's task done at the level of itqan** (excellence) "(Sahih Muslim 1976). The Quran states explicitly

"Verily, Allah enjoins justice, and *Ihsaan* and giving help to relatives, and He forbids immoral sins, evil and tyranny. He admonishes you, so that perhaps you may take heed." (Surah An-Nahl:90)

Ihsaan is a comprehensive concept. It includes doing things to your best ability, excellently, completely, artfully, methodically and doing them correctly in the right way according to the best standards and regulations (if relevant).A Muslim who practices Ihsaan throughout his life is a responsible person and a person who always does a high quality job in a timely manner. He is never satisfied with anything other than a very good quality job in all that he does, being timely not tardy, being reliable, right down to the most mundane chores. As commanded excellence is required for all actions.

Pursuit of excellence requires not only sincerity of intention but focus and commitment and a desire and passion to train and learn new skills and competencies. To develop the human capacity or potential to be versatile and excel in a particular skill or branch of knowledge is becoming a lost art as many have succumbed to mediocrity through laziness and lack of motivation. It is necessary for one to enhance personal productivity and as a community apply that for the benefit of the community and for the prosperity of a nation. Quran 95:4 states "Indeed, We have created man in the best of moulds". God is the one who gave us our capabilities, our intellect, physical strength, talent, work ethic and our ability to perform was given as a gift and trust from Allah. After receiving these gifts, is it not a violation and an act of ingratitude to not work to our full potential and do our best? Current Muslim failures are undoubtedly due to the majority having forgotten that the God they worship requests nothing less than the pursuit or striving for excellence in everything they do.

The concept of 'Itqan' was extended to all the actions of the Prophet which translated to 'operational excellence or effectiveness' in each activity that formed a cluster around the key strategic dimensions in order to create synergy and a 'competitive advantage' in relation to other corrupted/deviant beliefs and /or heresies. Unlike the corporate world the bases of competition of the Prophet's message were: the simplicity of its monotheistic creed; the appeal to reason and logic;

equality and justice; mercy and compassion; faith and righteous deeds; the reward in the hereafter of eternal life in perpetual bliss.

An important point to understand in this 'model' is contextual relevance. We can derive the principles of achieving excellence from the prophetic traditions which is not the same as blindly replicating elements of 7th Century or early Islamic practices of governance to modern day situations. For instance is the model of governance dictated by the Caliphate relevant for today? Certainly the moral integrity of the rightly guided caliphs are vital for any system of governance but the modalities of its operations and functioning is definitely open to question and it is the duty of scholars of both the text and context and Muslims in general to find solutions that work best in a given time and space.

To quote a French historian and educator: Alphonse de Lamartine -

"If greatness of purpose, smallness of means and astounding results are the three criteria of human genius, who would dare to compare any great man in history with Muhammad? Philosopher, apostle, legislator, warrior, conqueror of ideas, restorer of rational beliefs, of a cult without images, the founder of twenty terrestrial empires and one spiritual empire, that is Muhammad. As regards all standards by which human greatness may be measured, we may well ask, is there any man greater than he?"
[Historie de le Turquie, Paris 1854, Vol.11.Pages 276-77]

Jules Masserman a renowned US psychoanalyst wrote in the Time magazine in July 1974;
"Leaders must fulfil three functions:
a) provide for the wellbeing of the led;
b) provide a social organization in which people feel relatively secure,
c) provide them with one set of beliefs.

People like Pasteur and Salk are leaders in the first sense. People like Gandhi and Confucius, on one hand, and Alexander, Caesar and

Hitler on the other, are leaders in the second and perhaps the third sense.

Jesus and Buddha belong in the third category alone. Perhaps the grea-test leader of all times was Muhammad, who combined all three functi-ons. To a lesser degree Moses did the same."

In an extensive study by Jim Kouzes and Barry Postner, eminent researchers in leadership studies, conducted with over 1.5 milion par-ticipants over 6 continents in 2007, identified 7 characteristics of lead-ers, and the number one trait that was common across all sectors was credibility and integrity. This basically translates to 'truthful and trust-worthiness' or in Arabic "Saadiqul Ameen", the title that was conferred upon Muhammad in his early life before prophethood which he car-ried right through his exemplary life. A compilation of these traits leads to "The Kouzes-Posner First Law of Leadership`` which states that, ``if you don't believe in the messenger, you wont believe the message``. A statement that could not have been more apt and fitting than to the final Messenger of God, Muhammad (ﷺ). They go on to state or derive their Five Practices for exemplary Leadership and these can be clearly aligned with the `Seerah`` or the Prophetic life.

The five practices and examples of their application by Muhammad are listed under:

- *Model the Way*- Clarifying values and setting an example.
- *Inspire a Shared Vision*- Envisioning and articulating the future and enlisting others.
- *Challenge the Process*-Search for opportunities and Experiment and take risks.
- *Enable Others to Act*-Fostering collaboration and Strengthen Others.
- *Encourage the Heart*- Recognize Contributions and Celebrate the Value and Victories.

Modelling the way
- Emphasising and articulating the universal Message of Islam to mankind as the final divine revelation and inviting the whole of mankind to the straight path.
- Living a life that was the embodiment of the Quran and set an example of being a 'mercy to all of mankind'.
- Setting up a 'constitution' for governance and pluralism among Muslims, People of the book and others in the new city of Madinah.
- Estanblishing and implementing the 'Shariah' or the divine law.

Sharing the Vision
- Stressing upon the greater importance of the hereafter and vision of justice, good deeds/behaviour and seeking God's pleasure.
- Prophesising the spread of Islam to the great Roman and Persian empires at his time.
- Mentoring his companions and rooting them firm in faith and enlisting them in his mission.
- Aligning and matching the competencies and aspirations of his followers with the objectives and goals of his vision and giving the glad tidings of assurance of Jannah to ten of his closest companions.
- Profoundly concerned about the state of his people and their salvation in the afterlife and wellbeing in this life, and articulating this with passionate fervour.

Challenging the Process
- Initiating migration to Abbysinia for some of his followers during the Makkan persecution.
- Approaching the people of Taif to invite them towards Islam.
- Digging of the trench to defend Madinah against the vast enemy which was a novel strategy in the Arabian Peninsula.
- Sending invitations and delegations to foreign neighbouring lands to spread the word of God.

- Entering into a contract with the Makkans at Hudaibiyah which seemed to against the Muslims in the short term.
- Seeking to arrange a treaty with the people of Yathrib prior to migration.
- Mobilizing and orchestrating the strategy for the peaceful conquest of Makkah.

Enabling others to Act
- Collaborating and taking advice from his followers and companions even after facing setbacks in his mission.
- Instilling complete trust in him to his followers that enabled them to take on any formidable or ordinary task that was given.
- Empowering Abu Bakr, his closest and only companion during migration to act decisively on leadership after his demise.
- Placing in charge and trusting his companions to do the right thing in a crisis, like Jafar ibn Abu Talib's appeal to the king Negus of Abyssinia during the first migration.
- Strengthening the hearts of his followers before sending them on a mission with powerful yet reinforcing motivational advice and words of wisdom.
- Selecting the right person for a task based on intimate knowledge of his competencies and empowering them with the resources.

Encouraging the Heart
- Forgiveness granted to all Pagan Makkans after its conquest and leaving no place for revenge.
- Equitable and transparent distribution of the spoils of war.
- Winning the hearts of the newly converted Makkans by giving them the lion's share of the booty from the campaign of Hunayn in which they participated.Speaking kindly to the disobedient archers at Uhud and even seeking their consultation.
- Reinforcing the temporary reality of this life and the eternal life of the hereafter whilst encouraging excellence and diligence in their earthly tasks and pursuits.

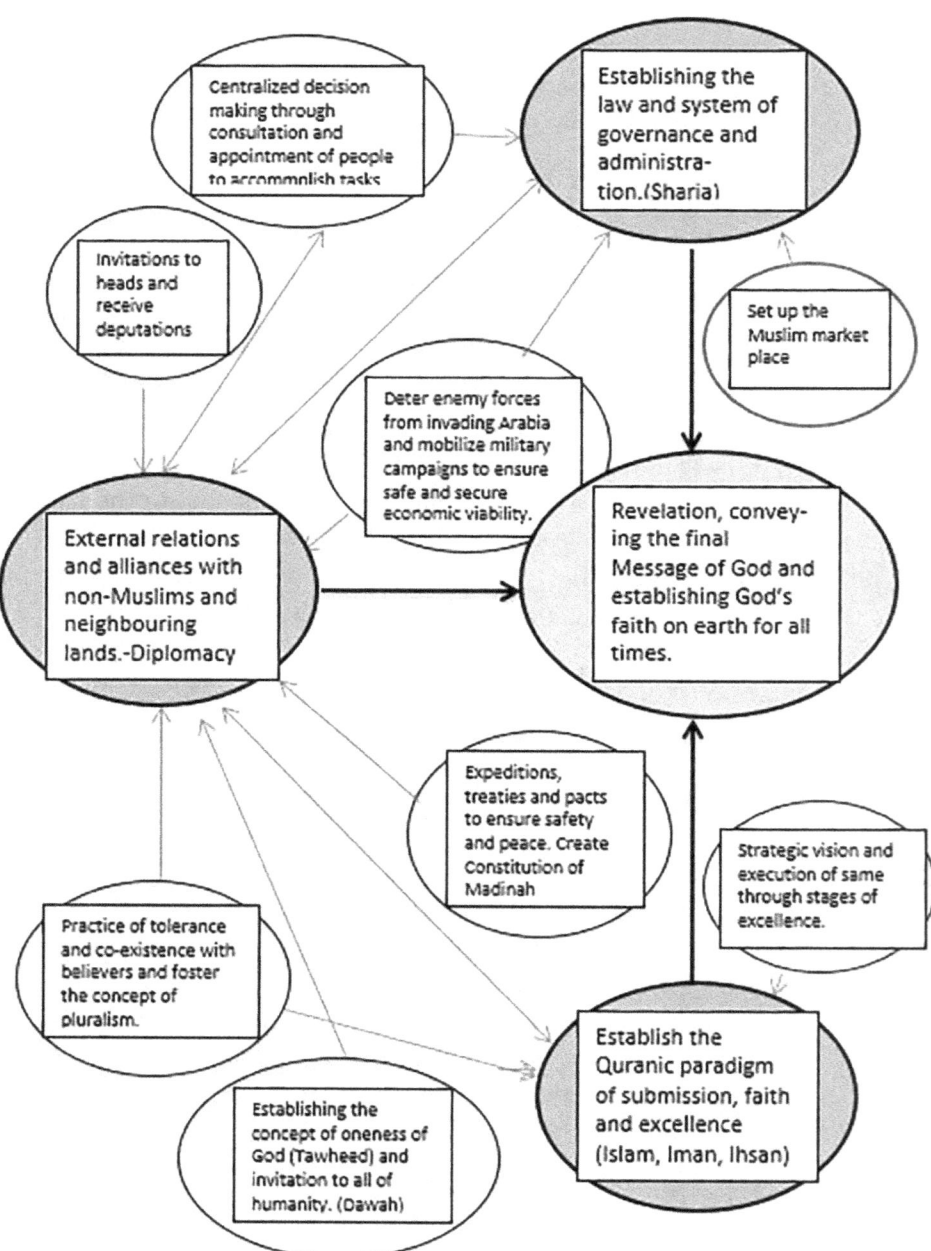

Centralized decision making through consultation and appointment of people to accomplish tasks

Establishing the law and system of governance and administration.(Sharia)

Invitations to heads and receive deputations

Set up the Muslim market place

Deter enemy forces from invading Arabia and mobilize military campaigns to ensure safe and secure economic viability.

External relations and alliances with non-Muslims and neighbouring lands.-Diplomacy

Revelation, conveying the final Message of God and establishing God's faith on earth for all times.

Expeditions, treaties and pacts to ensure safety and peace. Create Constitution of Madinah

Strategic vision and execution of same through stages of excellence.

Practice of tolerance and co-existence with believers and foster the concept of pluralism.

Establish the Quranic paradigm of submission, faith and excellence (Islam, Iman, Ihsan)

Establishing the concept of oneness of God (Tawheed) and invitation to all of humanity. (Dawah)

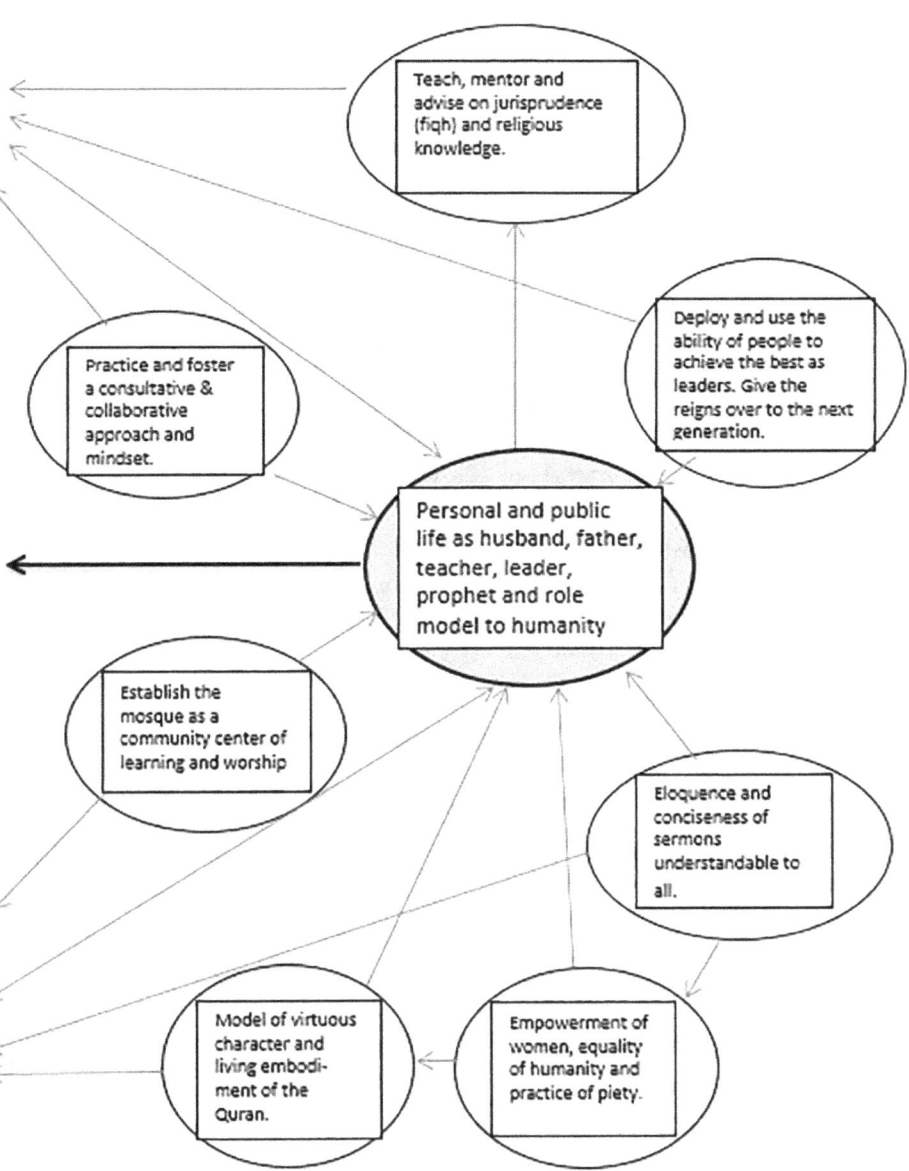

Teach, mentor and advise on jurisprudence (fiqh) and religious knowledge.

Deploy and use the ability of people to achieve the best as leaders. Give the reigns over to the next generation.

Practice and foster a consultative & collaborative approach and mindset.

Personal and public life as husband, father, teacher, leader, prophet and role model to humanity

Establish the mosque as a community center of learning and worship

Eloquence and conciseness of sermons understandable to all.

Model of virtuous character and living embodi-ment of the Quran.

Empowerment of women, equality of humanity and practice of piety.

231

Prof. Joel Hayward a contemporary historian and professor of strategic studies and specializing in the ``Seerah`` of the Prophet, summarizes and encapsulates in his insightful book, ``The Leadership of Muhammad-A Historical Reconstruction``, wherein he states;

``If someone wanted to strip away the historical content of Muhammad`s Arabia to see whether we might be able to identify from his fascinating life any enduring `lessons`` of how a leader might want to consider doing things today, I would write then a list much like the one I offer here:``

Character and Qualities

- Personify and exemplify the best human qualities and values.
- Do not be seen as ambitious or status conscious.
- Never adapt an air of superiority.
- Avoid any self interest or even the appearance of it.
- Be humble, flexible open to learning from others.
- Continously self reflect.
- Do not keep doing what does not work.
- Learn quickly from mistakes.

Strategic Vision

- Develop a vision for creating a better situation.
- If your vision is bold be prepared for resistance.
- Persevere and don't surrender that vision.
- Turn the vision into a meaningful set of goals.
- Create the sequence of steps needed to achieve them.
- Resource each of them sufficiently.

Strategic Communication

- Explain your vision to everyone who will play a role or be affected.
- Explain it frequently using a few carefully chosen key motifs.
- Be knowledgeble and assured to establish your credibility.

- But also be modest, steady and calm.
- Explain clearly why the vision mattersand how it will improve things.
- Explain clearly how your people will benefit.
- Explain clearly what you need them to accomplish.
- Remember to appeal both to the intellect and emotions.

Consensus building

- Identify any factions or potentially competing interests and needs among your people.
- Try to find cooperative solutions that will meetall parties interests and needs.
- Keep watching to ensure as you proceedthat everyonecan live with the likely outcome.
- Ensure that everyone will benefit.
- Ensure that everyone knows that they will benefit.

Learning from Others

- Consult others oftenand with an open mind and genuine desire for the critique of your ideas.
- Consult people who know what they are talking about and proven themselves trustworthy.
- Create an environment in which everyone knows they can approach you with ideas.
- Establish what the majority view is and if it is likely to move the team forwards towards the goals.
- If it is less likely to do sothan your own idea would, have the moral courageto explain why.
- Give credit and praiseto the person whose idea or plan you use.

Establishing Rapport

- Learn about your people's interests, hopes and anxieties.

- Search for common ground.
- Share in every difficulty that you ask your people to endure.
- Work as hard as your most productive team member.

<u>Managing People</u>

- Select the right people by looking for intelligence, passion, energy and reliability.
- Do this even if you do not especially like them.
- Never show anyone that you do not like them.
- Train them as fullyas you can through example.
- Trust them to undertake increasingly difficult tasks.
- Tell them what you want and why but not how they should do it.
- Reward them for accomplishment.
- Let a person`s success with one responsibility be the basis for receiving a larger responsibility.
- Always praise in public.
- Overlook imperfections.
- Forgive failure if a person has done his or her best.
- Never accept immorality.

All these leadership qualities or traits are part of an overall ethical framework within an Islamic or Quranic paradigm which are founded on the principles of Justice, Compassion, Wisdom and Human Welfare. This ethical framework informed by the Quranic teachings also forms the basis of the Prophetic Sunnah and hence Muhammad was the embodiment of the Quran in its practical manifestation as guidance to humanity.

Leadership - A Quranic perspective

The Prophet Muhammad stated as cited by Abu Dawoud (Vol. 2, 2273), that if there are three embarking on a journey, one of them should be appointed as a leader. This hadith underscores a significant facet of the Sunnah which is to appoint or elect a leader in any undertaking, venture, and task or team effort. **Behold everyone is a leader and you shall be asked about those you lead. Imam is a leader over the people and shall be asked about them, a man is leader over the house and shall be asked about the household, a woman is a leader over her children and shall be asked about them"***-reported by Abdullah ibn Omar in Bukhari and Muslim. On a more general vein the Prophet(s) said,* **"Each of you is a shepherd, and all of you are responsible for your flocks."** *(Saheeh Al-Bukhari 7138, Saheeh Muslim1829)*

The Quran echoes the allusion to leadership among humanity when it state, **"It is He Who hath made you (His) agents, inheritors of the earth: He hath raised you in ranks, some above others: that He may try you in the gifts He hath given you: for thy Lord is quick in punishment: yet He is indeed Oft-forgiving, Most Merciful***" (Al-An 'am 6: 165). Leadership in Islam is considered as an amanah (a trust) and a responsibility. A leader is required to meet his obligations to God, the Supreme Power as well as to discharge his duties towards the people or his followers to the best of his abilities. Hence to build leadership traits calls for building integrity, accountability, humility, mercy, wisdom and justice to name a few of the essential traits of leadership.*

Love for authentic leadership (not necessarily authority!) is a positive quality indicating a person's desire to mobilize resources and people towards a vision of the good, or to serve as a proper role model for present and future generations. As Allah said about the companions;

"You are the best nation to come forth for people. You enjoin what is good and forbid what is evil and have faith in Allah.*" (Sūrat Ālī 'Imrān 3:110.)*

All of the righteous companions are role models and 'leaders' in Islam, even if they never held authority in an official capacity like the Caliphs or governors.

What made them the best generation is that they were focused on maximizing good and minimizing evil and inspiring others to believe in Allah. They are spiritual models to follow. Such authentic leaders are worthy of our admiration. We should aspire to be moral exemplars for our families and children first, and for the rest of the Muslim community, as Allah said through the words of the believers, **"Our Lord, grant us comfort from our wives and children and make us a leader for the righteous."** (Sūrat al-Furqān 25:74)

Love of authentic leadership puts us on a difficult but traversable path of personal transformation that compels us to increase our knowledge and virtues. The two key qualities of authentic leadership are perseverance (al-sabr) and certainty in faith (al-yaqin**), "We made leaders among them, guiding by Our commands, when they were patient and certain of Our signs." (**Sūrat al-Sajdah 32:34)

A leader needs to ensure that their vision of the good, and their intentions and methods, are approved by Allah and then to persevere in bringing the good to fruition. Hence leadership from an Islamic perspective is considered a responsibility and a trust, and cannot be sought. Proponents of this viewpoint refer to the hadith cited in Muslim, **"Do not ask for a position of authority, for if you are granted this position as a result of your asking for it, you will be left alone and if you are granted it without asking for it, you will be helped".**

The help hear refers to the help from God and this hadith is cited as proof that people should not seek political office and that it should be by appointment. This position has profound implications in its relevance in contemporary society where the democratic process demands that one seeks election through canvassing and by touting one's suitability and capability.

It is important to discern between the reality and the wisdom behind the Islamic principle. They could be reconciled to work in harmony provided the seeking of an office or position is not tainted by false claims and deception.

Hence the principle essence of the wisdom behind not actively seeking a position of leadership appears to act as a deterrent against its negative behavioural responses that are anathematic to the ethical and moral orientation of Islam and the Message of the Quran. Hence if one sincerely believes that he or she can contribute towards a better society that upholds justice and human welfare with equality towards all without prejudice or bias then there could be a strong case for seeking leadership within a democratic framework. This was the situation in the case of prophet Yusuf (Joseph) who actually requested that he be appointed as head of the government treasury and agriculture because he knew what was coming and had divine guidance and knowledge on how to mitigate the ravaging effects of a famine.

In an article published in the The Global Studies Journal, Kasim Randeree of the University of Oxford, writes under the title 'Leadership- An Islamic Perspective"; (abridged and edited)

"Further, the qualities leaders need to possess are also essential, since these qualities will form the basis of the vision, effectiveness, function, productivity, development, momentum and growth of a society. In all, fifteen qualities are highlighted. These are;

(1) leaders must possess fitness for purpose,

(2) they must be trustworthy,

(3) they must engage in lifelong learning,

(4) they must know their followers,

(5) they must be mindful of the need for the professional development of their followers,

(6) they must possess and articulate a vision,

(7) they must exercise responsibility,

(8) they must provide training,

(9) they must display good communication skills,

(10) they must be patient,

(11) they must be a good role model,

(12) they must engage in consultation,

(13) they must exercise correct judgement,

(14) they must be good decision makers,

(15) they must display an appreciation for diversity and multiculturalism.

The first two qualities a leader must possess are fitness and trustworthiness. These are expounded in the Quran which essentially stipulates two criteria for employee selection, the first being strength (fitness) and the second trustworthiness. The Quran cites these in two places and in both cases in relation to the employment of Prophets. The first mentioned is Yusuf (Joseph) who was essentially appointed minister of finance, economy and planning. The Quran states:

Yusuf said: "set me over the storehouses of the land, I will indeed guard them with full knowledge." (12:55*)*

The second prophet was Moosa (Moses), who through his kindness to watering the sheep of two women in the Madyan region, was employed by their father, and believed to be the prophet Shuaib to work for him.

"And said one of them, 'O my father! Hire him! Verily the best of men for you to hire is the strong, the trustworthy." (28:26)

The commentary on this statement expounds this word "Al Qawi"(strong), stating that it is not limited to physical strength but rather fitness for purpose. Thus leadership is assigned accordingly. This is made clear by Muhammad who indicated Abu Bakr as leader of the faithful (Amir ul -Mumineen) as he possessed the best credentials for this role. However the Prophet appointed Khalid Ibn al Waleed as the the military commander for the Muslims as he demonstrated skills in warfare management and Musab ibn Umair as his viceroy to Yathrib, as he displayed qualities as a gifted preacher and Jafar ibn Abu Talib as the spokesman and leader for the immigrants to Abyssinia, as he possessed the best communication skills. Thus, it is both necessary for leadership to be assigned to those most fit to carry out a given task and for leaders themselves to recognize the qualities of future leaders and develop them accordingly.

Another quality of leaders is they must engage in lifelong learning and be seekers of knowledge. Society is a dynamic, living entity and as such leaders must be adaptive to work most productively. This attribute is emphasised by way of example, when Moses was asked by one of the Israelites if he knew who was the most knowledgeable person on earth, to which Moses replied that he was. However in response to this claim by Moses, it was revealed to him by God that there was another man more knowledgeable than Moses. Interestingly, Moses's response gives a profound lesson to contemporary leaders that the Quran expounds:

"And remember when Moses said to his boy servant, "I will not give up travelling until I reach the junction of the two seas or until I spend years and years in travelling." (18:60)

Moses thus embarked upon an arduous journey to find this more knowledgeable person so that he could learn from him. Having eventually found this man, whose name is given as Al-Khidr in the Quran, he proceeds to receive instruction, through a series of profound events along a journey, about fairness, equity, justice and patience, expounded in detail in sura Kahf in the Quran.

In addition to the knowledge a leader possesses, and developing that knowledge through continuous learning, leaders must also have knowledge of those they lead. Prophet Sulaiman or Solomon, for example was a king and given command and control by God over men, animals and the Jinn and his leadership is highlighted in the Quran as noticing the absence of a single bird, a hoophoe from a military lineup.

"He inspected the birds, and said: "What is the matter that I see not the hoophoe? Or is he among the absentees?" (27:20)

The illustration of a commander in chief over a vast force noticing this absence is a significant lesson for leaders being well acquainted with those they lead. In fact the Prophet Muhammad was so close to his companions that whenever someone did not turn up at the mosque for several days he used to inquire where so and so is. During the Tabuk expedition when around thirty thousand Muslims marched towards the northern frontier, someone told the Prophet that there was a lone rider *who was travelling fast behind them to catch up with the expedition and the Prophet said "I hope it is so and so", and when it turned out to be the person he mentioned he expressed his happiness. To notice the absence of a single companion among thousands is a remarkable trait of a leader that serves to exemplify the leader's responsibility, accountability and conscientiousness towards his subordinates.*

In addition to having a close knowledge of those you lead, even in a large corporation, Deming (1982) states, "A good leader is one that makes many leaders". This emphasizes that one of the qualities of leadership is to direct energies towards the development of those they lead. Muhammad ensured through his constant advice, counselling and example as a role model, he prepared those closest to him for leadership. This is the reason that AbuBakr the first leader of the faithful after the Prophet took on the role confidently and continued the prophetic legacy. Towards the end of the period of the rule of the rightly guided caliphs during the caliphate of Ali ibn Talib, one of the companions of the prophet asked Ali, "why is there so much conflict and differences among the Muslims now than in the early years after the Prophet's demise", and Ali replied promptly that it was the training and knowledge imparted to the close and senior companions by the Prophet that enabled them to resolve issue, keep the peace and ensure the spread of Islam among nations outside Arabia. At times the Prophet thrust leadership upon some like in the case of Osama bin Zayed who was barely eighteen years of age when the Prophet commanded him to lead an expedition to the Byzantine frontier and lead many who were much senior. This was a clear case of 'passing the baton' to the future generation and preparing them for the rigors of leadership.

Any organization must have a vision-a positive image of what it can become and an articulation of the path towards that goal. This was demonstrated in the Prophetic tradition when in the early days of propagation the Prophet sent a group of Muslims as immigrants to Abyssinia so that even if the Muslims in Makkah were wiped out by the pagan Makkans there would be a core of Muslims outside who would carry the flames of the faith. In another remarkable instance when the Muslims in Madinah were digging a trench to protect the city from a massive enemy onslaught, Muhammad too was in the trenches and as he hit upon a rock in the ground with his pick axe that produced sparks of fire, he exclaimed to the Muslims that the kingdom of both Rome and Persia shall soon come under the rule of the Muslims. Although this was a prophetic vision, Muhammad articulated it in such a dramatic manner at a time of such distress and anxiety that the Muslims felt a sense of greater purpose and calling that transcended the exertion of their physical effort. The treaty of Hudaybiyah that Muhammad entered to with the Quraysh was another classic example of the pursuit of a long term vision for the sacrifice of short term gains.

Another quality leaders possess is one of responsibility for those they lead. The Quran states in an emphatic tone the responsible and empathetic nature of the Prophet thus:

"Surely, a Messenger has come unto you from among yourselves; grievous to him is that you should fall into trouble; he is ardently desirous of your welfare; and to the believers he is compassionate, merciful." (9:128)

Muhammad felt deeply responsible for the welfare of the families of the martyrs among the Muslims and ensured they were taken care of and even married one of the widows whose husband had migrated to Abyssinia and had passed away there.

A leader must be a good communicator and different leaders through history have possessed various communication tools. The Prophet Muhammad communicated the Message of the Quran beyond Arabia by means of eight letters he had dictated and sent to eight leaders, including the empires neighbouring Arabia, inviting them to Islam. These letters reveal important leadership lessons, since their recipients were so diverse and had a variety of beliefs, attitudes and mindsets. Furthermore the Prophet Muhammad, in addressing different individuals used a variation in approach. Thus a leader needs to communicate orally and textually, in an appropriate manner with an understanding of the receiving audience.

A leader must be patient and forbearing and the story of Prophet Yusuf or Joseph is one of the best examples as expounded in the Quran. His patience extends through trials, which include attempted murder, being

241

separated from his parents, being sold to slavery, being wrongfully accused of a crime and imprisonment on false charges. However his patience paid dividends, ultimately being absolved of all crimes and being given a leadership role in Egypt. Patience is thus best tested in the crucible of trial and tribulation as the Quran states:

"And certainly, We shall test you with something of fear, hunger, loss of wealth, lives and fruits, but give glad tidings to the patient ones." (2:155)

Great leaders have the quality of being a role model to those they lead. Muhammad's characteristic as being a person worthy of being followed is articulated in the Quran;

"Indeed in the Messenger of God(Muhammad) you have a good example to follow for him who hopes in meeting with God and the Last Day and remembers God much." (33:21)

This verse indicates that not only the Prophet is a role model, but presents a reason for that in being an example of being followed. Thus the personality and character of a leader is more important than his formal position or status.

Another leadership quality expounded in the Quran is 'consultation'. Leaders must consult with those they lead in order to form a coherent consensus and have confidence in their decision making. The Quran underscores this point in sura Shuaara or 'Consultation'

"And those who respond to their Lord, and pray regularly, and conduct their affairs by mutual consultation and give of what We have provided them." (42:38)

Muhammad was instructed to engage in consultation after the battle of Uhud, when God revealed; **"It is by of grace from God that you were gentle with them. Had you been harsh, hardhearted, they would have dispersed from around you. So pardon them, and ask forgiveness for them, and consult them in the conduct of affairs. And when you make a decision, put your trust in God; God loves the trusting." (3:159)**

Thus consultation requires a soft approach to nurture obedience, motivate, and inspire followers. In a corporate context, this is synonymous with empowering a stakeholder, where participation is encouraged from all levels. This is evident in methodologies such as TQC, Change Management and Configuration Management, as well as suggestion systems, all of which are aimed at continuous improvement through consultation and employee participation and empowerment.

Often leaders are put into positions where decision making and exercising correct judgement is tested to the limit. In such circumstances, the consequences of a poor decision or judgement are likely to have repercussions in relation to the mission at hand. With regard to the Prophets, their mission of preaching a message of monotheism to nations largely steeped in ignorance and idolatry was all the more challenging. Prophet Muhammad made a number of crucial decisions during his mission which were designed not only to resolve a situation but provide a powerful teaching moment and a lesson to some. One striking case was after the battle of Hunayn when the Prophet distributed the 'spoils of war' to the Muslims. He gave generously to the newly converted Quraysh and the immigrants or 'Muhajireen' who had migrated to Madinah whilst leaving nothing for the "Ansars' or the Madinites who had given the Prophet shelter and protection when he migrated to Madinah. When the Prophet heard that the Madinites were expressing their disappointment and sense of deprivation, he gathered the Madinites together privately and told them one of his most profound statements, "Aren't you feeling content in the fact that whilst the others are going away with cattle and sheep whilst you are going back with the Messenger of God?" The gravity of this remark immediately dawned upon the Madinites and they exclaimed in unison, "Yes O Messenger of God we are happy to have you with us than all the wealth of the world"

The point here being that the judgement and decision of the Prophet was based on softening the hearts of the new converts and to give their fellow Makkans who had migrated leaving behind all their wealth the material gains of war whereas he knew that the Madinites had their homes and property to return to.

The Prophet's decision here also underscored the insignificance of material gains to the guidance and light of God that will be experienced by those close to him and the revelation. He wanted what was best for the people of Madinah whom he cherished and made a decision as to what was best for them both in this world and the hereafter.

Contemporary leaders must possess knowledge of the growing diversity in the global arena. This can be manifest in terms of cultural, ethnic, regional or gender diversity with a leader needing to exercise an inclusive approach to leadership. The Prophet Muhammad demonstrated these qualities of diversity and inclusion in his actions and behaviour when he embraced the freed black slave Bilal and brought him into his circle of confidantes and made him the official caller to prayer in the mosque of the Prophet. He also practiced inclusivity both in gender and race relations when he encouraged women to attend mosque to learn and ask questions and allocated a special time for them exclusively. He listened to and acted on the advice of Salman Al Farsi the Persian convert to Islam during the battle of the trench which proved decisive in a Muslim victory. The Prophet also spoke to the Arabs from different regions who visited Madinah in their local dialect so as to relate and resonate to them better instead of insisting upon the pure dialect of the Quraysh.

The fifteen leadership attributes discussed here and their references in the Quranic text and in the lives of the Prophets through history echoes a leadership paradigm that appears to be universal.

APPENDIX A- A tabulated narrative on the wives of the Prophet (Mothers of the Believers)

NAME	BACKGROUND	DATE OF MAR-RIAGE	REASON	ROLE	AGE YRS.
1) Khadija	Widow with 2 children and successful businesswoman with trade caravans. Employs the Prophet as an agent to manage caravan trade	595 CE 15 years before Prophet hood	First marriage of Prophet At the age of 25. Proposal initiated by Khadija.	Bore six children, 2 sons and 4 daughters, Provides security, comfort and nurturing during most difficult times and during first revelation from God. Dies in 619 CE in the 9th year of Prophet hood after 25 years of married life with the Prophet	35-40
2) Sawda	Widow with 5 children. First husband dies after migration to Abyssinia. First female migrant to Abyssinia.	619 CE 9 years after Prophet hood	2nd. Marriage after death of Khadija. First Muslim widow during Makkan period. Proposal made by a female marriage broker.	Provides companionship during year of grief and sorrow and migrates to Madinah and survives the Prophet.	40-42

3) Ayesha	Daughter of closest compan-ion Abu Bakr. The only virgin woman the Prophet mar-ries. She was betrothed to the Prophet 3 years before she actually moved in with the Prophet.	Engaged in 620CE and moves in with the Prophet in 623 CE after Migration to Madi-nah. (1 AH)	Revealed to Prophet by God in a dream. Seals and hon-ours friendship with Abu Bakr his closest companion and confidante.	First female Islamic scholar and records over 2000 traditions of the Prophet and educates women in matters of faith and teaches and counsels companions of Prophet after his death. She was not only eloquent and scholarly but confident and assertive.	9 Or 18 ?
4) Hafsa	Daughter of Omar and widowed after 1st.husband dies from injuries after fighting in Uhud. Omar became 2nd. Caliph after Abu Bakr.	622CE	To honour Omar after Omar complained to Prophet that both Abu Bakr and Uthman had declined his proposal of Hafsa to them.	Educated and eloquent she memorized Quran and was the custodian of the first compiled copy of Quran during Caliph Omar's time which was used by Caliph Uthman during stan-dardizing of the Quran. Extremely pious in worship.	23-25
5) Zainab bint Khu-zaima	She was not from the Quraysh and was from the Najd or central Arabia. She was first divorced when she became a Mus-lim and then re-married to a Muslim who was killed in the battle of Badr.	624 CE	She had no relatives to take care of her in Madinah as she was from a Najd tribe and was a noble and righteous woman	She was known as 'mother of the orphans' and was extreme-ly generous and pious and lived only 3- 4 months after her marriage to the Prophet. Supported the Prophet in his charitable acts.	30-32

6) Um Salama (Hind)	Belonged to the Quraysh tribe and immigrated to Abyssinia and returned early and was the first woman to migrate to Madinah. Husband dies from injuries after battle of Uhud.	Late 625 CE 3 AH	She had 4 children from earlier marriage and well respected for her lineage and wisdom. Many sought her hand but only agreed to when the Prophet proposed. Several companions of the Prophet married the widows of Uhud after the Prophet married her.	Advised and counselled the Prophet at critical times like at Hudaibiyah and was a spokesperson for the women in Madinah in relation to their rights and duties.	29-30
7) Zainab bint Jahash	Cousin of the Prophet from father's side and was proposed for marriage by the prophet to his adopted son and freed slave, Zaid. This marriage did not work and Zaid wanted a divorce despite Muhammad's request to Zaid to stay in the marriage.	627 CE 5AH	This marriage was commanded by God in the Quran between Zainab and theProphet to break the tradition and custom of treating adopted children as their own biological offspring.	She was referred to as the "mother of the poor" as she used to sew and make things and sell them and help the poor and orphans with her own money. First wife to pass away after the Prophet's death.	37-40

247

9) Ramla Um-Habib	Daughter of the Quraysh chief Abu Sufiyan and embraced Islam early with her husband and migrated to Abyssinia. Husband converts to Christianity whilst in Abyssinia after he befriends some priests but she remains a Muslim. He later passed away whilst over there.	629 CE 7 AH	The Prophet sensed her lonely desperate situation after her husband's death and requests King Negus of Abyssinia to arrange to marry her to the Prophet in his absence. She received a high dower from the Prophet to help her out in Abyssinia and honour her struggle	She recorded all events that took place in Abyssinia and because of her patience with the conversion of her husband to Christianity and the fact that she was from a noble lineage in Makkah but could not return to her family in Makkah	20-22
8) Ju-wairiya	Daughter of the chief of the Bani Mustalaq tribe who turned hostile and planned to attack the Muslims in Madinah. The Muslim's overcame them in a battle and could have taken all of them as prisoners. She was married previously and was divorced.	628 CE 6 AH	When the Prophet married her, the Muslims freed all the prisoners and gave back to them their property. The tribe itself converted to Islam when their chief tried to pay the ransom for his daughter and she refused and stayed back as the wife of the Prophet. Ayesha narrated that no tribe was blessed so much as Juwairiya's as a result of her marriage to the Prophet.	She was extremely pious and devoted to prayer and fasting and spiritual inspiration to the women in Madinah.	28-32

248

10) Safiya	She was Jewish and her tribe who had hostile intentions towards the Muslims were defeated. She was the daughter of the head of the Jewish tribe and had married twice before and her husband died in the battle with the Muslims.	629 CE 7 AH	To establish normative relations with the Jewish tribes and honour them and promote greater acceptance of Jews among Muslims. She also recognized the prophet hood of the Prophet before accepting Islam.	To build a bridge of peace with the Jewish tribes in Khyber and accept Jews as part of a larger pluralistic Arabia.	28-30
11) M a i - muna	She proposed to the Prophet through Uncle of the Prophet Al Abbas when the Prophet visited Makkah for the lesser pilgrimage. Sister in law of the Prophet's uncle Al Abbas and aunt of the great Muslim scholar Ibn Abbas who learnt Prophetic etiquette from her.	630 CE 8 AH	Build ties with the family of the Prophets Uncle who were part of the noble clan of Quraysh in Makkah. She was both a widow and a divorcee and thus married twice before.	Being the last of the Arabian wives the Prophet married, and the fact that she proposed to the Prophet made her keep excellent relations with all his wives. She also taught the Sunnah of the Prophet and narrated a number of hadeeth.	26-28

12) Maria the Coptic Christian	She was sent to the Prophet as a gift by the Coptic ruler of Egypt Muqawkis in response to the Prophet's letter of invitation to him to accept Islam. She was not sent as a slave but as a woman of noble birth.	629 CE 7AH	The Prophet took her as a member of his cohort of wives to honour the gesture by the Egyptian ruler and the people of the book. She embraced Islam after the Prophet's death.	She bore him a son who was named Ibrahim who passed away at an early age in infancy. She was respected and honoured by the companions and the Prophets family and led an ascetic life after the Prophets death.	20-22 yrs.?

NOTES:

- Although no reason or rationale need be given to justify the Prophet marrying the women he did, the purpose here is to understand for our own reflection the more profound nuances behind his marriages.
- In 7th century Arabia the customs and social norms were such that a woman found dignity through marriage and this union brought the families and clans and tribes together in mutual respect and closeness.
- Polygamy was an accepted cultural norm and any number of wives could be had without concern for equality and justice. Islam limited this to four wives and demanded strict equanimity in treatment of them. It prescribed only one wife in order to be fair and just.
- The Prophet's case was an exception as a Prophet and permitted by God to address and mould the nascent Muslim community and ensure the empowerment, engagement and education of women as an equal force.
- All of his wives distinguished themselves in some area of charity, kindness, or, as in the case of 'Aisha, erudition and knowledge. They were held to a higher standard and were informed that both their rewards and punishments were greater than of other women in the society. The Quran honours them as the "Mothers of the believers". Their marriages to the Prophet

were voluntary and they could initiate and ask for divorce if they so desired. The Quran and the Prophet made revolutionary changes in the status of women and his wives were in many ways exemplars of these changes. As the Prophet's dealings with his wives were based on love, affection, respect and dignity, others in the society were expected to follow his exemplary behaviour. Men and women were declared equal in the eyes of Allah. Compassion, equity, and justice were mandated. Rules were laid down for marriage and divorce. Laws regarding ownership of property were promulgated. The notion of the moral superiority of men over women was shot down. Men were told they had the duty to protect women and children. As mentioned earlier the Quran stresses the moral and spiritual equality of men and women in emphatic and unambiguous language.

The age of Ayesha at the time of her marriage to the Prophet.

There are fewer events from the life of the Prophet that has provided more grist to the mill for Islamophobes and polemics than that of the age of Ayesha when she married the Prophet. According to traditional sources based on a hadeeth reported in the most authentic collections, Ayesha is reported to have stated that she was betrothed to the Prophet when she was six and moved in with him when she was nine years old after she had attained puberty. The Prophet was of course 53 years old at this time. Tradition also confirms that God revealed Ayesha as the Prophet's future wife in a dream to the Prophet which is akin to revelation. Notwithstanding the attempts by Muslim apologists and scholars to expound the folly of projecting present day sensibilities in social and cultural norms on 7th century Arabia ("Presentism") and the physiological and psychological ambiguity of age related universality in establishing criteria for marriage suitability through the ages and cases of 'under age' marriages from more recent history in the 18th, 19th and even 20th century, this event still remains at the top of the arsenal of anti- Islam activists and by extension anti-Muhammad polemics, whose only desire is to place a slur on the life of the Prophet.

251

<u>Tradition vs. History</u>

Interestingly and from a historical perspective, a chronological analysis of events during the time of the Prophet and their occurrence in time and sequence would place Ayesha's age at no less than 18 years at the time of her marriage. Muslim historians have pointed out to the fact that events such as births and marriages were not registered and hence dates had to be deduced by placing other historic or famous and well acknowledged incidents in perspective to ascertain dates when things occurred. Sheikh Adil Salahi, a reputed and recognized scholar on Islam and writer on the life of the Prophet has pointed out to the following facts in his book, "Muhammad- His Conduct and Character", published by the Islamic Foundation in United Kingdom.

- Ayesha was suggested to the Prophet as a possible wife three years before the marriage actually took place, which would have meant that she was six when she was recommended to him? The woman suggesting her mentioned that he needed a wife to give him company and comfort after Khadijah, his first wife, had died. The Prophet had four daughters by his first marriage, the youngest of whom was over that age. He certainly needed a wife to give him support and comfort. Could a child of six or nine years give him that? Would not she be an added burden to him? Is it logical that Khawlah bint Ḥakīm, the woman who suggested that he should get married, highlighting his need for home support, should propose to him such a child? In fact, she suggested two women: a mature woman, Sawdah, who had already been married and a virgin, Ayesha. The disparity between the two in age, were we to accept that Ayesha was six, meant that Sawdah could have been Aye-ha's grandmother.
- Ayesha had already been engaged to Jubayr ibn Muṭ'im, and her en-gagement was broken off before she got engaged to the Prophet. Could she have been engaged at the age of five or six? It was a serious engagement, not a casual talk between families. Abū Bakr, Ayesha's father, needed to skilfully with-draw from that engagement when he realized that the

Prophet wanted to marry her. Besides, neither of her parents suggested that she was too young for marriage. Indeed, they would not have accepted her earlier engagement if she was too young. (Besides, why would Abu Bakr give his daughter in marriage to a polytheist when he had accepted Islam himself in 610CE and this engagement apparently took place in 619 CE? –author's comment)

- In the oldest biography of the Prophet by Ibn Isḥaaq, Ayesha is mentioned among the first fifty people to have accepted Islam in its early days (in fact, she is number nineteen on the list). On this list she is mentioned to have been young at the time, yet the list does not include any children. All those included in this report converted to Islam more than eight years before Ayesha's marriage. Most of them joined the immigration to Abyssinia in the fifth year of the start of Islam (i.e. eight years before the immigration to Madinah). This means that at that time, she was young, but old enough to accept a new religion. Could she have been less than ten at the time of her adoption of Islam? Would any historian include a child less than ten in any meaningful list of converts? If she was ten when she adopted Islam, then at the time of her marriage she was eighteen or older.

- Ayesha is authentically reported by Bukhārī to have been with the Muslim army in the Battle of Uhud, nursing the wounded. This battle took place eighteen months after her marriage, which means that had she been nine at the time of her marriage, so she would have been eleven at the time of the battle. Before the battle, the Prophet examined his troops and ordered every young man below fifteen years of age to go back home. Could he have allowed a girl of eleven to stay with the army?

- Ayesha was renowned for her indepth knowledge of Islam. Her knowledge was not that of someone who memorizes information and recounts it when needed: it was of the analytical and critical type, as is clear from her numerous arguments with other Companions of the Prophet over a wide range of questions. All her knowledge came directly from the Prophet. Such knowledge could not be acquired in adolescent years, which suggests that she was at a more mature age when she was married to the Prophet.

- According to existing reports her parents were married ten years before the start of Islam. Abu Bakr was twenty-eight at the time. He had two children by an earlier marriage and two by this marriage. In the absence of any effective methods of birth control at the time, it is reasonable to assume that the two children were born in the first five years of the marriage. If so, she would be twenty by the time of her marriage.

- A counter argument is always given on grounds that a ḥadīth related by al-Bukhārī gives her age at the time of the marriage as nine. However, this ḥadīth is attributed to Hishām ibn 'Urwah who learnt it from his father. Hishaam related it when he was in Iraq. Scholars of Ḥadīth mention that although Hishām was a reliable re-porter, he was less accurate with what he reported in Iraq from his father. This raises a question mark about the authenticity of this hadith. Another hadith, also related by Bukhari, quotes Ayesha as saying that by the time she was old enough to understand religion her parents were already Muslims. She puts that in historical perspective, mentioning the event when her father prepared to immigrate to Abyssinia. This was in the fifth year of the start of Islam and nine years before her marriage. If she was eight when this intention to immigrate took place, she would have been seventeen at the time of her marriage.

When we look at these facts, and bear in mind that several other Companions of the Prophet are given ages that could not in any way be reconciled with events in which they were prominent participants, we have to conclude that such figures are unreliable. These reported ages need to be approached critically, bringing in other factors in order to obtain a more informed idea of their status. As for the Prophet, he was the perfect model for humanity. Unfortunately, Muslims show him to have married an old woman when he was a young man and a child when he was approaching old age. This is unfair to the Prophet, because neither assumption can stand up to considered analysis. Notwithstanding this dichotomy between traditional narration and historical facts, Muslims have no issues with this as they believe that the Prophet would not have done something wrong in relation to the time he was living in or committed an injustice or immoral act in the context of the milieu he was living in. Although there exists a large number of scholars who take the position of tradition there are a growing number of scholars and people who accept the more rational explanation of historical facts as Muslims believe that only the Quran- the uncreated word of God is infallible and all other sources can contain errors of human judgement and fallibility. By a similar line of logic and argument it could be deduced historically that the age of Khadija, the first wife of the Prophet would have been closer to 35 than 40 years as popularly reported due to the fact that she bore six children over a space of ten years and there are narrations that indicate that she was closer to thirty than to forty when she got married to the Prophet who was twenty five at that time for certain. Strangely this discrepancy in age in the other direction is never reported as a virtue of the Prophet's character in marrying a widow who was at least ten years his senior.

The historical reports indicating that the age of Ayesha was several years older than nine at the time of the consummation of the marriage are numerous. They are supplemental evidences that cannot be considered stand-alone evidences. However, the evidences collectively form a clear and strong proof that cannot be ignored. Similarly, we cannot prefer what has been established from Ayesha over all of those evidences because when numerous evidences reach that level, they are stronger than the saying of one companion [of the Prophet ﷺ] who is not beyond confusion, error, or forgetfulness. While it is not possible that Ayesha would be negligent of such an important and special event in her life, it is not far-fetched that she could have experienced some forgetfulness due to her old age.

Arnold Yasin Mol in his scholarly paper published by Yaqeen Institute titled: "Ayesha: The case for an older age in sunni-hadith scholarship" (October 2018) states:

"The books of hadith are more authentic than the books of history. They are also more reliant on authentic chains of narrators and stronger in terms of knowing which narrations are confined to one narrator and which have multiple chains. This is something that is agreed upon. The issue here is not to compare the books of hadith to the books of history. Rather it is to compare one specific hadith established in the books of hadith through one companion to ten evidences from the books of hadith and the books of history. I have come to the conclusion that we must prefer the numerous evidences over the narration established from one companion in the books of hadith."

The case for the Traditional view on Ayesha's age of marriage

A majority of scholars from the traditional schools of Islamic sciences still maintain the authenticity of the hadith that gives Aisha's age as nine at the time of marriage as reported by Bukhari which is regarded as the most authentic collection of hadith. They provide compelling evidence to show that marriage at that age; provided a girl has reached puberty was a common and accepted custom and practice not just in the 7th century but up to the end of the 19th century. The laws of most countries did permit the marriage of women ranging in ages from seven to fifteen years subject to sexual maturity. In fact William Blackstone a renowned historian from England wrote commentaries on English Law where he has indicated that the age of consent for women in English law was the age of seven and he wrote this in the late 18th century. The additional fact that there was no criticism on this marriage of the Prophet to Aisha by writers from the medieval, renaissance, enlightenment period and even by the orientalist authors who were so critical about Islam, yet did not comment anything negative on this event is ample evidence that it was an accepted norm, tradition, cultural expectation or custom that women did get married at a younger age in the pre-modern era.

In fact in the US state of Delaware right until 1962, the legal age for women to be able to consent to marriage and get married was seven years!

It was only in the mid to late 20th century that evangelical right wing Christian missionaries looking for material to slander the Prophet Muhammad and malign his character started highlighting the marriage of Aisha and alluding to the difference in age as a moral defect in his character. They ingenuously and diabolically leveraged on the present day cultural and liberal trends in relation to women's rights and values and began a hate filled campaign of highlighting the age factor which appeared immoral and improper in the light of the evolving societal, cultural norms and expectations. This was a clear and blatant case of **'Presentism'** *where the social values and customs of today are projected back in to a time period where it was different and hence portraying the incident as repugnant in comparison to present day reality. Of course in today's socio-cultural milieu of the 21st century it would seem totally improper for a nine year old girl to get married even if she had reached puberty because of the expectations and defining values of the present time. However, if social mores and perceptions were different just a century ago, then what about 1400 years ago?!*

Who was Umm Ayman or Baraka?

She was the Abyssinian servant of Abdullah the Prophet's father who entrusted to her the care of his wife Amina when he went on his trade journey to Syria where he passed away during his return in Madinah. Baraka as she was then called, witnessed and aided in the birth of Muhammad and accompanied him and his mother on a trip to Madinah when he was five years old and whilst on their return, Amina passed away after entrusting the care of her young son to her. She brought the grieving Muhammad to his grandfather and cared for him until his marriage to Khadija twenty years later. Only after the Prophet's marriage did she get married to Ubaid and had a son named Ayman, hence her name Umm Ayman (mother of Ayman). The Prophet referred to her endearingly as his mother after his real mother and a woman of Paradise. Her husband was martyred in the battle of Khybar and her son Ayman at the battle of Hunayn. The Prophet's adopted son Zayed then married her and they had a son named Usamah whom the Prophet dearly loved. She took part in many expeditions and battles and remained close to the Prophet and his wives and the Prophet used to visit her frequently to ensure her welfare. After the demise of the Prophet when his two closest companions visited her and found her crying and they inquired after her sadness, she uttered her profound quote stated at the beginning of this book-and the inspiration behind the title of this book- hearing this; both Abu Bakr and Umar fell to their knees and wept with her.

Appendix B- The myth of slavery and concubines in Islam

As any article on this subject from the Islamic perspective would naturally point out, Islam didn't invent slavery but rather was itself born into a world wherein slavery already existed. This fact is true of every religion before Islam -including Judaism and Christianity and to coin a silly phrase like "Islamic slavery," as some Islamophobes are wont to do, is utterly preposterous.

There was simply slavery, full stop, and every culture and religion that existed up to that point in time more or less accepted it as an institution. Islam is unique among other religions in its attitude toward slavery; it can in some respects be seen as an abolitionist religion and stipulated restrictions and conditions on slavery that would eventually lead to the eradication of it altogether from Arabia and all its territories. In a sense what the Prophetic traditions and the Quran did was to stipulate "sunset clauses" that would ensure the progressive abolition of slavery in all its forms in the context of 7th century Arabia, a time when slavery was seen as the norm all over the world. In that context, it was a "subtle" abolitionist movement.

To this end, consider the following: One of the first things the Prophet Muhammad did as head of state was to organize and put forth a set of laws and ethics aimed at protecting the rights of slaves. He is recorded as saying:

"Feed them (slaves) with what you eat, clothe them with what you wear and do not impose duties upon them which will overburden them. If you so impose duties, then assist them." (Related in Sahih Muslim).

He even went so far as to prohibit calling them "slaves" by saying, "One of you should not say: 'My slave (abd) and my slave-girl (amati).' All of you are the servants of God and all of your womenfolk are (likewise) the female servants of God. Rather let him say: 'My (Ghulam) boy and my (jariyah) girl and my (fata) young boy and my (fatati) young girl.'" (Sahih Muslim).

Muhammad went even further, and prescribed a death penalty for anyone who killed a slave, saying, "Whoever kills his slave, we will kill him." (Narrated in the Musnad of Imam Ahmad and Abu Dawood). He also proscribed a penalty for anyone that beat their slaves, saying,

"Whoever slaps his slave or strikes him, his atonement (kaffara) is to free him." (Sahih Muslim).

As the years went on under Muhammad's leadership, freeing a slave went from being an optional laudatory act which brought reward in the afterlife, to a mandatory act for any number of offenses, included but not limited to, breaking the fast in Ramadan, involuntary manslaughter, breaking one's oath, violating the sanctity of the hajj pilgrimage, etc. etc. In other words, there were specific sins which mandated the freeing of a slave, and when ruminating on this fact I think it becomes obvious that Islam, in the context of its time, had within its framework and recurrent themes an obvious emancipatory strain.

Furthermore, Muslims believe that God has made it mandatory for slave owners to grant their slaves a manumission contract if they so requested, and to allot them the free time necessary to make the money that would have been agreed upon in the contract in order to purchase their freedom. (Relevant reference: The Quran 24:33, which states, **"If any of your slaves wish to pay for their freedom, make a contract with them accordingly, if you know they have good in them, and give them some of the wealth God has given you."**

The Prophet Muhammad first sought to humanize slaves in the eyes of society by giving them rights under law & by forbidding any public reference to them as "slaves," and then began a gradual process of eradicating slavery altogether. As to why he chose this route as opposed to ending it immediately, it seems he preferred to avoid upheaval in society by a gradual reduction rather than an immediate abolition (one need only look at the devastation wrought by the American civil war to get the point -and that, when many parties in the U.S. were in fact abolitionist... it still led to considerable bloodshed and suffering). It is a fact in history that the freed slaves in the Middle East during the spread of Islam became administrators, governors and even rulers.

A related but popular myth propagated by Islamophobes is the notion that the Prophet allowed the "rape" of slave women or women captured as prisoners of war who were then enslaved. They also refer to a Quranic verse that refers as follows:

"And all married women (are forbidden unto you) save those (captives) whom your right hands possess. It is a decree of Allah for you. Lawful unto you are all beyond those mentioned, so that ye seek them with your wealth in honest wedlock." (Quran 4:24)

This verse is also conflated with the accusation that Islam allows concubines from among the slave women. Again this a classic case of Quranic misrepresentation based on faulty understanding of the context and linguistic nuances of the Quran. Islamic scholars to a large extent concur on the fact that these verses revealed in the past tense were only relevant during that time in history when there were prisoners of war and the word 'lawful' here in Arabic does not mean they could have non- consensual relations. These regulations were clearly laid down by the Prophet and any 'relations' with the women taken prisoners in war and who were married had to be given the specified 'waiting period' or "iddah". An incident in recent history that validates this position was when Muslim Bosnian men who were defending themselves against the Serbian onslaught and genocide, captured Serbian women and wanted to apply this Quranic injunction to which all modern day schol- ars unequivocally issued a statement that this 'permission' only applied to a given situation in the past and it is effectively abrogated or does not apply now. Even classical scholars in Islam in the 8th century were majoritarian on this view and prescribed the death penalty for those guilty of rape of women whether they are slaves or free women at that time. However bizarre it may seem today, and however far removed we are from such a time, it is important that now, when looking back on this phenomenon, that we accept its reality without engaging in erroneous presentism, anachronism, or other historian's fallacies. In so doing we will see, for once and all, that the notion of "rape" of female captives being sanctioned by Islamic Law is among the most nefariously untruthful claims of all of the widespread Islamophobic talking points that are now, unfortunately, ubiquitous on the internet.

Within the general framework outlined by the religion, female slaves were further humanized by categorically forbidding their rape, as we have established. Even so, while rape was forbidden, consensual sexual intercourse with a female slave was not, for a number of reasons.viz;

1) The sexual relationship with female slaves and their male owners was also regulated in Islamic Law. For example, if the female slave became pregnant, she was immediately given the status of 'umm walad,' and henceforth freed. 2) Furthermore, during the waiting or 'iddah period, any relatives that were still living could pay her ransom price, typically a price set by the state or the general, surrounding culture- and she would be freed. 3) Also, per a hadith in Sunan Abu Dawood, # 5142, Muslims are commanded to sell slaves that displease them, and simultaneously cautioned against harming them. This would mean that, theoretically if a Muslim man wished to have intercourse with a female slave and she refused, his only recourse is either to bear this patiently, or else sell her. 4) This is especially true when one considers the fact that, in general, rape is considered "hiraabah" in Islamic Law -an offense that carries with it one of 3 punishments: Death by crucifixion, amputation, or permanent exile from a city, depending on the gravity of the offense.

It must also be remembered that should a female slave request an emancipatory contract at any time, it must be granted her, per sharia. In other words, there was no such thing as "accepting her fate" should she consider her servanthood to be a predicament or plight. She could simply set in motion the means to her freedom, should she so choose.

Now, another question one might ask would be, why not just free these women? Why take them as captives at all? And it's a fair question. The answer lies in simply recognizing the realities of the 7th century. This was a period in history before anything even remotely resembling feminism in the 21st century sense had even been conceived of. It was before any welfare states or coordinated governmental efforts were put in place to protect the weakest and most vulnerable. Add to that, it was very often a harsh and violent time. A woman without any sort of male guardianship would've been up the creek, to use a modern euphemism. And while it might seem more ethical to tell men to give up their wealth to protect the widows of their enemies, the reality is that most men weren't going to do this without some sort of reciprocal benefit. Islam is a spiritual tradition, yes, but it is also a utilitarian faith in that it recognizes the failings and weaknesses of human beings, and tries to take them into account. Given all of the above information with regard to the equitable treatment and humanization of captives, it's safe to say that the institution as it was re-organized under Islam was probably the best -or most utilitarian option at the time.

In a ten part series available on Youtube titled 'Islam and Concubinage' and presented by Dr. Shabir Ally's 'Let the Quran Speak' series, Dr. Ally in his concluding presentation responds to the many polemic comments on the Quranic phrase "that which your right hand possesses", by stating that this particular description applies to prisoners of war who are taken as slaves and then distributed among the victors as domestic help and should not be misinterpreted or conflated with buying slaves as 'concubines' for the express purpose of having intimate relations which amounts to fornication. In conclusion Dr. Ally emphasizes on the moral or spiritual thrust of the Quranic message that intended to prescribe an expedient and just way of dealing with the issue of female prisoners of war in the context of the time in which the Quran was revealed and not as a modality to be followed for all times. The greater or grander intent by God was to protect the rights of the most vulnerable within the epistemology of that time and not prescribe for Muslims a concept or paradigm for all ages to come which would limit the dynamism and effectiveness of divine text.

Appendix C - The case of apostasy and punishment in Islam

The way that the early Muslim community seems to have under-stood apostasy differs strikingly from the decisive rulings of the later schools of law. This is most clear in the rulings of the Prophet himself. There is no reliable evidence that the Prophet ever executed anyone for apostasy. When one of the Companions, ʿUbaydallah bin Jaḥsh left Islam and became Christian while the Muslims were seeking refuge in Ethiopia, the Prophet did not order him punished. The Treaty of Hudaybiyah, which the Prophet concluded with the Quraysh, stated that if anyone decided to leave the Muslim community in Madinah no harm would befall them. There was no mention of a punishment for apostasy. In fact, when a man who had come to the Prophet just the day before to pledge his loyalty to Islam wanted to be released from his oath, the Prophet let him go. Imam al-Shāfiʿī himself notes how, during the Prophet's time in Madinah, "Some people believed and then apostatized. Then they again took on the outer trappings of faith. But the Messenger of God did not punish them. This is equally clear in the conduct of the early caliphs. When six men from the Bakr bin Wāʾil tribe apostatized during a campaign in southern Iran, the leaders of the army had them killed. When the caliph Umar was informed of this, he upbraided the commanders. Had he been making the decision, the caliph explained, he would have offered the men "a way back in from the door they took out," or he would have put them in prison. When the pious Umayyad caliph Umar bin ʿAbd al-Aziz (d. 720) was told that a group of recent converts to Islam in northern Iraq had apostatized, he allowed them to revert to their previous status as a protected non-Muslim minority.

The Quran warns those who abandon Islam after embracing it that their good deeds will mean nothing in this life or the next (Quran 2:217). It mentions no worldly punishment. Even "those who believe, then disbelieve and then (again) believe, then disbelieve, and then increase in disbelief" are not given any earthly punishment by the Quran. Instead, God warns only that He "will never pardon them, nor will He guide them unto a way" (Quran 4:137). The Quranic verse that strikes the most stridently dissonant note with the death penalty for apostasy is the declaration that, "There is no compulsion in religion. Wisdom has been clearly distinguished from falsehood" (Quran 2:256).

What the Prophet considered punishable by death was not the personal decision to cease believing in and practicing Islam but rather the betrayal of the Muslim community by joining the ranks of its enemies. One of the main pieces of evidence for the death penalty for apostasy, the Hadith narrated by Ibn Abbas that the Prophet ordered "Whoever changes their religion, kill them," is invoked by Ibn Abbas in the context of a group of Muslims who had rejected Islam and then began preaching and even setting down in writing "heretical" ideas (these apostates are described as heretics), seeking to challenge the caliph Ali. The Arabic word used to describe what they had done, irtaddū, was understood in the early Islamic period to be a public act of political secession from or rebellion against the Muslim community. Hence the famous two years of the Ridda Wars fought during the caliphate of Abu Bakr (632-34 CE), the very name of which shows the conflation of ridda as apostasy with ridda as rebellion and secession from the Muslim polity (in Hadiths the word was used with both meanings).

The second main piece of Hadith evidence for the apostasy ruling leaves a similar impression. When the Prophet says that a Muslim cannot be killed except as punishment for murder, adultery or leaving Islam, he qualifies the apostate here as one who "leaves his religion and forsakes the community or, in another version, one who "makes war on God and His Messenger.

Based on the Prophetic, Quranic and decisions of the early generations of Muslims, scholars explained that Islam does not punish disbelief (kufr) with death. What is punishable by death, they concluded, is "fighting the Muslims, attacking them and trying to split them away from their religion. "Scholars like Yusuf al-Qaraḍāwī have therefore compared the punishment for apostasy to the modern crime of treason. Al-Qaraḍāwī explains that there is no punishment for an individual's decision to stop believing in Islam, since the Quran makes clear that "there is no compulsion in religion". Only those who combine their leaving Islam with a public attempt to undermine the stability of the Muslim community can be punished for ridda. Al-Qaraḍāwī introduces the distinction between 'transgressive apostasy and 'non-transgressive apostasy. The former, in which a Muslim renounces their faith in a way that actively encourages others to do so or that undermines stability, is subject to the apostasy punishment. One who simply leaves Islam or embraces another religion privately is left alone.

> *Historically and traditionally the punishment for apostasy (accompanied with treason and /or blasphemy) in Islam was not intended to restrict the freedom of conscience of an individual but more to preserve and protect the integrity of the Muslim state and community.*

In the final analysis, apostasy as understood by the Prophet and the early Muslims was more than simply renouncing ones faith but an act accompanied by treason and blasphemy designed to cause sedition and disruption to public order. Hence in the Sharia, the aim of punishing apostasy from Islam is to protect the communal faith and social order of a Muslim state. For Muslims living in states whose laws provide protection for freedom of religion, this issue is simple. It is thanks to such legal protections that Muslims have come to reside in these countries and to enjoy the protection of their laws. It would be totally unacceptable to violate the pact, implicit or explicit, made by our residence in these states by working to undermine the freedom of religion of other citizens.

Blasphemy

The Quran states in sura 3, verse 186;

"You are sure to hear much that is hurtful from those who were given the scripture before you and from those who associate others with God, but if you are steadfast and mindful of God, that is the best course." (3:186)

Despite verses such as above and the tolerant spirit of the Quran, Islamic jurisprudence developed a harsh verdict for blasphemy- in particular blasphemy against the prophet Muhammad. Classical jurists sometimes conflated blasphemy with apostasy thus treating it as meriting capital punishment. Unfortunately to this day, this medieval juris-diction is still influential in some Muslim majority countries. Worse, at the hands of militants and extremists blasphemy laws turn into vigi-lante violence against "those who insult Islam".

Ironically, when the Quran encounters blasphemy, it responds to it with rational arguments. At most it threatens blasphemers with God's wrath in the afterlife, but it decrees no punishment in this life. When the blasphemy is of a nature you cannot reason with and amounts to sheer insult? In this case too, the Quran does not decree any violent or coercive response.

"And when you come across those who ridicule our revelation, do not sit with them unless they engage in a different topic." (6:68)

For those who argue that this verse was revealed during the pas-sive phase of temporary restraint in Makkah during the early period of revelation, God repeats the same commandment in a later Madinan sura;

"He has already revealed to you in the Book that when you hear God's revelations being ridiculed or denied, then do not sit in that company unless they engage in a different topic or else you will be like them." (4:140)

If the Quran does not support the severity with which Muslims react to blasphemy, then where does it come from? Like in the case of apostasy, the source is certain narrations about the Prophet Muhammad as recorded in his biographical accounts or Al Sira al Nabawiyya written by Muslim chroniclers about a century after the Prophet. There are no clear hadiths ordering violence against acts of blasphemy but there are stories in the 'Seerah' that narrate about the targeted assassination of several individuals who wrote hostile or blasphemous poems against the Prophet. Those who take these stories in their literal sense without its critical nuance and out of context with the historicized reality fail in an epic way in understanding and interpreting its relevance and reason. The most notorious and iconic 'blaspheming poet' was Kaab ibn al Ashraf who was a leader of the Jewish tribe of Bani Nadir who lived in Madinah and signed the 'Constitution of Madinah' with the Prophet Muhammad soon after the latter's arrival in Madinah. The early Muslim chronicler al-Waqidi narrates in his book 'Kitab al- Maghazi'; "When the Messenger of God arrived in Madinah he desired to establish peace for them and he reconciled with all of them, including the polytheists and Jews. Some of the latter hurt the Prophet and his companions grievously with their bitter words, but God most high commanded His prophet and the Muslims to be patient and forgiving". Yet still, Ibn al -Ashraf proved growingly intransigent and hostile. Following the battle of Badr and the manifest victory of the Muslims over the Makkan pagans, he not only mocked and belittled the victory but swore to incite the polytheists to fight the Muslims again and even wept with the Makkans for their dead. His anti-Muslim vitriol reached a wide circulation there rousing the Makkans to grief and anger and the desire for revenge. There are also reports that he plotted with his tribesmen to assassinate the Prophet. Only after all this, Ibn al-Ashraf was reportedly killed by a group of Muslims acting on the orders of the Prophet.

Most of the other 'blaspheming' poets seem to have combined their offensive words with their active enmity and a point that may explain the dark side of offensive and hate filled poetry in early seventh century Arabia wasn't just poetry but 'invective poetry' where the poet could lead his people into battle, hurling his verses as he would hurl a spear. In other words there were no clear lines between verbal denigration and physical aggression and Muslims might have conflated the two.

Appendix D- Does the Quran permit spousal abuse?

The Quran's chapter 4, verse 34, has been widely acknowledged by classical interpreters and modern translators as meaning that a man, with cautions and limitations, may beat his rebellious wife. Many Muslims minimize the problem by emphasizing limitations on the sort of beating, and the sort of crime that would merit such a measure. They would also insist in a sequence of lighter measures the exhaustion of which would lead to the beating as a last resort. Such approaches, however, do not completely satisfy modern concerns about domestic violence. Others have attempted a solution by seeking out alternative yet legitimate meanings of the verb *daraba* whose most usual meaning is 'to beat, hit, or strike'. The Quran uses the word *daraba* in different contexts as in 'We *struck* forth an example' or 'We *blocked* their ears' and hence in the context of 4:34, the word *wadaribuhuna* would simply mean *'strike* a further distance from them' rather than *'strike* or beat them lightly'. On linguistic grounds, such attempts remain unconvincing. On the other hand Khaled Abou El Fadl, working with the obvious meaning of the verb, argues that the addressees of the verse are not husbands, but Muslim authorities. In his recent book, The Search for Beauty in Islam, El Fadl argues that the verse is not an instruction for men to beat their wives, but for state authorities to redress sexual impropriety. And if this verse prescribes measures against women in particular, other verses specify measures against men and women more generally (for example 4:16; and 24:2) thus maintaining equity.

"Men are the upholders and maintainers of women by virtue of that in which God has favoured some of them above others and by virtue of their spending from their wealth. Therefore the righteous women are devoutly obedient, guarding in [their husbands'] absence what God has guarded. As for those from whom you fear discord and animosity, admonish them, then leave them in their beds, then strike them. Then if they obey you, seek not a way against them. Truly God is Exalted, Great." (4:34)

Yusuf Ali translates: *"As to those women on whose part ye fear disloyalty and ill-conduct, admonish them (first), (next), refuse to share their beds, and (last) beat them (lightly)."* Ali's parentheses enclosing the words 'first', 'next', 'last' and 'lightly' reveal them to be insertions into an otherwise literal translation. They nevertheless reflect the common interpretation that only a light beating is permitted, and only as a last resort.

Abdel Haleem, while maintaining Ali's sequencing, drops the parentheses: *"If you fear high-handedness from your wives, remind them [of the teachings of God], then ignore them when you go to bed, then hit them. If they obey you, you have no right to act against them." (Quran 4:34)*

While Dr. Jamal Badawi and Dr. Tariq Ramadan accept the traditional interpretation in principle, they emphasize the limitations and cautions. But such an approach fails to completely satisfy modern concerns about domestic violence. Seeking an alternative meaning of 'ḍaraba', Abdulhamid Abusulayman in a recent paper found the instruction to mean that a man is to move away from his wife rather than beat her. Aside from the question of the validity of this reinterpretation, however, it retains for men the authority to judge the actions of their wives and to impose some reform measures.

On yet other grounds, Riffat Hasan likewise denied that the verse allows for wife-beating. To her, the verse is addressing not husbands, but state authorities, and the imperative means not 'beat them' but 'imprison them'. This would be the appropriate measure against women if they collectively refuse to bear children in a manner that threatens the survival of Muslim communities.

This alternative meaning of the verb is not convincing. But Hasan seems to have correctly identified the addressees of the verse. Whatever the instruction, it is given not to husbands, but to Muslim authorities. And this can make all the difference.

She argues for this on textual grounds. She sees the instruction as being to both men and women since the Arabic text uses the male plural which grammatically accommodates both genders. But her argument seems inadequate, for in the same chapter, such as verses 3, 19, and 20-25, in which the same grammatical form dominates, the address is certainly to men only.

For El Fadl, likewise, the verse addresses the state authorities. However, his justification for this identification is mainly on the moral ground that the verse could not possibly assign to men the position of judge and enforcer over their wives. This argument may not satisfy those Muslims who would insist on text-based judgements.

However, the argument can be saved. The identification can be made on textual grounds. The Quran's fourth chapter is a connected whole. In a series of rhetorical shifts, the chapter turns to address believers in general in verse 29. Verse 32 is clearly addressed to both men and women telling them to not covet the shares of inheritance assigned to each gender earlier on in the same chapter. Verse 34 continues the same point by pointing out that the two genders have corresponding responsibilities. The extra share of inheritance men receive is to be spent in support of females. Righteous women are to be devout, guarding in privacy that which God would have them guard. As for those women whose licentiousness is in question, the authorities should apply the three measures as appropriate to the specifics of the crime under consideration.

What definitely decides the issue in favour of the legal authorities as the addressees of the verse, however, is the continued address into the following verse, 4:35. That this verse continues the discourse is indicated by its beginning with the conjunction "and" (wa). In verse 34 the addressees are told: "As for those women whose licentiousness you fear (takhāfūna) . . . ." In verse 35 they are told: "And if you fear (khiftum) a breach between the two of them . . . ." Verse 35 cannot possibly address the husband or the wife. In verse 35 the instruction is for community leaders to appoint two persons, one related to each side of a failing marriage, as arbiters to find out who is wrong, whether the husband or the wife, and to impose measures to deal with the conflict.

Hence the discourse is continuous, and the addressees are the same throughout. It is only after turning to verse 35, however, that Imam al-Razi in his exegesis asks who the addressees of this latter verse could be, and answers that the authorities are meant. But he did not return to his commentary of the previous verse to correct the assumption made there that husbands were being instructed to beat their wives. In this method of verse by verse commentary, which Fazlur Rahman referred to as atomic, the exegetes sometimes failed to step back and see the big picture.

Likewise, having already translated verse 34 on the assumption that it addressed husbands, Abdel Haleem had to make clear to his readers that verse 35 no longer addresses husbands. To accomplish this change of addressee, Abdel Haleem inserted the word 'believers' in brackets as follows:

"If you [believers] fear that a couple may break up, appoint one arbiter from his family and one from hers. Then, if the couple wants to put things right, God will bring about reconciliation between them: He is all knowing, all aware."

There is, of course, nothing in the Arabic text to indicate a change of addressee. And since the addressees in verse 35 are admittedly believers in general, they are the addressees in verse 34 as well. Once the addressee of verse 34 is properly identified as the believers in general, as represented by their Imam or Qāḍi, the verse can no longer be about wife-beating, and a new meaning for its instructions must be sought. The crime which merited the three measures was represented by the Arabic word nushūz. El Fadl depended on a hadith to explain nushūz as licentious behavior. But we need not make selective appeals to hadiths to reach this conclusion. The Quran can explain itself on this point. In the verse those whose nushūz is feared are in contradistinction to the righteous devout women who guard that which Allah would have them guard. The idea of guarding one's private parts is replete in the Quran, mentioned in verses such as 23:5; 24:30-31 etc. In the very chapter, verse 15 spoke of those women who commit lewdness (wa-l-lātī ya'tīna bi-fāḥishah). Verse 34 speaks of those whose nushūz is feared (wa-l-lāti takhāfūna nushūzahunna). The parallelism is obvious. The same basic idea of a woman committing something reprehensible is stated in each verse. It is lewdness (fahishah) in one verse and a related form of licentious behavior (nushūz) in another.

The Quran generally states the same thing several times in various ways, whether it is dealing with stories of the prophets or with current legislation. One has to compare similar texts to discover the added details and varying emphases. In chapter 4 alone, the idea of sexual impropriety is mentioned in vss. 15, 16, 19, 24, 25, 34, and 128. When these verses are interpreted in the light of each other it is clear that the Quran is dealing with different aspects of the same topic. In this case the corporal punishment prescribed in vss. 15 and 16 is related to the measures prescribed in v. 34, and the crime is likewise related. Moreover, the one hundred lashes which are prescribed for fornicators in 24:2 are said in 4:25 to be halved in the case of slave-women. It is not unusual that the Quran returns to the point in 4:34 to add some details to the legislation about corporal punishment for an adulteress. In short, El Fadl had depended on a hadith to prove that the crime in 4:34 was not simply a wife's disobeying her husband, but lewdness (fāhisha). To avoid a selective use of the hadith whose other implications are incompatible with our conclusion, however, we have here been able to identify the crime as being fāhisha on the basis of the Quran alone.

It will suffice to say that Quran 4:34 and other verses such as 4:15, 16, 19, 32, 128, and 24:2 should be seen together. These verses, interpreted in the light of each other, yield the meaning that Muslim authorities can beat those men and women who are guilty of promiscuity when lesser deterrents such as warnings and house arrest are deemed inadequate. There is nothing in this interpretation to favor any one gender. This will provide some relief to those who, like El Fadl, find it troublesome that men should be permitted by the Quran to beat their wives. But, unlike El Fadl, it was not this moral compass that pointed to our conclusion, which we have reached on textual grounds mainly after noticing how commentators misidentified the addressees of 4:34. Seeing that in the following verse the addressees remain unchanged, we agreed with al-Rāzi and Abdel Haleem that these are the Muslim court authorities. From this it followed that 4:34 does not in any way allow for men to beat their wives.

Appendix E- The concept of "Abrogation" in the Quran

One of the most contentious issues in the sciences of the Quran is the doctrine of 'abrogation' (naskh). The English term abrogation implies that a previous rule or teaching in a verse was completely cancelled by a new verse. Critics of Islam have seized on this notion to argue that the Quran is contradictory and, therefore, cannot be of divine origin. But is this how the early Muslims understood the phenomenon of Quranic abrogation? Did Allah change His mind? Or is there a deeper wisdom as to why some rules should change?

The truth is that abrogation is further evidence of the divine origin of the Quran because it has delivered appropriate rules to be applied in different situations, reflecting the Wisdom of the Creator who intended Islam to be applicable to all times, places, and people. If the text had a rigid set of rules, it would have been too inflexible for modern people, let alone the early Muslims, to follow its guidance in their lives. Abrogation occurs by the Will and Wisdom of Allah, Who knows what teachings people need in the precise moment that they need it. It can occur between verses of different divine books or within the same divine book.

Allah declares:" *We do not abrogate a verse and allow it to be forgotten but that We bring what is better than it or like it. Do you not know that Allah has power over all things?"* (Quran 2:106)

Some specific rules in the previous revelations contained in the Torah, Psalms, and Gospel were abrogated by rules laid down in Islam, although the spirit of all the divine books is the same. For example, Jews celebrate the Sabbath on Saturday, Christians celebrate their holy day on Sunday, and Muslims perform al-Jummah prayers on Friday. We believe that Allah guided us to single out Friday for the weekly sermon instead of other days. Should Muslims, then, impose their religious law on all others by force?

The Quran states: *"To each among you We have made a law and a way. If Allah had willed, He would have made you into a single nation, but He tests you in what you have been given. Thus, race towards what is good. Unto Allah will all of you return and He will tell you about that in which you differed."* (5:48)

The religion of the Prophets is the same single religion, while the laws they followed changed over time and place. Allah could have commanded Muslims to force all people to follow a single code of law but He did not, instead urging us to "race towards what is good," which is to compete with each other in good deeds. We believe Islam is the final religion, abrogating and perfecting all that came before it, so we should invite others to it by way of good example, behaviour, and persuasion, but never by compulsion or deception.

In addition to inter-revelatory abrogation is the issue of intra-revelatory abrogation, that is, understanding why some verses of the Quran seemed to contradict each other and how they can be properly reconciled. Critics claims that abrogation is simply a tool used to explain away confused and contradictory verses. Does the Quran contradict itself?

The Quran declares: *"Do they not reflect upon the Quran? If it had come from another besides Allah, they would have found much contradiction within it."* (4:82)

Muslims often argue that Islam is a religion of peace by pointing to the dozens and dozens of Quranic verses that encourage compassion, forgiveness, and good deeds. However, critics of Islam and even some radicalised Muslims have an unsophisticated argument to explain away anything in the Quran that contradicts their views: the peaceful verses have allegedly been abrogated by the 'verse of the sword.' Needless to say, their argument falls apart upon closer scrutiny. Although proponents of sword-verse abrogation disagree over which verse is actually the verse of the sword, it is often cited as verse 9:5:

"When the sacred months have passed, then kill the idolaters wherever you find them, besiege them and lie in wait for them in every place of ambush. But if they repent, establish prayer, and give charity, then let them go on their way. Verily, Allah is Forgiving and Merciful."

It is important to appreciate that the term 'verse of the sword' appeared later in the classical tradition. The sword, of course, was considered to be a symbol of justice and not aggression or violence. Regardless, such terminology does not originate with the Prophet (ﷺ) and his companions. The clause 'kill the idolaters wherever you find them' is usually singled out by critics and extremists as the final command regarding relations between Muslims and non-Muslims, as if it were a declaration of all-out permanent holy war on all non-Muslims everywhere. Besides the absurd infeasibility of such a teaching, to interpret this clause as absolute only makes sense if one cynically ignores all of the surrounding verses in the same chapter. The subsequent verses 9:10 through 9:13 state unequivocally that the 'idolaters' under discussion are those who habitually broke their peace treaties. The purpose of fighting them is to stop their aggression and, even so, the door of repentance remains open for them:

"They do not observe for a believer any kinship or covenant. It is they who have transgressed. If they repent, establish prayer, and give charity, then they are your brothers in religion. We make clear the signs for people who know." (9:10-11)

"If they break their oaths after their treaty and defame your religion, then fight the leaders of unbelief. Verily, nothing is sacred to them, that they might cease. Will you not fight people who violated their oaths and determined to expel the Messenger and yourselves and they attacked you first?" (9:12-13)

The clause 'that they might cease' clarifies that the aim of fighting is to stop their aggression, and 'they attacked you first' explains what caused the conflict to begin in the first place. Moreover, the immediately following verse 9:6 grants asylum and immunity to any idolater who lays down their weapons whether or not they individually accept Islam:

"If one of the idolaters seeks your protection, then grant him protection that he may hear the word of Allah, then deliver him to his place of safety. That is because they are people who do not know." (9:6)

As expressed elsewhere in the Quran, war is only justified as a response to unprovoked aggression. That principle still holds true when the entire passage surrounding the sword verse is read and interpreted consistently. It becomes evidently implausible to imagine that a single line from verse 9:5 has completely abrogated all of the verses around it and hundreds of verses in other chapters. Verses revealed earlier about peace and warfare were likewise understood by the companions as still operative and legally valid even after the revelation of the sword verses. At least three key verses disprove the idea that Islam advocates a permanent state of war against non-Muslims or that the peaceful verses were invalidated.

The Quran declares:

"Fight in the way of Allah those who fight you, but do not transgress. Verily, Allah does not love transgressors." (2:190)

This verse is relevant to both the justification for starting a war (jus ad bellum) and the lawful limits of conduct during war (jus in bello), both of which are based upon the Islamic principle of non-aggression. It warns against transgressing the rules of war, as there can never be a time when Allah loves transgression, indicating that the effective legal cause will remain eternally unchanged. It is also consistent with the authentic statement of the Prophet

"Verily, the most tyrannical of people to Allah Almighty is one who kills those who did not fight him," among many others.

Al-Tabari records several narrations from the early Muslims who did not consider this verse to be abrogated. The distinguished commentator Ibn Abbas explained the import of the verse this way:

Do not kill women, children, the elderly, or whoever comes to you with peace and he restrains his hand (from fighting), for if you did so you would have certainly transgressed.

Another key verse commands Muslims to conduct peace treaties with their enemies if they are offered reasonable terms of peace. The Quran states:

278

"If they incline to peace, then incline to it as well and put your trust in Allah. Verily, Allah is the Hearing, the Knowing." (8:61)

According to Ibn Kathir, this verse cannot be abrogated because the Prophet (ﷺ) continued to act upon it as a legal precedent. Thus, it is not invalidated, nor is it abrogated, nor is it restricted." He supports his argument with the statement of the Prophet (ﷺ), "Verily, after me there will be conflicts or affairs, so if you are able to end them in peace then do so." This verse and its accompanying traditions demonstrate that peace is preferred whenever possible. In other words, the Muslim leader has broad permission to conduct peace treaties if it serves the welfare (maslahah) of the Muslim community. Therefore, this verse cannot be abrogated and, in fact, it places limits on the sword verses.

Lastly, a third key verse articulates the general rule governing relations between Muslims and non-Muslims. Like the other verses, this rule also has not been abrogated or invalidated.

The Quran states:

"Allah does not prohibit you from those who do not fight you for religion and do not expel you from your homes, that you be benevolent to them and generous to them. Verily, Allah loves those who are fair. Allah only prohibits you from those who fight you for religion and expel you from your homes and assist in your expulsion, that you take them as allies. Whoever takes them as allies, then they are the oppressors." (60:8-9)

The wording of the verse is stated comprehensively such that it applies to all people, regardless of their religion, anyone who can be accurately described as a non-aggressor. Each set of verses, whether discussing compassion or justice, peace or war, are applicable to their appropriate situations. The verses of compassion and forgiveness were revealed first to express the default stance, then the sword verses created an exception to this general rule. Peace is the desired state of affairs, but war is sometimes necessary to defend the innocent. Forgiveness is the right attitude to have, but not at the expense of justice for victims. The peaceful verses and the sword verses do not contradict each other, nor do they cancel each other out. Each set of verses serves its own purpose, in its own time and its own conditions, with peaceful, just, and positive relations between human beings as the desired end goal. Or as it is said in the Bible, "For everything there is a season, and a time for every matter under heaven... a time for war and a time for peace." (Ecclesiastes 3:1-8).

The claim that the peaceful verses of the Quran were abrogated, or invalidated, by the 'verses of the sword' is based upon a lack of awareness of the nuanced manner in which the term was employed by early Muslims. Several classical scholars, including the Quran's earliest commentators, rejected the claim that the peaceful verses were abrogated in part or in whole. Those who did claim the peaceful verses were abrogated intended by that partial abrogation, that warfare involves rules that are exceptions to the otherwise general rules of peace, tolerance, and forgiveness. *(adapted from the Yaqeen Research article,`` Abrogated rulings in the Quran: discerning their divine wisdom.`` by Justin Parrott Nov. 15th 2018)*

Appendix F- The dynamism of divine script-tradition, reason and intellect and towards an Islamic Worldview

It was the Christian historian and theologian, Jaroslav Pelikan who once stated that, "Tradition is the living faith of the dead and traditionalism is the dead faith of the living". He went on to elucidate how 'traditionalism' that is fossilized in history and manifests as blind ritualistic and literalist adherence to dogma that gives 'tradition' a bad rap. Abdul Hakim Murad the dean of the Cambridge Muslim College states in his 'Commentary on the Eleventh Contentions',contention 89; 'Only through tradition are we an umma semper reformanda', meaning a community constantly reformed. Reform in Islam is not to be a reshaping, for it is known by Ijma that the shape is complete in the Sunna; instead it is to be islah or reforming and setting right. Following the final Prophetic revelation, throughout Islamic history, God in His Mercy has inspired many who excelled in piety and knowledge and showed a true and deep understanding of Islamic orthodoxy and tradition or the prophetic way. They were 'Reformers' and 'Revivalists' (Mujtahids and Mujaddids) of the Muslim mindset and based their scholarly works without betraying orthodoxy and tradition but in context and relevance to the reality of time and place in history and its evolving dynamics. Some contemporary scholars refer to them as 'Renovators' as they do not see the need for the kind of reformation that Christianity went through. Islam needs no revision or modification since the Divine instructions carried within them the very principles to ascertain and accommodate changing social circumstances. Social customs ('urf) can affect the implementation of subsidiary social rulings under particular circumstances and more importantly, human reason and the intellect play a critical role in deriving and changing laws so that they echo universal and objective ethical values founded on beauty, justice and excellence.

They were able to navigate through the pitfalls of 'traditionalism' and free the Muslim minds from being trapped in the dungeons of the past. These great personalities in Islam who came after the Prophet continued the true prophetic methodology of reasoning and analogical deduction (Ijtihad) and provided a powerful scholarly framework for Islam and Muslims to be productive and relevant through the vicissitudes of time. In fact this is an enduring and integral part of the Prophetic legacy and the Prophet is reported to have stated: *"Surely, Allah will send for this Ummah at the advent of every one hundred years a person (or persons) who will renovate its religion for it."*

God declares in the Quran,

"Ye are the best of peoples, evolved for mankind, enjoining what is right, forbidding what is wrong, and believing in Allah." (Quran 3:110)

Tariq Ramadan referring to the above verse in his book 'Essentials of Islam', states that, "the notion of favour on the Muslims flows from the condition of exemplary morality that is the visible expression of faith. However, the Muslim spiritual community can be favoured only insofar as it stands as a moral example for humanity by transmitting and teaching the Message, but above all by applying and living it." It is at this critical juncture, that Muslims fail as they apply outmoded concepts founded on 'traditionalism' together with a sense of 'absolutism' where they raised the 'favouring' of God attributable to the sole fact of being Muslim: the same temptation of declaring ones identity as being 'chosen people of God', and hence restricting God's universal Message to Humanity to a people based on religious, racial or ethnic lines.

Hence, true dynamic tradition circumvents fallacious attempts to reinvent Islam on the edifice of Western liberalism. At the other end of the spectrum, Islam through its inbuilt traditional methodologies is able to avoid the pitfalls of 'modernism' and 'progressivism' as such mechanisms suffer from arbitrary judgments about the constitutive elements of the allegedly universal (though inevitably westernized) moral philosophy, hermeneutical indeterminacy whereby any conceivable concocted reinterpretation can be justified, and finally, a failure to find any theological or rational justification as to why it should be taken as more authoritative than the traditional faith of fourteen centuries of scholarship upheld by 1.6 billion Muslims who revere God's revelation and His Prophet.

In his insightful and reformative book "Canadian Islam- belonging and loyalty", Imam Zijad Delic asserts that what is required to showcase the eternal beauty and relevance of Islam and its compatibility with what is good and beneficial(maslaha) for humanity, co-existing harmoniously with fellow citizens and living up to the expectations of the social contract of citizenship is: "A more informed reading of Islam's foundational text, the Quran, along with the examples and recorded teachings of Prophet Muhammad which reveals a mindful, generous, and holistic approach to life whose core values emphasize respect, mercy, compassion, love understanding, cooperation, consultation, equality, family and- essential in today's conflicted world- an enduring concept of peace through justice that emphasizes repentance and forgiveness. Islam is far away from the harshness meted out in many places under the false pretext of following Islamic principles."

Today, there are around 1.6 billion Muslims around the world living in lands that are Islamic and endeavouring to apply Islamic values and mores; living in lands that are only Islamic in name but governed by monarchies and dictators and values that are anathema to Islam; living in non-Muslim lands that are governed by values enshrined in their constitution that resonate with Islam and finally living in non-Muslim lands that are hostile to Islamic beliefs and practices (like atheism or communism). In this light it is critical than ever before in history that the global Muslim Ummah or community develop a worldview narrative or Weltanschauung which would include a person's philosophic, moral, and religious orientation based on the foundational principles as elucidated by Imam Zijad Delic above. Both classical and contemporary scholars have identified the defining principles or criteria on which this foundation and its accompanying jurisprudence should be structured which are public benefit (Maslaha), justice (Adala), wisdom (Hikma) and mercy (Rahma). It was the practice of mercy that resulted in the Ottoman Empire over its 400 year history not sentencing capital punishment for a single soul.

Tariq Ramadan also expounds in his aforementioned book the wider meaning of the word 'Ummah' or community which can be understood at two levels; "on the plane of faith, the Ummah is a spiritual community, whose believers share a common religion, rites and aspiration towards the Transcendent. ... but the idea of Ummah is also that of a community of shared principles, which may well be more than the Muslims alone and may even turn against them should they betray it. It was in this light the Prophet considered the Jews of Madinah as members of the Ummah he founded, fulfilling the same duties and enjoying the same rights as the Muslims. Likewise the revelation obliges the Muslims, in the name of their higher principles, to struggle against Muslims who are oppressors."

The afore-mentioned is especially of significance for Muslims living as minorities in western lands or for that matter anywhere on earth. Dr. Zijad Delic goes on to state in his afore-mentioned book: "The key defining elements of Muslim identity are characterized by openness and regular social interaction. These attributes help Muslims to acclimatize successfully in different cultural contexts while remaining faithful to their religious values. By returning to their scriptural sources, Muslims can establish a positive distinction between the religious principles that define them and the acquired cultural norms that identify or reflect the various societies in which they live. When Muslim identity is consciously based on religious principles, Muslims can live and thrive anywhere."

Imam Delic goes on to propose the 'constructive integration model' for Muslims living as minorities in lands that may be defined as abodes of peace and trust (Dar-ul Aman, Dar ul Ahad, or Dar-ul Sulh). Islam does not prescribe utopia for Muslims in this world but a more balanced and nuanced "Optopia" where the defining and operative words are engagement, participation and contribution to the greater society and country for optimal performance. This view leads to the concept of the social contract of citizenship which is sacred in Islamic jurisprudence and hence unlawful to break or violate. Imam Delic, specifically referring to the Canadian experience goes on to state, "For Muslim reformers, being part of Western society means facing reality, with all its challenges, head on. It means reforming themselves individually and collectively within the positive context of their adopted liberal democratic cultures, while remaining faithful to the basic religious principles that define their core religious identity as Muslims. Thus when they settle suitably and reconcile effectively, they can productively live in harmony amid new environments and contribute to the well-being of all."

He also argues that; "choosing the option of mere transplanting of cultures or ideologies from their place of origin has been shown to render Muslims uncreative and incapable of coming up with original solutions; incapable of devising independent analytical methodologies, unable to think outside of current stereotypes, fragmented in outlook, alienated from the major issues of the society around them, and unaware of their true identity within the context of contemporary history and milieu."

Muslim communities who adopt the "ghetto" or "ethnocentric" mentality and isolate themselves in a bubble by importing religio-cultural symbols of their life back in their country of origin do a great disservice to the younger generation of Muslims who face a serious cognitive dissonance as they grapple to come to terms with the new reality. One of the most regressive and harmful manifestation of this 'ghetto' mindset is to bring on a temporary basis Imams from their home countries who have no commitment to or understanding of the Canadian or host country experience and lack fluency in language to interact with the youth in a meaningful way resulting in a complete disconnect of the individual from the mosque or community centre.

"Verily, God will not change the (good) condition of a people as long as they do not change their state (of goodness) themselves." (13:11)

In the introduction to their book "Agenda to Change our Condition", Hamza Yusuf and Zaid Shakir, capture the essence of personal and community or inner and outer transformation:

"In order for us to realize our God given potential within our lifetimes, we must break the cycles of stagnation by abandoning methods that have proven ineffective in fulfilling our responsibilities as people committed to Islam. We can accomplish this only by changing our current condition- this requires courage, commitment, and above all, critical introspection."

In conclusion of their book the authors state that such a change if implemented will engender Muslims with a healthier relationship with God, and a healthier relationship with God will lead to a healthier relationship with our neighbours. That enhanced relationship will in turn lead to a change in our collective condition. God willing.

Khaled Abou El Fadl, emeritus chair in Islamic studies and Professor in Islamic law at the University of California in Los Angeles states in his ground breaking book and magnum opus "Reasoning with God"

"There is a serious problem with arguing that God intended to lock the epistemology of the 7th Century into the immutable text of the Quran, and then intended to hold Muslims hostage to this epistemological framework for all ages to come. Among other things, this would limit the dynamism and effectiveness of divine text because the Quran would be forever locked within a knowledge paradigm that is very difficult to retrieve or re-create."

This penetrating and insightful statement by Dr. Fadl defines the essence of ijtihad or 'critical reasoning' but unfortunately a large part of the orthodox traditional Islamic thinking today have placed upon them self-imposed constrictions and barriers that limit their ability to engage in such reasoning and bring out the best in the beauty, excellence and ethical behaviour that the Quran directs us towards.

On the closely related subject of righteousness or 'Taqwa', the Prophet said,

"Righteousness is in good character, and wrongdoing is that which wavers in your soul, and which you dislike people finding out about." [Muslim]

And on the authority of Wabisah bin Ma'bad, a companion of the Prophet who narrated;

"I came to the Messenger of Allah and he said, 'You have come to ask about righteousness.' I said, 'Yes.' He said, 'Consult your heart. Righteousness is that about which the soul feels at ease and the heart feels tranquil. And wrongdoing is that which wavers in the soul and causes uneasiness in the breast, even though people have repeatedly given their legal opinion [in its favour]'" (Imam Ahmad)

Allah has created us with a pure, innate disposition that is called fitrah also referred to as the primordial natural normative disposition which all humans are endowed with. This means to love the truth and the good, and to hate falsehood and evil. Consequently, good believers with pure fitrah should never confuse truth with falsehood.

To develop the capacity of knowing right from wrong in your heart, you have to realize that what's good in your heart can be affected by what you consume in terms of ideas and knowledge. So the more you know about the Prophet - who he was, how he acted in different situations - the more you will be able to distinguish right from wrong. Get to know the Prophet so you know how he will act in any context. The second hadith guides us to consult our heart regarding doubtful matters. If the heart is tranquil, that implies that it has 'Bir' or righteousness. If the heart is not tranquil when approaching an act, one should abstain from carrying out the act or doubtful matter. However, it should be noted that fitrah is subject to corruption and can be darkened due to the influence of a bad environment - a person may start to like and appreciate what is bad or evil, and dislike truth and goodness. Here, the heart is diseased or even dead. Such a person cannot use his heart as a measure to judge what is good and bad because the fitrah is already corrupted.

The core essence of this reasoning lies in the concept of 'Taqwa' or God consciousness which is the ability to discern good from bad and develop the capacity to ascertain moral responsibility for one's actions instead of projecting the burden of morality onto the law. However, as anyone familiar with the Islamic tradition may know, what taqwa came to mean in Islam is "God-fearing piety," often expressed as meticulous observation of the Sharia. Taqwa, in this more established sense, is an internal drive for doing the right thing, rather than a capacity for figuring out the right thing.

In the final analysis Muslims have to reconcile and harmonize tradition, reason, intellect with divine revelation to align with the fitrah in developing an internal guidance controlling system and be a beacon of divine illumination based on the dynamism and perennial relevance of divine scripture and the divinely endowed faculty of intellect embedded in the 'fitrah' of mankind.

Appendix G- The 'People of the Book' and earlier Revelations in the Quran

It is a fundamental article of faith for Muslims to believe in the Prophets who came before Muhammad and to also believe in the revelations that were sent down to them. The Quran refers to those to whom God sent down Revelations before the Quran as 'People of the Book' or "Ahl al Kitaab", and in numerous verses of the Quran, addresses, exhorts, admonishes and warns them. Those directly referred to as people of the book are the Jews and the Christians and the scriptures sent down to them were the Taurat (Torah) and the Injeel (Gospel) to Moses and Jesus respectively and the Zaboor (Psalms) to David. The Quran and its revelation to Muhammad symbolize the culmination of revelation from God and the completion and perfection of His religion in Islam. In a sense all the Prophets of God followed Islam and were Muslims as they submitted to the one true God and delivered the monotheistic faith to the people. The Quran is not just a continuation of the earlier scriptures but a replacement and a correction of the deviation and corruption of them with a promise by God to protect it as it is the 'uncreated' word of God. The Quran declares:

"It was We who revealed the law [to Moses]: therein was guidance and light. By its standard have been judged the Jews, by the prophets who bowed [as in Islam] to God's will, by the rabbis and the doctors of law: for to them was entrusted the protection of God's book, and they were witnesses thereto: therefore fear not men, but fear me, and sell not my signs for a miserable price. If any do fail to judge by [the light of] what God hath revealed, they are [no better than] unbelievers." (5:44)

And addressing the Christians God declares:

"And in their footsteps We sent Jesus the son of Mary, confirming the Law that had come before him: We sent him the Gospel: therein was guidance and light, and confirmation of the Law that had come before him: guidance and an admonition to those who fear God. Let

288

the people of the Gospel judge by what God hath revealed therein. If any do fail to judge by [the light of] what God hath revealed, they are [no better than] those who rebel." (5:46-47)

The above verse seems to suggest that, instead of calling Christians to convert to Islam, the Quran rather asks them to follow their own scripture firmly. But then in the following verse God reveals the ultimate betrayal of God's chain of guidance:

"Then woe to those who write the Book with their own hands, and then say: "This is from God," to traffic with it for miserable price! - Woe to them for what their hands do write, and for the gain they make thereby." (2:79)

From the Muslim perspective this corruption of the Book is largely reflected in the books of the New Testament where we have several gospels written by different evangelists whereas the Quran speaks of a single "Gospel" given to Jesus. This begs the question, is the original gospel revealed to Jesus still out there?

Mustafa Akyol, author, journalist and columnist to the New York Times and several international publications, in his new book 'The Islamic Jesus' refers to the famous "Q Gospel" which 'saw the light of day' in the 19th century, when some German scholars of the Bible noticed a formerly unknown interconnection between the three synoptic gospels- Mark, Mathew and Luke. Mustafa goes on to say;

"First, they realized that the earliest among these was Mark -not Mathew as the traditional view held. Second, they realized that Mathew and Luke borrowed heavily from Mark. Third and most important they also realized that Mathew and Luke have many identical parts that do not appear in Mark. Since Mathew and Luke were most probably written around the same time but in different places, these scholars reasoned their 'common material' must have come from a separate source. One of the scholars, theologian Johannes Weiss (d.1914) called this source the Q Gospel, Q standing for the German word Quelle, which means "source". Since then this theory has been widely accepted. This hypothetical Q Gospel, which scholars constructed by mapping out the common material in Mathew and Luke, has been published as a text in itself and has taken on a life of its own. Many books have been written about it, with titles calling it "the earliest gospel" or "the lost gospel"."

The most fascinating and interesting feature of the Q gospel is a possible answer to the question posed earlier about the original gospel taught by Jesus. The Q source appears to be a sayings gospel which contains nothing but the sayings of Jesus. Included in its contents are some of the most fundamental moral teachings of Jesus that resonate so clearly with the Quran, such as the Sermon on the Mount, the Lord's Prayer, loving one's enemies, turning the other cheek, the Beatitudes, the parables of the mustard seed, the yeast, the invited dinner guests, the golden rule, the tree known by its fruit, the lost sheep, giving the shirt off one's back and the list goes on. There is nothing in Q that is attributable to Paul and hence the entire Pauline theology about the crucifixion, atonement and resurrection of Christ are absent in this source. A cursory reading of Q gives an impression of Jesus as a reformer within Judaism who emphasizes the spirit of the law over its letter. Q would have been the earliest recorded teaching of Jesus's sayings and collected in Aramaic writing and then also in Greek the prevalent language at that time producing the 'source' that both Mathew and Luke used as the basis of their texts.

Paul's thirteen letters in the New Testament has nothing about Jesus's sayings and was all about the crucifixion and resurrection of Jesus. For him, -as Mustafa observes in his book- "the Good News for Paul was not the teachings of Jesus but the teachings about Jesus." So to answer the question about whether the original teachings of Jesus are present now, the Q seems to match with the Injeel that was revealed to Jesus and referred to in the Quran both in form and theology. This perspective would make a selective reading of the New Testament an arguably correct reading of the scriptures revealed to Jesus.

The message to the Christians in the Quran that cannot be stated in a more concise and clear manner is;

"O People of the Scripture, do not commit excess in your religion or say about Allah except the truth. The Messiah, Jesus, the son of Mary, was but a messenger of Allah and His word which He directed

to Mary and a spirit [created at a command] from Him. So believe in Allah and His messengers. And do not say, "Three"; desist - it is better for you. Indeed, Allah is but one God. Exalted is He above having a son. To Him belongs whatever is in the heavens and whatever is on the earth. And sufficient is Allah as Disposer of affairs." (4:171)

Here in one unambiguous verse, God calls upon the Christians to not transgress the bounds of truth and engage in speculative mysterious theology in attributing to God things that are patently false and conjecture like shared divinity and the triune Godhead and attributing a son to Him. God also affirms here Jesus's messianic mission and the special way of his creation through God's word and a spirit proceeding from Him.

In the same verse God affirms that Jesus is only a messenger and God is only one i.e. He does not share His divinity with anyone or anything and to Him belongs the dominion of the heavens and earth and He is sufficient as a disposer of all affairs whether it be truth or falsehood.

James D Tabor a scholar of Christian origins and ancient Judaism states in his book, 'The Jesus Dynasty: The hidden history of Jesus, His Royal family, and the Birth of Christianity';

"There are two completely separate and distinct Christianities embedded in the New Testament. One is quite familiar and became the version of the Christian faith known to billions over the past two millennia. Its main proponent was the apostle Paul. The other has been largely forgotten and by the turn of the first century A.D. had been effectively marginalized and suppressed by the other.... Its champion was none other than James the brother of Jesus."

In the conclusion of his book, Dr. Tabor makes one of the most ecumenical statements in the history of the Abrahamic faiths;

"An understanding of the Jesus dynasty also offers new avenues of understanding between Jews, Christians, and Muslims. Christian persecution of Jews has understandably done much to marginalize Jesus within Jewish history. Over the centuries Jews found it difficult to think about Jesus without associating him with the bad conduct of those who acted in his name. In the last century, and into our own time, much of that is changing with a recovery of the Jewishness of Jesus and a fruitful

attempt by historians to place Jesus in his proper historical context. As Martin Buber, the great Jewish philosopher of the 20th century, put it, "I do not believe in Jesus but I believe with him. I firmly believe that the Jewish community in the course of its renaissance will recognize Jesus; not merely as a great figure in its religious history, but also in the organic context of a Messianic development extending over millennia, whose final goal is the Redemption of Israel and of the world." What Jews have rejected is not so much Jesus as the systems of Christian theology that equated Jesus with God that nullified the Torah and that displaced the Jewish people and their covenant. Jews are acutely aware of the unredeemed nature of the world. If Jesus can never be the Messiah for Jews, as a descendant of David who inaugurated a yet unfinished messianic program, he is surely, by historical measures, a messiah. That seems to be Buber's great insight. A recovery of the perspectives of James and Jesus' other original followers, who continued to hope and strive for messianic redemption, and who espoused a set of biblical ethics based on the Hebrew Prophets, even after Jesus' death, offers a point of unity and understanding hitherto neglected between Jews and Christians. For Christians an understanding of the Jesus dynasty opens a way for recovering and appreciating the Jewish roots of Jesus.

There have been significant developments along these lines in recent years across a wide spectrum of Christian groups— whether traditionally "liberal" or "conservative." More and more Christians have become familiar with basic Jewish customs and holidays in an effort to understand Jesus better as a Jew in his own time. It is not uncommon for Passover observances to be conducted in churches, with rabbis invited in to teach, in an effort to better understand Jesus in his own time and place. In the academic study of Christian origins at any major college or university the Jewishness of Jesus is a given, and courses on the New Testament and early Christianity approach Jesus and his movement as an integral part of the history of the varieties of Judaism in Roman Palestine. If Christians can give James his rightful place as successor to Jesus' movement, and begin to realize that his version of the faith represents Christianity with claims to authenticity that override those of Paul, even more doors of understanding between Christians and Jews will be opened. But just as important, in terms of Christian mission and purpose in the world, the unfinished agenda of John, Jesus, and James can find new life and relevance in modern times.

Muslims do not worship Jesus, who is known as Isa in Arabic, nor do they consider him divine, but they do believe that he was a prophet or messenger of God and he is called the Messiah in the Quran. However, by affirming Jesus as Messiah they are attesting to his messianic message, not his mission as a heavenly Christ. There are some rather striking connections between the research I have presented in The Jesus Dynasty and the traditional beliefs of Islam. The Muslim emphasis on Jesus as messianic prophet and teacher is quite parallel to what we find in the Q source, in the book of James, and in the Didache. To be the Messiah is to proclaim a message, but it is the same message as that proclaimed by Abraham, Moses, and all the Prophets. Islam insists that neither Jesus nor Muhammad brought a new religion.

Both sought to call people back to what might be called "Abrahamic faith." This is precisely what we find emphasized in the book of James. Like Islam, the book of James, and the teaching of Jesus in Q, emphasizes doing the will of God as a demonstration of one's faith. Also, the dietary laws of Islam, as quoted in the Quran, echo the teachings of James in Acts 15 almost word for word: "Abstain from swine flesh, blood, things offered to idols, and carrion"(Quran 2:172). Since Muslims reject all of the Pauline affirmations about Jesus, and thus the central claims of orthodox Christianity, the gulf between Islam and Christianity on Jesus is a wide one. However, there is little about the view of Jesus presented in this book that conflicts with Islam's basic perception. The prophet Muhammad was in contact with Christian groups in Arabia, and there is evidence to suppose that the Christians he met might have been closer in their beliefs to the Ebionites than to the Western church. If that be the case then one of the most fascinating turns of history would be that the view of Jesus represented by the Jesus dynasty, has survived, ironically, in aspects of Islamic tradition as well. The Christianity we know from the Q source, from the letter of James, from the Didache, and some of our other surviving Jewish Christian sources, represents a version of the Jesus faith that can actually unite, rather than divide, Jews, Christians, and Muslims. If nothing else, the insights revealed through an understanding of the Jesus dynasty can open wide new and fruitful doors of dialogue and understanding among these three great traditions that have in the past considered their views of Jesus to be so sharply contradictory as to close off discussion."......

I have discovered over the last forty years that there are countless others who share the quest for the historical Jesus and who want to know the truth, wherever it may lead. Our conclusions might differ but I hope that my journey will help them to better glimpse Jesus as he was in his own time and place. I truly believe that an understanding of Jesus and his family, and the dynasty that perpetuated his message, is one of the most important keys to completing our quest to know the historical Jesus and the origins of Christianity."

In the Quran, God repeatedly engages polemically with the people of the book and admonishes, warns, appeals to their reason and exhorts and invites them to the clear truth of the final revelation that has no crookedness, conjecture or contradiction in it. This message is best, succinctly and sublimely captured in the most emphatic manner:

Say, 'He is God the One, God the eternal. He begot no one nor was He begotten. No one is comparable to Him.' (112:1-4)

The word used by God to declare that He is 'One' in Arabic is 'Ahad' which resonates with the word 'Akhad' used in the Torah in Hebrew. This word in Hebrew is found in the most fundamental creed of the Jewish Torah in the 'Shema Yisrael':

"Hear O Yisrael The Lord our God, the Lord is [the Only] One." (Deut:6)

God uses the same root word to declare his unity and oneness so that the Jews will be able to relate to the message in the Quran, yet they reject it.

With regard to the Christians, God declares using the same words in the later Nicene Creed that is part of the Christian belief by negating and rejecting the 'begotten' nature of God, yet they persist in the greatest blasphemy on the nature and attribute of God. Christian apologists resort to a host of explanations steeped in linguistic and theological manoeuvring and hermeneutical waterboarding to surmount this issue in vain.

As Dr. Tabor states 'the quest for the historical Jesus is becoming ubiquitous'; and one can surmise that the truth is plain to see in the Quran if the Christians open their minds and hearts to the possibility of God reaching out to humanity after Jesus to establish His final message free of human corruption and distortion as a testament to His Grace and Mercy.

Appendix H- Towards a productive and meaningful inter-faith relationship and dialogue between Muslims and Christians

In a provocatively and unconventionally titled book "Was Jesus a Muslim?" Prof. Robert F. Shedinger analyses and questions categories in the study of religion and challenges fundamentally entrenched concepts that may appear radical to some. Of course for Muslims the question posed is a no brainer as they believe that all Prophets and Messengers of God were Muslims by definition as they all 'submitted to the one true God' which is the essence of what a Muslim is. Shedinger states in his book that he believes that the life and work of Jesus as recorded in the Gospels resonate more with particular interpretations of the nature and essence of the Islamic tradition than with common Western articulation of the nature and essence of Christianity. It is in this hermeneutical sense that he concludes that Jesus was really a Muslim.

Shedinger goes on to state that "Today more than at any time in recent history we need a global movement of solidarity to emerge between Christians and Muslims, a movement with the promise to promote a just world order. But a new world order of justice and peace will not rise from a clash between Islam and the West; the "clash" mentality of the neoconservative political movement will lead only to greater levels of violence and injustice as it tends to create the very clash that it seeks to analyze. Rather the world is in dire need of a movement of Christian- Muslim solidarity. I am hopeful that such a movement is possible, but only if Christians and Muslims are willing to rethink in fundamental ways long held assumptions about the relationship between Islam and Christianity and between religion and politics more generally. Positioning Jesus as a point of commonality between Muslims and Christians may be a first step towards this goal."

Despite many areas of scriptural overlap, the Quran is diametrically opposed to the central Christian affirmation of Jesus as the literal son of God, a person with a uniquely divine nature and the second person of the trinity. Thus at the end of the day Jesus stands more as a point of contradiction than commonality between the two traditions. This means that dialogue between Muslims and Christians revolving around doctrinal and theological issues at best serves to clarify areas of theological difference and at worst runs the risk of devolving into theological debate or apologetics that undermine the stated goal of dialogue, which is to promote mutual respect and understanding. In a broad survey of formative Islamic history along with an analysis of the works of contemporary Muslim thinkers, Shedinger shows that Muslim self- definition resists letting Islam be categorized as a religion in the Western sense of something possessing a unique essence embodied in an institutional structure distinct from the political, economic and social structures of the larger society. There is a unifying tendency to view Islam as an inherently political movement designed to promote just and egalitarian communities in accord with divinely revealed principles. Specifically he goes onto show how an Islamic Worldview conceives of the political and spiritual as mutually reinforcing aspects of an overarching unity rooted in the concept of "Tawheed" that cannot be adequately understood via the sacred-profane dualism that is so deeply embedded in the Western worldview and that defines the Western concept of religion.

Shedinger then analyses the life and ministry of Jesus placed outside the framework of the discourse of a 'generic' religious definition. He argues and convincingly demonstrates how recent years have witnessed a movement in New Testament scholarship that emphasizes the effect of Roman imperial politics as reflected by the writers of the New Testament books, on life in first-century Palestine. There is a growing recognition that Jesus must be understood within the context of Jewish resistance to Roman Imperial domination where Jesus emerges as more of a political rather than a traditionally religious figure. On this basis Shedinger concludes that as a prophet of resistance against the injustices perpetrated by the Roman Imperial system, the historical Jesus is more consistent with the later Islamic interpretation of him as a prophet of the Islamic message of justice than with the later Christian understanding that transformed Jesus into the central theological concept of an essentially depoliticized religious tradition that has in too many cases acquiesced to systems of global domination and injustice. It may be that Christianity has lost the spirit of Jesus by allowing itself to become 'religionized'.

This realization argues Shedinger, should return Jesus to a position of commonality rather than contradiction between Christians and Muslims and lead to a movement of Christian-Muslim solidarity against injustice. In fact a joint Jihad against economic, political, social, gender and environmental injustices! What a tantalizingly audacious and provocative global movement that would be!

To achieve this Christians and Muslims should engage in what Shedinger describes as a 'meta-religious ' dialogue, dialogue that positions the nature of religion itself and its relationship to the larger political, economic and social order as the primary forces of discussion. Meta-religious dialogue has the potential to help Christians understand contemporary Islamist movements not as a threatening politicization of a normative peaceful Islam but as movements of struggle against systems of globalized injustice, a struggle that is entirely consistent with the fundamental nature of the mission of Jesus and therefore a struggle Christians must join. When Muslims and Christians begin to dialogue on the meta-religious question of the very nature of religion, creative ways to conceive of the relationship between religion, politics and economics will undoubtedly emerge. Potentially this will lead to a Christian -Muslim movement of solidarity in which we work together toward the shared goal of a more just and peaceful world. Arguing for a Muslim identity for Jesus may become a liberating lesson for Christians and a key piece in the struggle to improve relations between Christians and Muslims in a fractured and unjust world.

Freed from the distorting influence of interreligious dialogue, meta-religious dialogue has the power to liberate an authentic Muslim voice and bring it into dialogue with a Christian voice. Meta-religious dialogue promotes not only mutual respect for and appreciation of the tradition of the other, but also a movement whereby Christians and Muslims stand side by side in addressing and resisting the injustices of the world. Meta-religious dialogue also makes the nature of religion itself and its relationship to the larger social order the topic of discussion and has the potential to return Jesus to a position of commonality and to foster a movement of solidarity.

In an article published in the 'Renovatio' journal of Zaytuna College, in December 2017, Maria Massi Dakake of George Mason University proposes what one might call a set of Quranic "rules of engagement" for interacting with Jews and Christians in peaceful and dialogic contexts and argue that, from a Quranic perspective, demonstrations of virtue and good manners (adab) in such interactions are ultimately as important as, or perhaps more important than, the eloquence of words and the rigor of arguments. She suggests four attributes for dialogue,

Disputing in "The Most Beautiful Way'

The idea of Islamic adab—meaning good manners, proper comportment, and even social ethics—is frequently based upon or connected with the concepts of ĥusn or îĥsān. These are terms with a wide semantic range, entailing the notions of beauty, goodness, and virtue.

And dispute not with the People of the Book, save in the most beautiful way, unless it be those of them who have done wrong. And say, "We believe in that which was sent down unto us and was sent down unto you; our God and your God is one, and unto Him we submit." (29:46)

Call unto the way of thy Lord with wisdom and goodly exhortation. Surely thy Lord is He Who knows best those who stray from His way, and He knows best the rightly guided. (16:125)

Thus, we can say that when the Quran instructs Muslims to engage the religious other, even in dispute, in "the most beautiful way" and "with wisdom," it is asking them to conduct themselves in a manner that is not only beautiful and wise in their own view, but that will be recognized as beautiful, good, virtuous, and wise by their interlocutors.

Finding common ground

Another Quranic rule of engagement for interreligious dialogue or even dispute, therefore, is to strive as much as possible to find common ground and then to speak on the basis of shared religious principles. Yet it is in relation to Jews and Christians that the Quran is the most engaging in this regard. In Quran 3:64, the Prophet (ﷺ) is instructed to directly invite the People of the Book to enter into a religious discussion with him and to do so by asking them first to acknowledge a "common word" between them on fundamental religious matters:

Say, "O People of the Book! Come to a word common between us and you, that we shall worship none but God, shall not associate aught with Him, and shall not take one another as lords apart from God." And if they turn away, then say, "Bear witness that we are submitters (muslimūn)." (3:64)

This verse became the verbatim basis of an invitation to dialogue issued by a group of Muslim religious scholars to the Roman Catholic Church, as well as other Christian denominations, in 2003—an invitation that has been the inspiration for a series of productive inter-religious exchanges. The Quranic invitation to dialogue on the shared religious principle of monotheism articulated in this verse thus has continued to invite dialogue between Muslims and Christians across fourteen centuries of Islamic history and into the contemporary world. The effectiveness of the Muslim scholars' invocation of this verse—for both Muslims and Christians involved in the dialogue—seems to belie the idea that such inviting Quranic approaches were applicable only in an early period of the Prophet's mission and have no usefulness or purpose after the revelation of later verses enjoining a more confrontational approach to Jews and Christians.

Responding to Exclusivist Claims

Some of the religious competition and conflict—especially between Jews and Christians—is reflected in and commented upon critically by the Quran. Yet the Quran's immediate response to expressions of religious exclusivism on the part of Jews and Christians is to critique these attitudes themselves as baseless, or else as unbecoming of scriptural (and therefore knowledgeable) religious communities, rather than to answer them with an exclusivism of its own. Although it is quite clearly expressed in other Quranic passages that Islam should be recognized by all as the true religion, or dīn al-ĥaqq, destined to prevail over all religion, its response to the exclusivist claims of other religious communities is typically to broaden the basis for salvation beyond any specific religious community and to ground it instead in religious sincerity and righteousness. One clear example of the way the Quran countenances exclusive religious claims can be found in 2:111–12:

"And they said, "None will enter the Garden unless he be a Jew or a Christian." Those are their hopes. Say, "Bring your proof, if you are truthful." Nay, whosoever submits his face to God, while being virtuous, shall have his reward with his Lord. No fear shall come upon them, nor shall they grieve." (2:111-112)

Here, the Quran dismisses the claims of Jews and Christians that they alone will enjoy the garden in the hereafter as merely their "hopes" (amāniyyuhum). The Arabic word here translated as "hopes" is related to the word for longing or intense desire and is used throughout the Quran to designate false hopes or false religious ideas that one comes to believe are true out of an intense desire that they should be true. They are beliefs, in other words, based on a kind of self-delusion generated by desire. Even worse than this, the Quran suggests that such false ideas and desires are the work of Satan himself. In another passage, the Quran responds to an implied claim on the part of the People of the Book that they alone will enter the garden by dismissing these claims merely as the desires or false hopes (amānī) of the People of the Book and refuting them by widening the field of those who might earn paradise:

"But for those who believe and perform righteous deeds, We shall cause them to enter Gardens with rivers running below, abiding therein forever. God's Promise is true, and who is truer in speech than God? It will not be in accordance with your desires (amāniyyikum) nor the desires (amānī) of the People of the Book. Whosoever does evil shall be requited for it, and he will not find any protector or any helper apart from God. And whosoever performs righteous deeds, whether male or female, and is a believer, such shall enter the Garden, and

they shall not be wronged as much as the speck on a date-stone. And who is better in religion than the one who submits his face to God, and is virtuous, and follows the creed of Abraham, as a ḥanīf? And God did take Abraham for a friend." (4:122-125)

The desires or false hopes (amānī) associated here with the People of the Book are said to refer to their claims that their religion is superior to that of others or that they will be granted a special leniency in judgment on that day, and the verse is clear that God's judgment will not proceed in accordance with their desires or hopes.

Monotheistic religions have often been thought to be more exclusivist in their religious claims than polytheists, who were more accepting of other religious views—such as the pagan Makkans, who were reportedly content to allow followers of various religions to worship at the Kaaba. The Quran, however, is particularly critical of exclusivist rhetoric among those monotheistic communities whose religion is based on scripture, and suggests that being in possession of revealed scripture grants one access to a kind of spiritual knowledge that should prevent such unwarranted exclusivist claims:

The Jews say, "The Christians stand on nothing," and the Christians say, "The Jews stand on nothing," though they [all] recite the Book. Just so did those who know not speak words like theirs. God will judge between them on the Day of Resurrection concerning that wherein they differed. (2:113)

Here, each group rejects entirely the validity of the other's religion and its tenets. Neither group is willing to recognize the shared beliefs, practices, or values on the basis of which they might better appreciate the other and against which their religious disagreements on other issues can be clearly articulated. The Quran rejects this approach as unacceptable, precisely because both groups "recite the Book"; that is, both have access to divine scripture, and both have knowledge of religious truth. Thus, while they might criticize or dispute with each other on certain points, even important ones, they have no basis for rejecting the other's views as entirely without merit. Such total rejection of the religious other and a refusal to listen to their views and arguments, the Quran suggests, is the hallmark of "those who know not"; that is, those who do not have access to the religious knowledge that comes with scripture.

Leaving Judgment to God

This brief review of Quranic passages relating to interreligious dialogue and dispute suggests that disagreements between religions are to be expected but must be approached with respect because religious devotion and sincerity can be found in different religious communities, even if one believes, on the basis of one's own scripture, that the doctrines of these other communities are false. Such respect is especially due when one is engaging adherents of scriptural faiths, particularly Jews and Christians. As noted at the outset, the ambiguity of many Quranic verses dealing with the People of the Book is such that the question of their ultimate judgment by God or the possibility of their salvation cannot be resolved with certainty or to the satisfaction of all. But the Quran is clear that one should not expect such a resolution to this issue, and it seems to reject the idea that human beings can make claims regarding the salvation of themselves or others with any certainty at all. A verse regularly cited as an indication of the Quran's pluralistic ideal suggests that such certainty can come only in the hereafter:

"And We have sent down unto thee the Book in truth, confirming the Book that came before it, and as a protector over it. So judge between them in accordance with that which God has sent down, and follow not their caprices away from the truth that has come unto thee. For each among you We have appointed a law and a way. And had God willed, He would have made you one community, but [He willed otherwise], that He might try you in that which He has given you. So vie with one another in good deeds. Unto God shall be your return all together, and He will inform you of that wherein you differ." (5:48)

This verse articulates the primary bases for an Islamic pluralism: the Book sent to the Prophet (ﷺ) is meant to confirm and protect (usually understood to mean "correct") previous scriptures, not to reject them; God has ordained a particular law and way for each religious community; and had God wished, He could have made all humankind follow a single religion, but He providentially allowed multiple religious communities to exist as a test for them.

The verse thus ends with an explicit injunction to engage and even challenge other religious communities through acts of goodness and virtue rather than by seeking a human resolution of religious differences in this life. Indeed, the Quran suggests that those very acts of engaging the religious other in dialogue or even dispute, when done with proper adab (decorum) and respect, earnestly seeking common ground, and avoiding chauvinistic or exclusivist claims that reject the religious knowledge and virtues of the other, can be opportunities to demonstrate the religious sincerity, virtue, and goodness that the Quran indicates in several places are the ultimate determinant of divine judgment.

The apparent death and resurrection of Jesus (peace be upon him)

The Quran is very explicit on this point as it asserts:

"And for boasting, "We killed the Messiah, Jesus, son of Mary, the messenger of Allah." But they neither killed nor crucified him—it was only made to appear so. Even those who argue for this ˥crucifixion˥ are in doubt. They have no knowledge whatsoever—only making assumptions. They certainly did not kill him." (Quran 4:157)

Christians typically respond to this in a totally perplexed manner claiming that, "thousands were eye witnesses to the crucifixion of Jesus and it is documented in historical records!" Some Christians even exclaim in bewilderment, "who then was crucified, was it a hologram?!", more in mock sarcasm than serious query. The Quran nor the Prophet Muhammad gives any further details or elaboration on this point except that the Quran also states,

"Rather, Allah raised him to Himself. And ever is Allah Exalted in Might and Wise." (Quran 4:158)

From an Islamic perspective, Jesus was therefore neither killed nor crucified but was raised alive to God. Muslims also believe that Jesus shall return to earth during the end times and die a natural death after a period of time during which he shall usher in an era of peace and justice after slaying the anti-Christ and affirming the true monotheistic message of God as revealed to the Prophet Muhammad. One has to hasten here to clarify that according to the Muslim belief, Jesus shall return not as a prophet but as a servant of God and a follower of His final testament in the Quran. Details of the second coming of Jesus and his role are found in the several authentic 'hadeeth' or the narrations of the Prophet and is also explicitly but indirectly alluded to in the Quran;

"And he,(Jesus, son of Mary) shall be a known sign for (the coming of) the Hour (Day of Resurrection...)[Quran 43:61].

As for the events surrounding the crucifixion of Jesus, Islamic scholars offer several possible explanations that support the Quranic position;

1. *Jesus's physical form was transposed on to another in the garden of Gethsemane before the Roman soldiers took him away (substitution theory) and ironically it could have been Judas who assumed Jesus's appearance (punitive substitution)and was crucified instead. An alternative plausibility is that Judas or another of Jesus's disciples volunteered (voluntary substitution) to take the place of Jesus on the cross in return for the promise of the companionship of Jesus in the kingdom of God and hence God transfigured him to appear like Jesus and raised Jesus unto Him.*

2. *When Jesus was brought before Pontius Pilate there was another person named Jesus Barabbas convicted of a crime befitting crucifixion and it was customary to set free one sentenced to death before Passover and it was Jesus the Messiah who was set free and Barabbas who presumably had the physical appearance of Jesus was crucified. (substitution/ switch theory)*

3. *Although Jesus was placed on the cross, he did not die by crucifixion but was brought down alive early and he appeared lifeless and practically dead to observers. Jesus would have felt no physical pain as God would have placed him in a deep state of unconsciousness. (swoon theory). Subsequently, Jesus would have been 'raised alive to heaven' either from the tomb or after the live Jesus came out of the tomb, through 'assumption' rather than 'resurrection'. (This presumes that crucifixion means death by being hung on the cross and since Jesus did not physically die, he was never crucified or killed as the Quran asserts)*

4. *Jesus of Nazareth was never captured or betrayed, the person who was crucified was Jesus Barabbas who was neither a switch or substitute but a convicted insurrectionist who was arrested on Pontius Pilate's orders and held over till Passover to be crucified anyway. Jesus Barabbas's crucifixion together with two other fellow criminals sparked rumours among the Jewish community and followers of Jesus of Nazareth that it was Jesus the Messiah who had been crucified. The entire passion narrative in the Gospels is a fictional narrative based on 'Hellenic literary mimesis' where the Gospel writers who were heavily influenced by Pauline Christology presented a totally fabricated*

story replete with literary mimesis from both the Tanakh and Homeric epics and abounding with historical implausibility that gave the world the impression that Jesus had been crucified. Further elaboration on this can be found in the book "The Cross & The Crescent", by Dr. Jerald F. Dirks a deacon of the Church and a graduate of the Harvard School of Divinity.

Dr. Ali Ataie, professor of comparative religion and theology at Zaytuna College in Berkeley California and a scholar of sacred languages and Biblical hermeneutics has recently(on the Blogging theology, YouTube under the title "Jesus was not crucified-the evidence") proposed a plausible narrative of the crucifixion that aligns with the Quranic assertion.

Dr. Ali Ataie's contends that, "despite the evangelist's (authors of the synoptic gospels and John's gospel)inclusion of real historical persons and their passion narratives such as Jesus of Nazareth, Pontius Pilate, Jesus Barabbas and Herod, these passion narratives are most likely not historical. The evangelists attempted to historicize the passion of their savior and the mention of several real figures gave their stories a strong sense of verisimilitude. The Evangelist's in essence created a simulacrum or substitute Jesus of Nazareth which they subsequently tortured and killed with their pens. The Jesus of Christian faith countless exceeding generations of Jews Christians and pagans were made to believe that Jesus of Nazareth was crucified due to these writings. This gives new insight into the Quranic statement that states that Jesus was made to appear to be crucified". Dr. Ataie also cites in the above presentation the scholarship of Dr. Dennis McDonald, professor of New Testament and Christian origins at Claremont Graduate University who in his book called 'Mythologizing Jesus from Jewish teacher to epic hero', highlights a major blind spot in New Testament historical scholarship and that is Hellenistic literary mimesis or more specifically Homeric literary mimesis. This is the notion that the Gospel writers are borrowing stories and events from the lives of Homeric Greek heroes like Odysseus revising these stories to fit their narratives and replacing those heroes with Jesus. In other words these events never happened and their educated Greek audiences knew that these events probably never happened. Mark the alleged author of the Gospel of Mark for instance was a highly educated Greek convert who definitely studied Homer, Hessian and Heroditus.

At his time the passion narratives in the gospels were written as literary works of art they were written to make theological and philosophical points okay for Mark. Historical accuracy was very much in the background and when he does present history he does it through the lens of his Christology and of course Mathew and Luke heavily depended upon Mark.

Dr. Ataie in his conclusion states that the problem for the historians and Christians is that the specific events surrounding the alleged crucifixion of Jesus and the gospels are highly implausible which makes one question the historicity of the entire event so after all of this if someone doesn't admit there is a reasonable doubt about the crucifixion or if they don't admit that it is at least historically plausible that he wasn't crucified, then we must question their intellectual honesty.

*An interesting point to note in the Bible narrative of the crucifixion is of Jesus praying to the Father in the garden of Gethsamane with the words, "Father, if you are willing, take **this cup** from me; yet not my will, but yours **be** done."(Luke 22:42).*

Assuming that the above verse was not a concocted mimetic fabrication, Jesus was alluding to his impending capture by the Roman soldiers leading to the crucifixion. From an Islamic perspective, the sincere prayers of a Prophet of God are surely answered if the prophet is not guilty of disobedience. Besides why would a merciful God allow His righteous servant to be subjected to the humiliation and agony of crucifixion for carrying out God's command? Since God is capable of all things and is the best of planners, the Quranic narrative of God raising Jesus up to Himself and "making it appear to them" that Jesus was crucified whereas he was neither crucified nor killed is a straightforward notion for a Muslim to believe. The true methodology and stratagem employed by God will be known best to Him alone. When sincere Christians are confronted with this Quranic narrative of the crucifixion, their reaction borders on sheer bewilderment as they attempt to process the logical contradiction behind God's justice and mercy on one hand and the Pauline doctrine of vicarious atonement and blood sacrifice as the wages of sin on the other. For many thinking and reasoning Christians the crucifixion presents a deeply problematic area of cognitive dissonance both theologically and rationally.

Are the Biblical Ten Commandments found in the Quran?

The ten commandments that was revealed to Moses as part of the To-rah is followed by the adherents of both the Jewish and the Christian faiths as a cornerstone of their scriptures with minor variants between the different sects. These well-known Ten Commandments form the backbone of the moral and ethical thrust of the Torah and the Bible and since the Quran asserts that the revelations from God carry the same moral message and that what is stated in the Quran is found in the earlier scriptures, are these commandments or their moral equivalent found in the Quran?

Not surprisingly we see the Quranic equivalent of the Ten Command-ments in chapter 6 verses 151 to 153:

"Say, Come! Let me tell you what your Lord has forbidden you: Do not associate anything with Him; be good to your parents; do not kill your children because of poverty- We shall provide sustenance for you and for them; do not even come near any shameful deeds whether openly or secretly; and do not kill the soul whom God has made sacred, ex-cept for a just cause. This is what He commands you to do so that you may use your reason."- (6:151)

"And do not touch the orphan's property, except to improve it, until he (or she) attains the age of maturity; give full measure and full weight with equity- We do not burden any soul with more than it can bear; and whenever you speak, speak justly even if it concerns a close rel-ative; and always fulfill any covenants you made in God's name. This is what He commands you to do so that you may remember."-(6:152)

"And this is My straight path: follow it and do not follow other paths-They will separate you away from His path. This is what He commands you to do so that you may remain conscious of Him." (6:153)

The Quranic Ten Commandments are divided between the three verses as follows: The first verse (6:151) contains the following five command-ments (abbreviated):

1. Do not associate anything or partners with God

2. Be good to your parents

3. Do not kill your children because of poverty

4. Do not even come close to shameful deeds

5. Do not kill a human soul except for a just cause

The second verse (6:152) contains the next four commandments:

6. Do not touch the orphans' property, except to improve it

7. Give full measure and weight with fairness

8. Speak justly even if it is against a close relative

9. Fulfill your covenant with God.

And finally the tenth or the 'capstone' commandment is contained in the third verse (6:153);

10. Follow My straight path and do not follow any other path.

These commandments are given further expression and substance in the rest of the Quran and the Hadeeth of the Prophet and are codified in the Islamic law or "Shariah".

The Quranic recognition of the truth and essential unity of the revealed Scriptures is not confined to Christianity and Judaism but extends to all the Prophets preceding Moses and Jesus and their teachings. Allah says:

"Say: We believe in God and in what has been revealed to us and what was revealed to Abraham, Ishmael, Isaac, Jacob, and the tribes and in the scriptures that God sent to Moses and Jesus, and the Prophets. We make no distinction between them. And for Him do we surrender ourselves." (3:84)

This verse essentially captures the universality and completeness of the final testament of God i.e The Quran.

Pause for reflection

In comparing and contrasting the three great Abrahamic faiths, it has been said that Judaism emphasized God's law and justice whereas Christianity epitomized His mercy and love, whilst Islam revealed the "balance of perfection" in God's final message to humankind.

A concise summary of the different worldviews of the three Abrahamic faiths gives a clearer perspective on their essence, form and substance:

The Christian worldview proclaims;

"We have all <u>sinned</u> and deserve God's judgment. <u>God</u>, the Father, sent His only Son to satisfy that judgment for those who believe in Him. <u>Jesus</u>, the creator and eternal Son of God, who lived a sinless life, loves us so much that He <u>died</u> for our sins, taking the punishment that we deserve, was <u>buried</u>, and <u>rose from the dead</u> according to the <u>Bible</u>. If you truly believe and trust this in your heart, receiving Jesus alone as your Saviour, declaring, "<u>Jesus is Lord</u>," you will be saved from <u>judgment</u> and spend eternity with God in heaven."

Here we observe a worldview that is Jesus centric and its theological foundations resting on a single event i.e; the death and resurrection of Jesus without which all of the Christian's belief is in vain according to Paul, the alleged author of the bulk of the New Testament.

Judaism's worldview is that, "there is only one God who has created the whole universe including all living things and our lives are all planned by God and He has chosen the children of Israel as the blessed people to prevail upon this world. They believe that the 'Mashihah', a man from God will one day come down to tell us the era of peace. Jewish people say that their bodies are possessing of a soul which will receive a judgement from God when they are dead. Judaism's worldview is basically about the commandments from God and the covenant with God to strictly keep the law".

Here the Jewish worldview is race centric and emphasizes the law and the commandments and the oneness of God as the central foundation of its faith.

The Islamic worldview is a more comprehensive concept and can be articulated as:

"Mirroring the _unity and unicity of God_ in all of God's creation in the unity of the human family through the chosen role of being God's _vicegerent_ on earth; and to manifest His _Mercy_ and Grace to all beings through _compassion_, moderation and knowledge; and be an agent of _human welfare_ and blessing whilst upholding _justice_ and the overarching ethical _Quranic principles_ to all of mankind, through the practice of _beauty and excellence_ in deeds and behaviour, whilst embracing the spirit of _pluralism & tolerance_, love and peace to all beings; and doing so with the sincerity of intent of seeking God's love for which the promise is eternal life and felicity in the hereafter."

The Islamic worldview is a holistic framework that underscores the unity of God, purpose of and guidance for life in this world and for success in the hereafter with the promise of eternal life for those who have faith, do good works and turn in repentance and humility to God.

As such, transformation of the world system is a human responsibility, a responsibility wrapped up in the mutual transformation of the material and spiritual in Islam. This understanding grows out of the centric Islamic concept of Tawheed but is virtually irreconcilable with the dualistic sacred-profane worldview of Western Christian thought.

Although the central themes of monotheism, salvation and righteousness run through all three faiths, the theological and jurisprudential nuances of the different faiths colours their practice and its followers.

In this context Judaism may be referred to as the religion of prophecy and law, Christianity the religion of a person and salvation and Islam the religion of God and faith.

Appendix I - Analysis of Quranic Composition

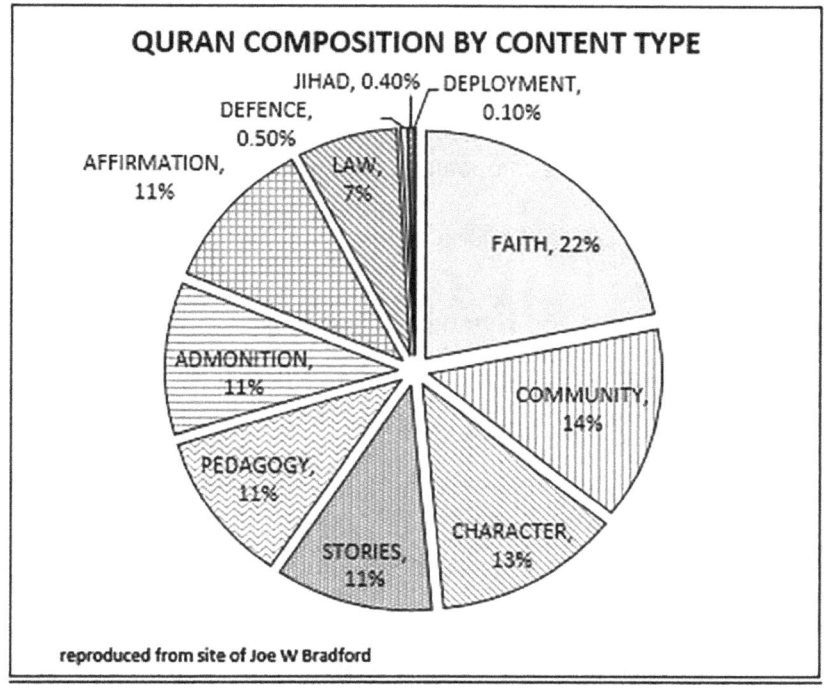

QURAN COMPOSITION BY CONTENT TYPE

JIHAD, 0.40%
DEPLOYMENT, 0.10%
DEFENCE, 0.50%
AFFIRMATION, 11%
LAW, 7%
FAITH, 22%
ADMONITION, 11%
COMMUNITY, 14%
PEDAGOGY, 11%
STORIES, 11%
CHARACTER, 13%

reproduced from site of Joe W Bradford

It is quite common to find Non-Muslims and anti-Islamic elements claiming that the Quran mainly contains law and legislation in order to allude that Islam is more of a political force than a spiritual faith and hence has a hidden agenda of conquering and establishing a Caliphate or system of government. Nothing could be further from the truth as the chart above shows that out of the 6236 verses in the Quran less than 9% is about law or a legal system. A broader classification would be to infer that 80% of the Quran is about faith or 'Imaan' and 20% constitutes 'Islam' as a system of law and submission to God. Hence the major thrust of the Quran is to instill faith in the hearts of humanity and for God to reveal His love, mercy and forgiveness through His revelation. It is sometimes incongruent to find modern books on Islamic topics focus more on the 'hardware' than the 'software' leading to an overemphasis on differences and methodologies rather than an emphasis on faith (Iman), beauty, and excellence (Ihsaan).

Appendix J- Order of Quranic Verses

All the information below is sourced at hp://tanzil.net/docs/rev-elaon_order The chronological order of suras (i.e., the order in which Quran suras are revealed to the holy prophet) is specified in several reliable sources, most of which are based on the narrations received from the great prophet's companion and cousin, Ibn Abbas.

Chronological Order of Suras

Order	Sura Name	Number	Type	Note
1	Al-Alaq	96	Makkan	
2	Al-Qalam	68	Makkan	Except 17-33 and 48-50, from Madinah
3	Al-Muzzam-mil	73	Makkan	Except 10, 11 and 20, from Madinah
4	Al-Muddath-thir	74	Makkan	
5	Al-Faatiha	1	Makkan	
6	Al-Masad	111	Makkan	
7	At-Takwir	81	Makkan	
8	Al-A'laa	87	Makkan	
9	Al-Lail	92	Makkan	
10	Al-Fajr	89	Makkan	
11	Ad-Dhuhaa	93	Makkan	
12	Ash-Sharh	94	Makkan	
13	Al-Asr	103	Makkan	
14	Al-Aadiyaat	100	Makkan	
15	Al-Kawthar	108	Makkan	
16	At-Takaathur	102	Makkan	
17	Al-Maa'un	107	Makkan	Only 1-3 from Makkah; the rest from Madinah

Order	Sura Name	Number	Type	Note
18	Al-Kaafiroon	109	Makkan	
19	Al-Fil	105	Makkan	
20	Al-Falaq	113	Makkan	
21	An-Naas	114	Makkan	
22	Al-Ikhlaas	112	Makkan	
23	An-Najm	53	Makkan	Except 32, from Madinah
24	Abasa	80	Makkan	
25	Al-Qadr	97	Makkan	
26	Ash-Shams	91	Makkan	
27	Al-Burooj	85	Makkan	
28	At-Tin	95	Makkan	
29	Quraysh	106	Makkan	
30	Al-Qaari'a	101	Makkan	
31	Al-Qiyaama	75	Makkan	
32	Al-Humaza	104	Makkan	
33	Al-Mursalaat	77	Makkan	Except 48, from Madinah
34	Qaaf	50	Makkan	Except 38, from Madinah
35	Al-Balad	90	Makkan	
36	At-Taariq	86	Makkan	
37	Al-Qamar	54	Makkan	Except 44-46, from Madinah
38	Saad	38	Makkan	
39	Al-A'raaf	7	Makkan	Except 163-170, from Madinah
40	Al-Jinn	72	Makkan	
41	Yaseen	36	Makkan	Except 45, from Madinah
42	Al-Furqaan	25	Makkan	Except 68-70, from Madinah

Order	Sura Name	Number	Type	Note
43	Faatir	35	Makkan	
44	Maryam	19	Makkan	Except 58 and 71, from Madinah
45	Taa-Haa	20	Makkan	Except 130 and 131, from Madinah
46	Al-Waaqia	56	Makkan	Except 81 and 82, from Madinah
47	Ash-Shu'araa	26	Makkan	Except 197 and 224-227, from Madinah
48	An-Naml	27	Makkan	
49	Al-Qasas	28	Makkan	Except 52-55 from Madinah and 85 from Juhfa at the time of the Hijra
50	Al-Israa	17	Makkan	Except 26, 32, 33, 57, 73-80, from Madinah
51	Yunus	10	Makkan	Except 40, 94, 95, 96, from Madinah
52	Hud	11	Makkan	Except 12, 17, 114, from Madinah
53	Yusuf	12	Makkan	Except 1, 2, 3, 7, from Madinah
54	Al-Hijr	15	Makkan	Except 87, from Madinah
55	Al-An'aam	6	Makkan	Except 20, 23, 91, 93, 114, 151, 152, 153,
56	As-Saaffaat	37	Makkan	
57	Luqman	31	Makkan	Except 27-29, from Madinah
58	Saba	34	Makkan	
59	Az-Zumar	39	Makkan	

Order	Sura Name	Number	Type	Note
60	Al-Ghaafir	40	Makkan	Except 56, 57, from Madinah
61	Fussilat	41	Makkan	
62	Ash-Shura	42	Makkan	Except 23, 24, 25, 27, from Madinah
63	Az-Zukhruf	43	Makkan	Except 54, from Madinah
64	Ad-Dukhaan	44	Makkan	
65	Al-Jaathiya	45	Makkan	Except 14, from Madinah
66	Al-Ahqaf	46	Makkan	Except 10, 15, 35, from Madinah
67	Adh-Dhaari-yat	51	Makkan	
68	Al-Ghaashiya	88	Makkan	
69	Al-Kahf	18	Makkan	Except 28, 83-101, from Madinah
70	An-Nahl	16	Makkan	Except the last three verses from Madinah
71	Nooh	71	Makkan	
72	Ibrahim	14	Makkan	Except 28, 29, from Madinah
73	Al-Anbiyaa	21	Makkan	
74	Al-Mumi-noon	23	Makkan	
75	As-Sajda	32	Makkan	Except 16-20, from Madinah
76	At-Tur	52	Makkan	
77	Al-Mulk	67	Makkan	
78	Al-Haaqqa	69	Makkan	
79	Al-Ma'aarij	70	Makkan	
80	An-Naba	78	Makkan	

Order	Sura Name	Number	Type	Note
81	An-Naazi'aat	79	Makkan	
82	Al-Infitaar	82	Makkan	
83	Al-Inshiqaaq	84	Makkan	
84	Ar-Room	30	Makkan	Except 17, from Madinah
85	Al-Ankaboot	29	Makkan	Except 1-11, from Madinah
86	Al-Mutaffifin	83	Makkan	
87	Al-Baqara	2	Madinan	Except 281 from Mina at the time of the Last Hajj
88	Al-Anfaal	8	Madinan	Except 30-36 from Makkah
89	Aal-i-Imraan	3	Madinan	
90	Al-Ahzaab	33	Madinan	
91	Al-Mumtah-ana	60	Madinan	
92	An-Nisaa	4	Madinan	
93	Az-Zalzala	99	Madinan	
94	Al-Hadid	57	Madinan	
95	Muhammad	47	Madinan	Except 13, revealed during the Prophet's Hijrah
96	Ar-Ra'd	13	Madinan	
97	Ar-Rahmaan	55	Madinan	
98	Al-Insaan	76	Madinan	

Order	Sura Name	Number	Type	Note
99	At-Talaaq	65	Madinan	
100	Al-Bayyina	98	Madinan	
101	Al-Hashr	59	Madinan	
102	An-Noor	24	Madinan	
103	Al-Hajj	22	Madinan	Except 52-55, revealed between Makkah and Madinah
104	Al-Munaafiqoon	63	Madinan	
105	Al-Mujaadila	58	Madinan	
106	Al-Hujuraat	49	Madinan	
107	At-Tahrim	66	Madinan	
108	At-Taghaabun	64	Madinan	
109	As-Saff	61	Madinan	
110	Al-Jumu'a	62	Madinan	
111	Al-Fath	48	Madinan	Revealed while returning from Hudaybiyya
112	Al-Maaida	5	Madinan	Except 3, revealed at Arafat on Last Hajj
113	At-Tawba	9	Madinan	Except last two verses from Makkah
114	An-Nasr	110	Madinan	Revealed at Mina on Last Hajj, but regarded as Madinan sura

Appendix K- Testaments to the life of Muhammad (ﷺ)

Bosworth Smith (d. 1908), a reverend schoolmaster and author, wrote:

"By a fortune absolutely unique in history, Muhammad is a three-fold founder of a nation, of an empire, and of a religion... Head of the State as well as the Church; he was Caesar and Pope in one; but he was Pope without the Pope's pretensions, and Caesar without the legions of Caesar, without a standing army, without a bodyguard, without a police force, without a fixed revenue. If ever a man ruled by a right divine, it was Muhammad, for he had all the powers without their supports. He cared not for the dressings of power. The simplicity of his private life was in keeping with his public life.

The renowned leader of Indian independence, Mahatma Ghandi wrote:

"I wanted to know the best of the life of one who holds today an undisputed sway over the hearts of millions of mankind... I became more than ever convinced that it was not the sword that won a place for Islam in those days in the scheme of life. It was the rigid simplicity, the utter self-effacement of, the scrupulous regard for pledges, his intense devotion to his friends and followers, his intrepidity, his fearlessness, his absolute trust in God and in his own mission. These and not the sword carried everything before them and surmounted every obstacle."

Adam Smith (d. 1790), the 18th century English economist.

"The Empire of the Caliphs seems to have been the first state under which the world enjoyed that degree of tranquility which the cultivation of the sciences requires. It was under the protection of those generous and magnificent princes, that the ancient philosophy and astronomy of the Greeks were restored and established in the East; that tranquility, which their mild, just and religious government diffused over their vast

empire, revived the curiosity of mankind, to inquire into the connecting principles of nature"

Edward Gibbon (d. 1794), a historian and member of England's Parliament, wrote,

"The good sense of Muhammad despised the pomp of royalty. The Apostle of God submitted to the menial offices of the family; he kindled the fire; swept the floor; milked the ewes; and mended with his own hands his shoes and garments. Disdaining the penance and merit of a hermit, he observed without effort or vanity the abstemious diet of an Arab." In other words, he not just endured the coarseness of an austere life, but it flowed naturally from him. He was not trying to encourage monkhood or self-deprivation, nor was he faking this minimalism to earn praise from the people. Gibbons continues, *"On solemn occasions, he feasted his companions with rustic and hospitable plenty. But, in his domestic life, many weeks would pass without a fire being kindled on the hearth of the Prophet."*

William Montgomery Watt (d. 2006), a Scottish historian and Emeritus Professor in Arabic and Islamic Studies, wrote,

"His readiness to undergo persecution for his beliefs, the high moral character of the men who believed in him and looked up to him as a leader, and the greatness of his ultimate achievement – all argue his fundamental integrity. To suppose Muhammad an imposter raises more problems than it solves. Moreover, none of the great figures of history is so poorly appreciated in the West as Muhammad... Thus, not merely must we credit Muhammad with essential honesty and integrity of purpose, if we are to understand him at all; if we are to correct the errors we have inherited from the past, we must not forget that conclusive proof is a much stricter requirement than a show of plausibility, and in a matter such as this only to be attained with difficulty."

Scottish philosopher and historian Thomas Carlyle (d. 1881) wrote:

"It goes greatly against the imposter theory, the fact that he lived in this entirely unexceptional, entirely quiet and commonplace way, till the heat of his years was done. He was forty before he talked of any mission from Heaven. His ambition,' seemingly, had been, hitherto, to live an honest life; his 'fame,' the mere good opinion of neighbours that knew him, had been sufficient hitherto. Not till he was already getting old, the prurient heat of his life all burnt out, and peace growing to be the chief thing this world could give him, did he start on the 'career of ambition;' and, belying all his past character and existence, set up [by others] as a wretched empty charlatan to acquire what he could no longer enjoy! For my share, I have no faith whatever in that [imposter theory]. The lies (Western slander) which well-meaning zeal has heaped round this man are disgraceful to us only"

Michael Hart- The 100 -A Ranking of the Most Influential Persons in History. (1989)

"My choice of Muhammad to lead the list of the world's most influential persons may surprise some readers and may be questioned by others, but he was the only man in history who was supremely successful on both the religious and secular levels…….Since there are roughly twice as many Christians as Muslims in the world, it may initially seem strange that Muhammad has been ranked higher than Jesus. Firstly, Muhammad played a far more important role in the development of Islam than Jesus did in Christianity. Although Jesus was responsible for the main ethical and moral precepts of Christianity, Paul was the main developer of Christian theology, its principal proselytiser and the author of a large portion of the New Testament."

"The most we know of him is that he is a man, and yet without exception he is the best of God's creation.

My Lord send boundless prayers and greetings upon your beloved, the best of mankind always and forever."

- from the Burdah (cloak) by Imam Al Busri

Selected Bibliography

Ataie, Ali. "Jesus was not crucified:The evidence",
https://www.youtube.com/watch?v=eU02_xwZlDg&ab_chan-
nel=Bloggi ngTheology

Akyol, Mustafa. The Islamic Jesus: How the King of the Jews Became a Prophet of the Muslims. St. Martin's Press, 2017.

Anjum, Ovamir "Prophetic Ethics: A Model for those Seeking God and Eternal Life" Yaqeen Institute for Islamic Research,14 July 2022,edited 15July 2022.

Alkiek, Tasneem, Brown, Jonathan, Suleiman,Omar " Islam and Violence Against Women: A Critical Look at Domestic Violence and Honor Killings in the Muslim Community" Yaqeen Institute for Islamic research, 17 May 2022.

Ally, Shabir. "Revisiting the tradition on wife-beating",
https://shabirally.com/articlesnblogsdetails?pId=30

Ally, Shabir. " Let the Quran Speak- Concubinage in Islam"
https://www.youtube.com/watch?v=2Bxg3_A85nU

Armstrong, Karen. Muhammad: A Prophet for Our Time. HarperOne, 2007.

Arnold, Yasin Mol: "Ayesha: The case for an older age in sunni-hadith scholarship". Yaqeen Institute, October 2018.

'Iyad, Qadi, "Ash- Shifa of Qadi 'Iyad", translated by A.Bewley. Diwan Press Ltd. Norwich U.K. 2011.

Badawi, Jamal. "Muhammad's Prophethood-An Analytical View". Islamic audiobooks central, 2020.

Brown, Jonathan. "The Issue of Apostasy in Islam". Yaqueen Institute for *Islamic* Research, 2017, https://yaqeeninstitute.org/wp-content/uploads/2017/07/FINAL-The-Issue-of-Apostasy-in-Islam-1.pdf.

Cole, Juan. Muhammad: Prophet of Peace Amid the Clash of Empires . Illustrated ed., Bold Type Books, 2018.

Dakake, Maria Massi. "Guidelines for rules of engagement", Renovatio, Journal of Zaytuna College, December 2017.

Delic, Zijad. Canadian Islam: Belonging and Loyalty. Kirtas Publishing, 2014.

Dirks, Jerald. The Cross and The Crescent. Amana Publishers, 2001.

El Fadl, Khaled Abou. Reasoning with God: Reclaiming Shari'ah in the Modern Age. Rowman & Littlefield Publishers, 2014.

ElShinawi, Mohammad. "Proofs of Prophethood", Yaqeen Institute for Islamic Research, 5 May 2020, https://yaqeeninstitute.org/series/proofs-of-prophethood.

ElShinawi, Mohammad and Suleiman Omer. " How the Prophet rose above enmity and insult",Yaqeen Research Institute,2017.

Hamid Ali, Abdullah bin. "Feminism & Recalibrating Faith According to an Islamic Epistemic". Muslims in Calgary, 7 Nov. 2016, https://muslimsincalgary.ca/feminism-recalibrating-faith-according-to-an-islamic-epistemic/.

Haykal, Muhammad Husayn. The Life of Muhammad. Revised ed., Islamic Book Service, 1976.

Hayward, Joel. The Leadership of Muhammad- A Historical Reconstruction. July 31, 2021 by Swansea: Claritas Book.

Hayward, Joel. *The Warrior Prophet Muhammad and War*, January 2022, Claritas Book.

Kouzes, J.M & Posner B.Z ,The Leadership Challenge(4th ed) 2007, Jossey-Bass.

Lings, Martin. Muhammad: His Life Based on the Earliest Sources. 5th ed. Inner Traditions, 2006.

Muhammad, Ghazi Bin. A Thinking Person's Guide to Islam. White Thread Press, Turath Publishing, 2017.

Murata, Sachiko, and William Chittick. The Vision of Islam. I. B. Tauris, 2006.

Nasr, Seyyed Hossein. The Study Quran: A New Translation and Commentary. HarperOne, 2017.

Ovamir, Anjum. "The Constitution of Madinah; Translation, Commentary and Meaning today", The Yaqeen Institute for Islamic Research 2021.

Parrott, Justin. "Abrogated Rulings in the Qur'an: Discerning Their Divine Wisdom". Yaqueen Institute for Islamic Research, 15 Nov. 2018, https://yaqeeninstitute.ca/read/paper/abrogated-rulings-in-the-quran-discerning-their-divine-wisdom.

Qadhi Yasir, The Sirah of the Prophet, The Islamic Foundation, Markfield. U.K. 2023.

Ramadan, Tariq. Islam: The Essentials. Pelican, 2017.

Randeree, Kasim. "An Islamic Perspective on Leadership: Quranic view on the quality of Leaders", University of Oxford, The Global Studies Journal-Vol.2 Number 1. 2009

Safi, Omid. Memories of Muhammad: Why the Prophet Matters. HarperOne, 2010.

Salahi, Adil. Muhammad: Man and Prophet. The Islamic Foundation, 2010.

Salahi, Adil. Muhammad: His Character and Conduct. The Islamic Foundation, 2014.

Shedinger, Robert F. Was Jesus a Muslim?: Questioning Categories in the Study of Religion. Fortress Press, 2009.

Suleiman, Omar. "Slavery in Islam". Yaqeen Research Institute, 2017, https://yaqeeninstitute.ca/omar-suleimanhadith-30-there-is-no-slavery-in-islam-except-to-the-most-high.

Tabor, James. The Jesus Dynasty: The Hidden History of Jesus, His Royal Family, and the Birth of Christianity. Illustrated ed., Simon & Schuster, 2007.

Yakup, Adem. Miracles of Prophet Muhammad. Ta-Ha Publishers, 2006.

Yusuf, Hamza, and Zaid Shakir. Agenda to Change Our Condition. 2nd ed., Sandala, 2013.

Yusuf, Hamza. The Life of the Prophet Muhammad. Islamic Study School, 2016.

The sources cited in the bibliography are all post-modern writings ranging from the early 20th century to today and are based on the primary sources and early authors on the life of the Prophet and world history or derived from classical and authoritative works of Islamic/religious scholarship and research.

About the Author

Ifthikar Hassen worked for over twenty five years in the Middle East as Finance Director and CFO of several private organizations and as a senior lecturer and visiting academic on the MBA courses in Accounting, Finance and Strategic Management in the United Arab Emirates campus of University of Strathclyde Graduate Business School and was also senior lecturer and the Programme Director for the MBA post-graduate degree at Middlesex University, London, Dubai Campus.

His other articles and publications include, "The Balanced Scorecard of the Believer"; "The Islamic Worldview and the role of Muslim Minority Communities" and the Muslim Charter of Commitment".

He currently resides in Toronto, Canada and is actively engaged in inter-faith dialogue and over the last 15 years attended numerous knowledge retreats, conferences and seminars conducted by leading Islamic scholars and organizations in North America. He is the CEO of a company in the hospitality industry which he co-owns with his wife.